IMAGES
of America

NORTHERN PINE COUNTY

On the Cover: In 1885, William H. Grant discovered a formation of high-quality sandstone along the Kettle River and established a quarry. Workers used a variety of tools and machines to separate large chunks of sandstone from the cliff walls and shape them into everything from pavers to building stones to decorative artwork.

IMAGES
of America

NORTHERN PINE COUNTY

Earl J. Foster and Amy Troolin

ARCADIA
PUBLISHING

ISBN 978-0-7385-8344-0

Published by Arcadia Publishing
Charleston, South Carolina

Printed in the United States of America

Library of Congress Control Number: 2010937080

For all general information, please contact Arcadia Publishing:
Telephone 843-853-2070
Fax 843-853-0044
E-mail sales@arcadiapublishing.com
For customer service and orders:
Toll-Free 1-888-313-2665

Visit us on the Internet at www.arcadiapublishing.com

Contents

ACKNOWLEDGMENTS

The pictures used in Images of America: *Northern Pine County* are drawn primarily from the collections of the Hinckley Fire Museum, Sandstone History and Art Center, Pine County Historical Society, Arla Budd, Gordon Jacobson, and Richard Berglund. The Pine County Genealogical Society also contributed photographs and research assistance, and Richard VanDerWerf provided many wonderful stories.

The authors would like to thank the staff at Proex Portraits in Coon Rapids, Minnesota, Melanie, Kris, Rose, Leslie, Lee, Rich, and John, for their efficient service.

Earl J. Foster would also like to acknowledge his grandchildren, Peyton, Chloe, and Earl III, who love to look at his photographs and listen to him explain them.

A special thanks goes out to T. J. Duchene for his invaluable help with editing the manuscript and solving a whole bevy of computer problems.

Finally, the authors would like to offer a special thanks and tribute to LaJune Troolin for her thorough research, editing, proofreading, organizational skills, excellent advice, and overall patience. We would not have been able to write this book without you!

INTRODUCTION

According to the Minnesota Preservation Center, Pine County is one of the most interesting and unique counties in the entire state of Minnesota. Over the years, Northern Pine County has been home to Native American camps and burial grounds; logging endeavors; quarrying operations; a military road; railroads; agricultural activities; popular forests and lakes; and countless businesses, schools, churches, and organizations. All of these have contributed greatly to the growth and sustainability of this part of the county. In Images of America: *Northern Pine County*, we will examine each of these features through the lens of the experiences of the county's people. We will present pictures and stories that relate the successes, sorrows, joys, and trials of Northern Pine County's residents, all the while placing the county within the wider historical context of the state and nation.

Each of this book's nine chapters will consider a specific aspect of life in Northern Pine County. We will begin with a tribute to area photographers, without whom this book would not be possible, and continue with an examination of the earliest days of Northern Pine County. Early explorers traversed the region, possibly leaving behind evidence of their visits, as we shall see when we examine the authenticity of a stone bearing the date 1679 and the name "Du Luth." From the 1860s through the mid-1890s, logging dominated the area, which was covered with majestic White, Norway, and Jack pines that proved highly profitable for logging companies. Loggers interacted, sometimes less than happily, with Native Americans, who did not approve of the destruction of the pines. Logging continued, however, and as the years passed, the government recognized Pine County as a prime location for investment in transportation.

In 1851, a crew from St. Paul set out to survey one of five military roads ordered by Gov. Alexander Ramsey and the U.S. War Department. The 185-mile-long Point Douglas to Superior Military Road was completed (at least as much as it ever would be) in the mid-1850s and quickly became the primary mail route between St. Paul-Minneapolis to the south and Duluth-Superior to the north. Stagecoach lines began using the road in 1861 to carry passengers, provisions, and mail through East Central Minnesota.

The military road, portions of which are still used today, was mostly supplanted by the coming of the railroads in the early 1870s. The Lake Superior and Mississippi Railroad was the first to lay tracks across the county. It later became the St. Paul and Duluth Railroad and was joined by James J. Hill's Eastern Minnesota Railway. These lines were renamed the Northern Pacific and the Great Northern Railways as the years passed.

As the railroads were laid and logging operations cleared the land and moved on, numerous settlers arrived, seeking farmland and community life. Towns were incorporated along the rail lines, including Hinckley in 1874 and Sandstone in 1889, and railroad stations were built in Friesland, Miller Station (later Groningen), Partridge (later Askov), Finlayson, Rutledge, Willow River, and Sturgeon Lake. Other settlements, driven by logging, the expansion of the railroads, or farming, were founded throughout the county, including Beroun, Brook Park, Bruno, Denham, Cloverdale, Nickerson, Kerrick, Duquette, Cloverton, Markville, Kingsdale, and Belden.

As the towns grew, so did local industries such as quarrying and farming. Businesses, schools, churches, organizations, and recreational activities developed to serve the employment, educational, religious, and social needs of residents. Photographs of these institutions and activities will tell the stories and depict the daily lives of the people who called Northern Pine County home.

Life was not always peaceful in Northern Pine County. On September 1, 1894, a massive fire storm swept through a large portion of the area, killing hundreds of people and destroying towns, businesses, homes, bridges, and nearly every other human-built structure. Through photographs, we will tell the story of this fire and its survivors, including the Samuelson family, who lived just north of Friesland and were saved, almost miraculously, in a root cellar. We will also present the fire of 1918, which devastated the northern tier of the county, and a variety of smaller, yet still significant, disasters, including train wrecks and the 1909 Sandstone school fire.

Finally, we will feature photographs of a few of Northern Pine County's citizens and families, once again emphasizing the successes, sorrows, joys, and trials of Northern Pine County's people.

SUGGESTED READINGS

Bjorkman, Edna, and Robert David Olson. *Courage in a Rugged Land: Bruno, Minnesota.* St. Cloud, MN: Northstar Press, 2005.

Brown, Daniel James. *Under a Flaming Sky: The Great Hinckley Firestorm of 1894.* Guilford, CT: The Lyons Press, 2006.

Cordes, Jim. *Pine County . . . and its Memories.* North Branch, MN: Jim Cordes, 1989.

Johnson, Lois E. *Sturgeon Lake: 100 Years of History.* Sturgeon Lake, MN: Lois E. Johnson, 2001.

Langseth, Muriel, ed. *Sandstone, the Quarry City.* Sandstone, MN: Sandstone History Club, 1989.

Larsen, Lawrence H. *Wall of Flames: The Minnesota Forest Fire of 1894.* Fargo, ND: The North Dakota Institute for Regional Studies, 1984.

Manni, Edwin E. *Kettle River, Automba, Kalevale and Surrounding Area History.* n.p.: Edwin Manni, 1977.

Popowitz, Coral. *Willow River: Flowing through the Centuries.* Mora, MN: Kanabec Publications, 1991.

Swenson, Grace Stageberg. *From the Ashes: The Story of the Hinckley Fire of 1894.* St. Cloud, MN: Northstar Press, 1988.

Walker, Ellen. *Early Sandstone and Its Schools.* Sandstone, MN: Ellen Walker, 1979.

Ziegler, Frank. *Ken-a-Big: The Story of Kanabec County.* Ed. Robert H. Beck. Mora, MN: B&W Printers, 1981.

One

The Earliest Days

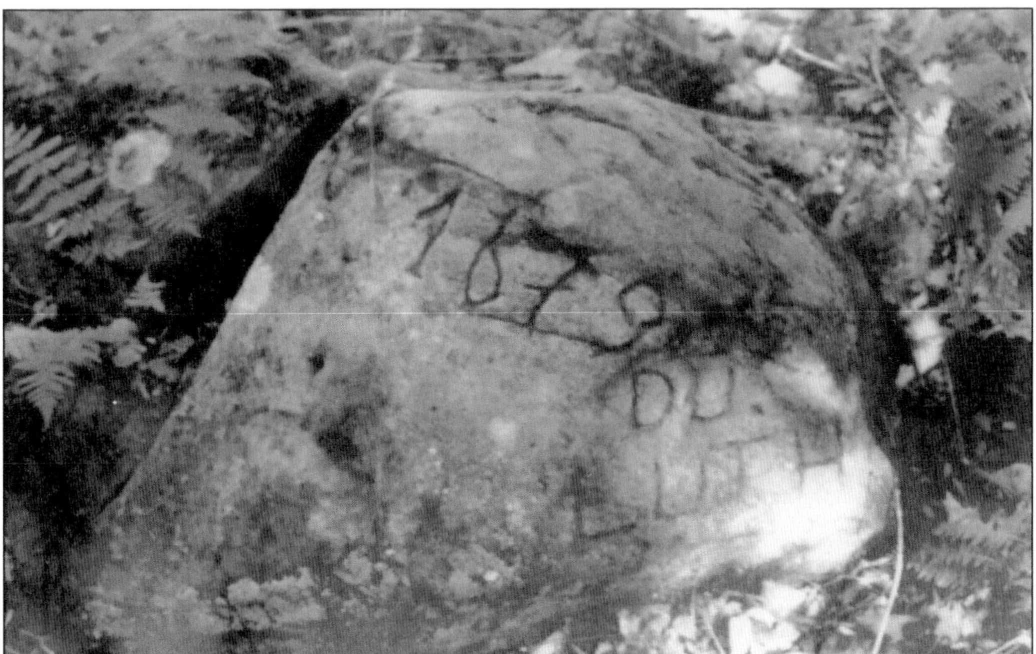

Early explorers traversed Northern Pine County, learning about the new world and interacting with native people. Daniel Greysolon, *Sieur du L'hut*, left his mark on a boulder in a forest east of Askov. The name "Du Luth" and date "1679," the year of the expedition, were carved into the stone, which was recently authenticated by American Petrographic Services.

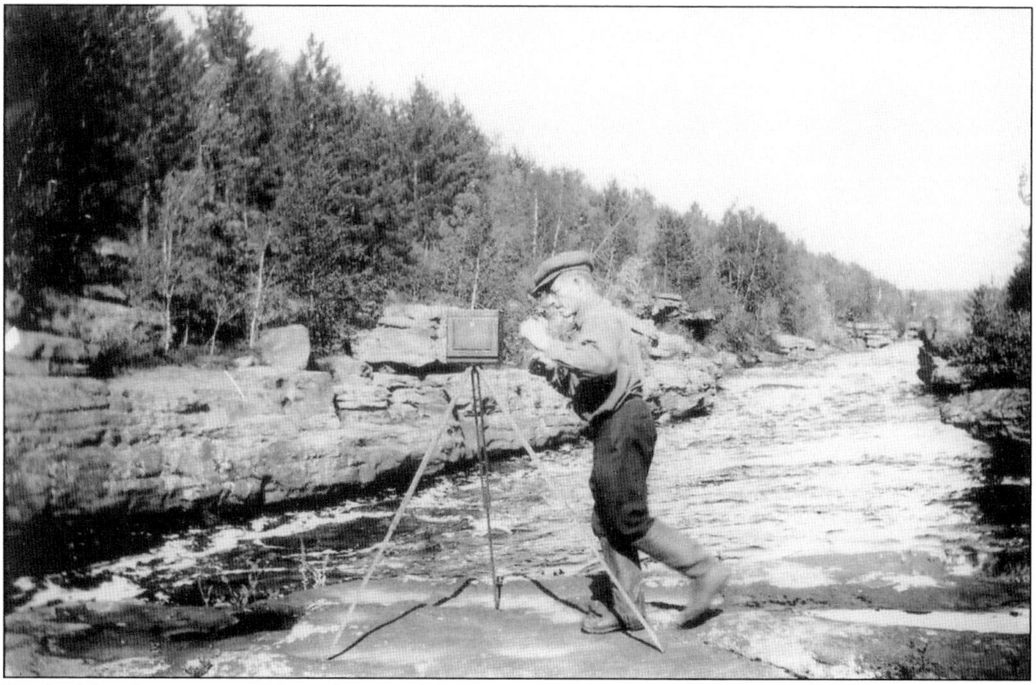

Books like this one would not be possible without the photographers of the past who recorded their world on film. In this 1910 photograph, Philip Hansen was preparing his camera to capture a scene on the Kettle River near Sandstone.

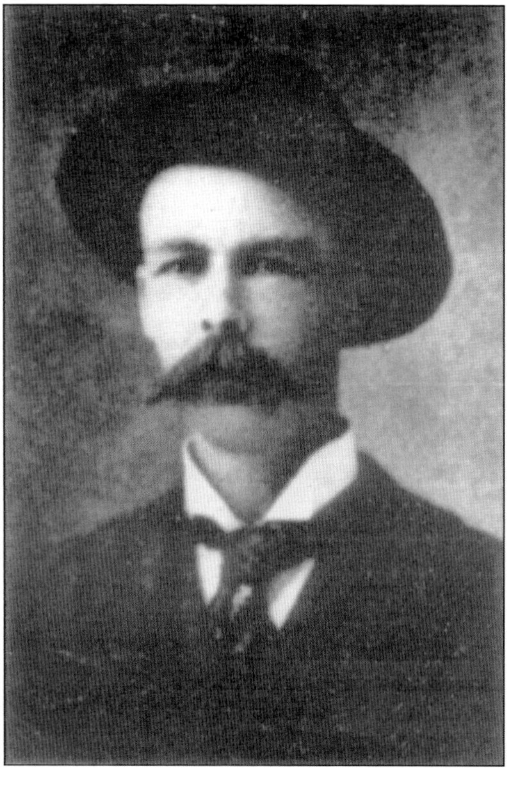

William Poole was another Northern Pine County photographer who took countless pictures and contributed to the preservation of the area's history. Poole owned two photograph galleries in Pine City and even traveled through Minnesota in a photo wagon.

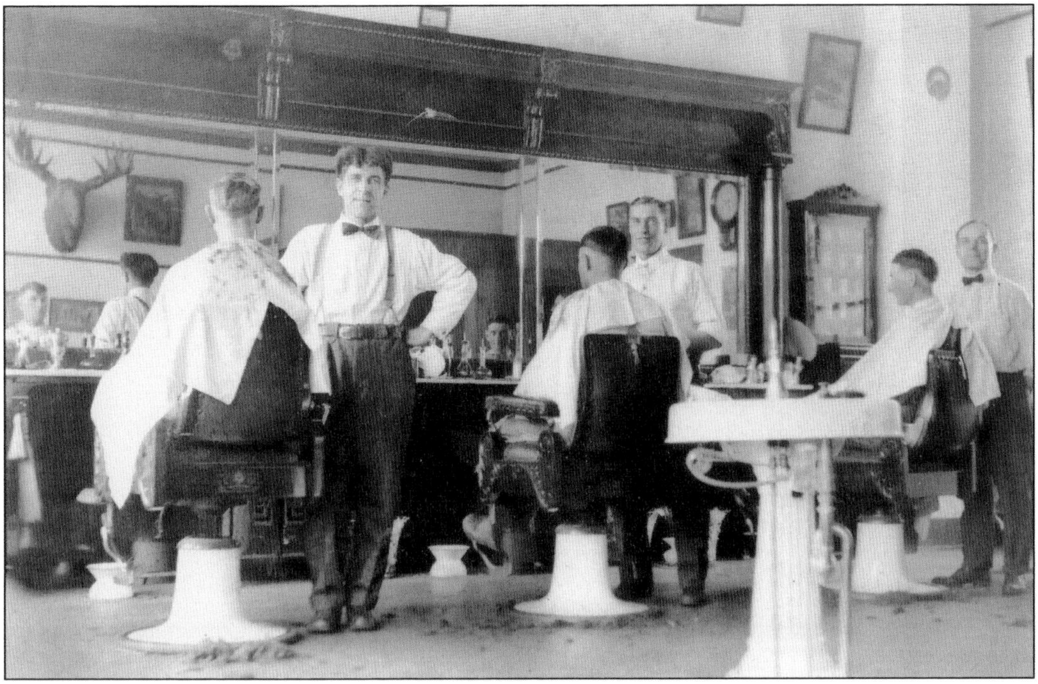

Bill Bantleon, a Pine City barber, was an amateur photographer, a rarity in the age before cameras were common in every home. He was quite the character with his red bow tie, red suspenders, and pompadour hairstyle.

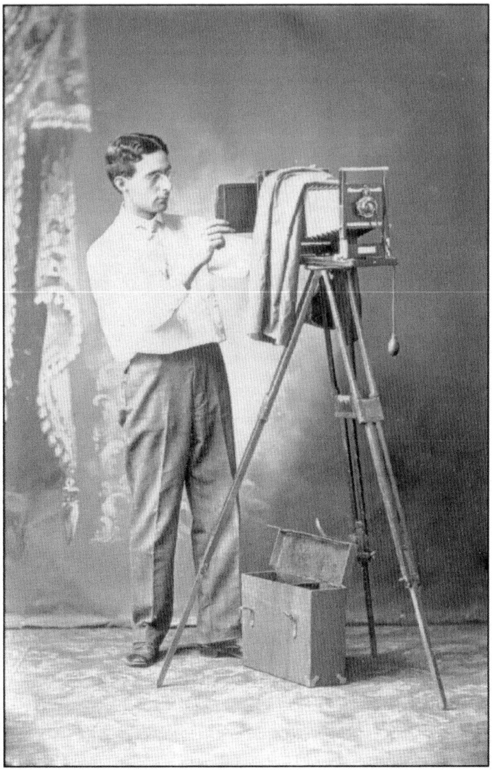

Ross Daniels was a Sandstone photographer for many years. He specialized in postcards and seemed to have a knack for setting up his camera at just the right moment to capture exciting events, including the 1909 Sandstone school fire. This photograph was taken at Daniels's Pine City studio.

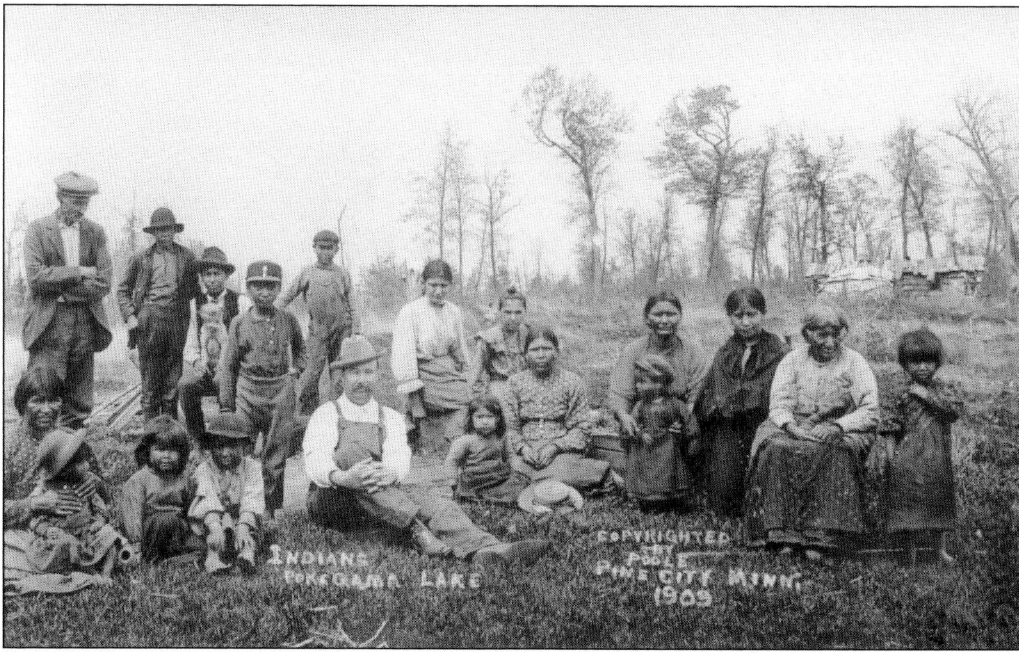

The Anishinabeg people, today called the Ojibway, have lived in Northern Pine County for hundreds of years. Their traditional name means "spontaneous or original people" and refers back to their creation stories. This group posed near Pokegama Lake in 1909. Note the birch bark wigwam and log cabin in the background.

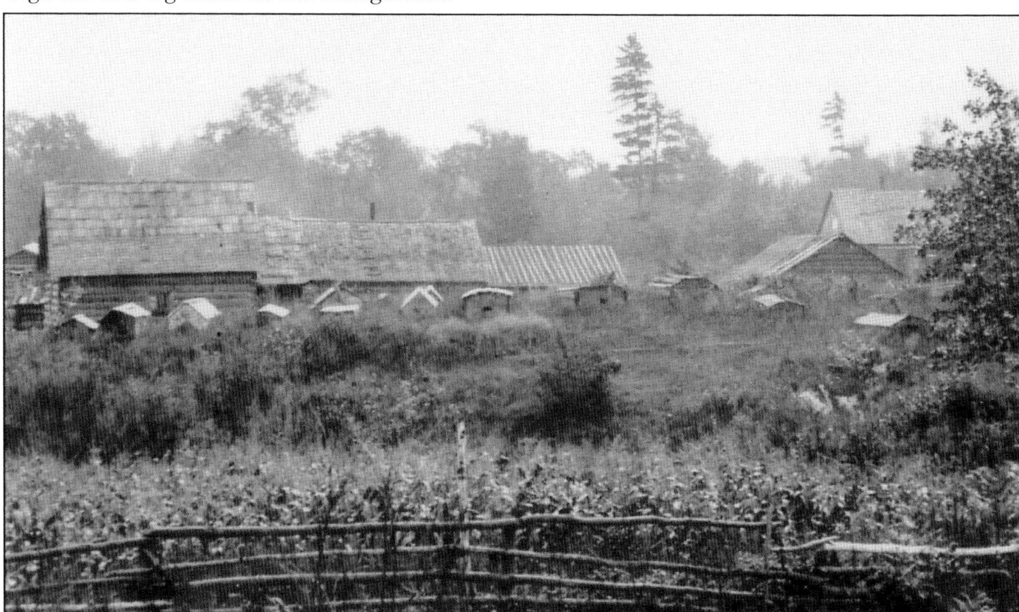

This 1910 picture of the Upper Tamarack Indian Village shows the village burial grounds. The miniature houses were individual grave sites. Each "soul house" covered a shallow grave and had a small window with a ledge where relatives of the deceased placed foods, like maple sugar or cooked berries, as gifts. The graves were typically marked with the deceased's totem, which showed his or her family connections.

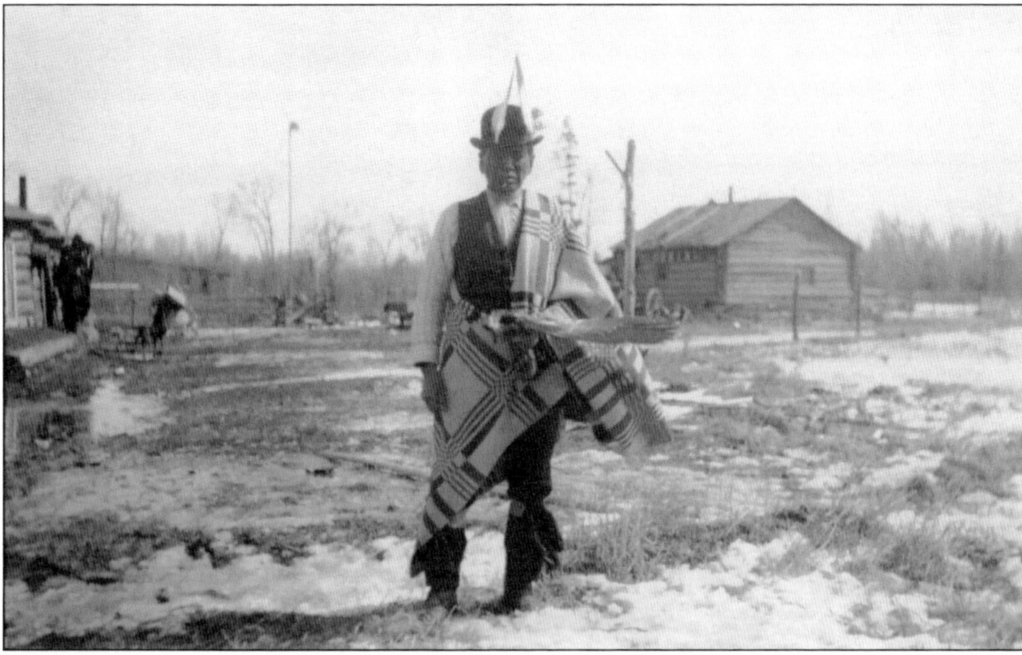

Chief Songkatay lived in a village north of Markville. He was 100 years old when this picture was taken. Note his feathered headdress and intricately beaded bag.

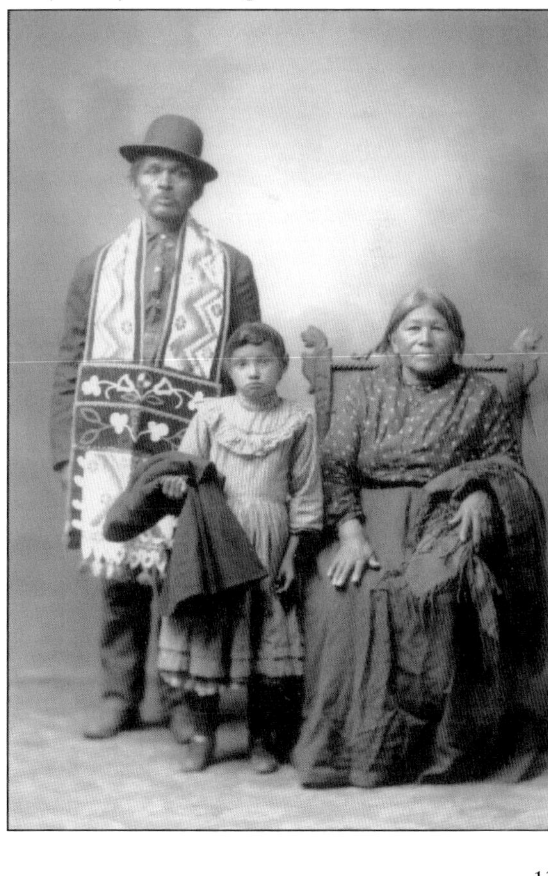

Sam Clark, Julia Clark, and Anna Tewasusch Clark posed for this photograph in 1912. By this time, the Anishinabeg had adopted many of the white man's customs. The blend of cultures is shown clearly in the clothing styles chosen by the Clark family.

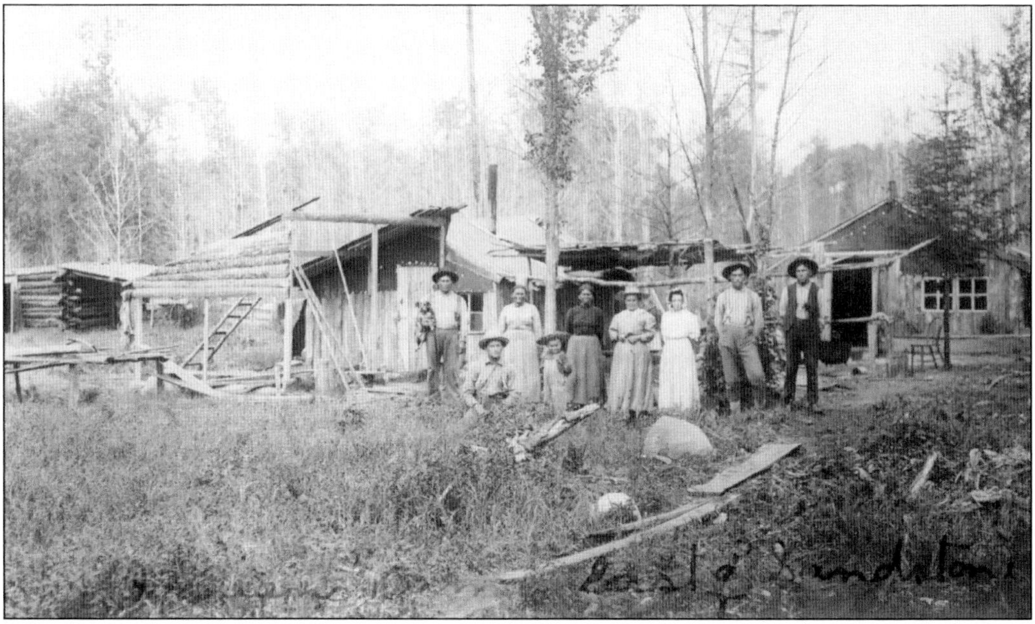

Anishinabeg villages were made up of log buildings, birch bark wigwams, and canvas tents. Numerous Anishinabeg communities still existed throughout Northern Pine County around 1900. Residents generally lived off the land: maple syrup and maple sugar in the spring; fish, gardening, and berries in the summer; wild rice and wild game in the fall; and wild game in the winter.

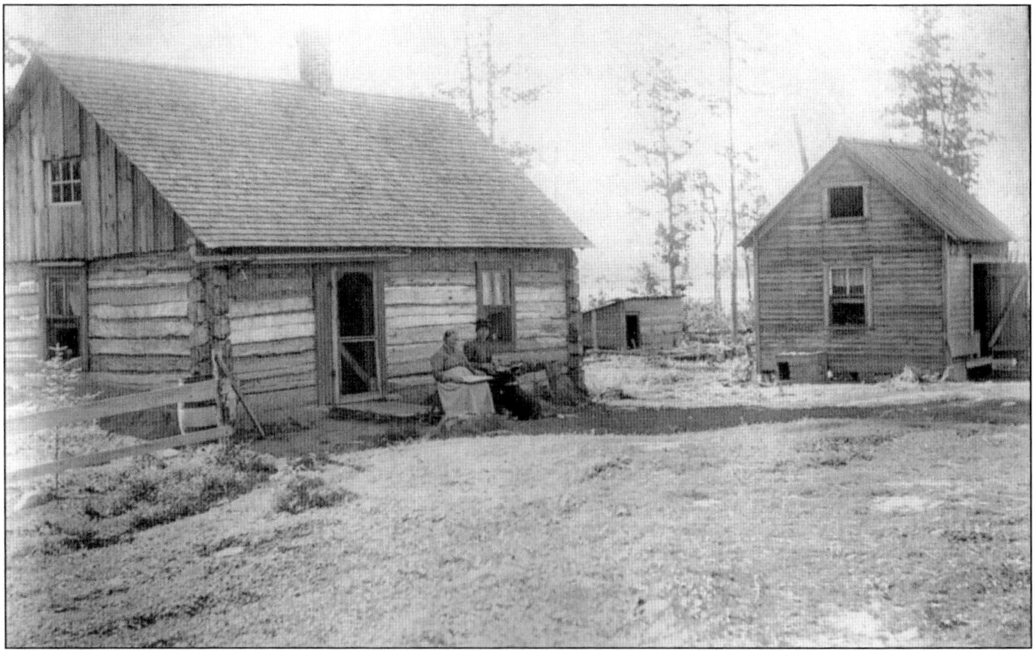

While the Anishinabeg dwellings look pretty primitive by modern standards, the homes of Northern Pine County's European settlers were not much different. Settlers generally did not move into the northern regions of the county until after 1870 when the railroad had been built and logging companies had begun clearing the land. This photograph shows a typical late-19th-century log home and outbuildings near Hinckley.

Pine County was established in 1856, two years before Minnesota became a state. It once included all or part of Kanabec, Mille Lacs, Carlton, and Aitkin Counties in East Central Minnesota. The county was organized with its current boundaries in 1872. Notice the temporary Doty and Superior Counties in Northern Minnesota. These existed for only a short time.

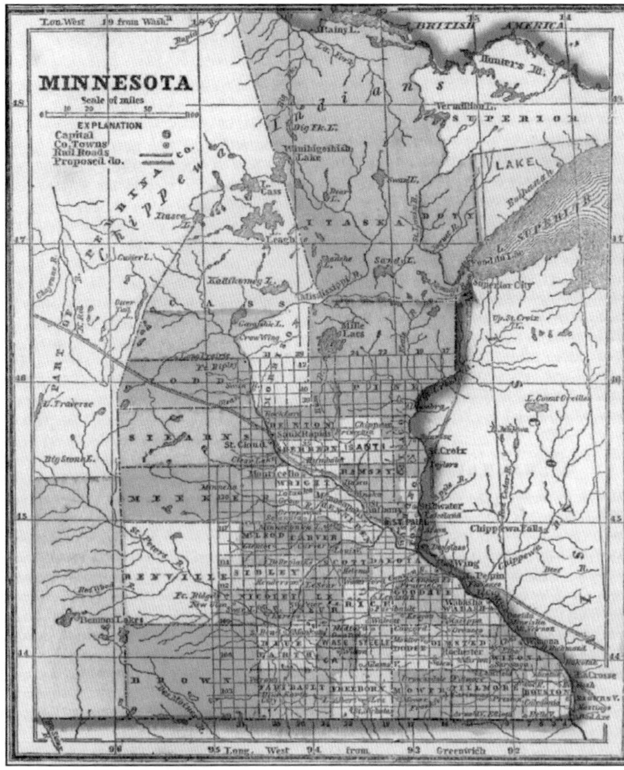

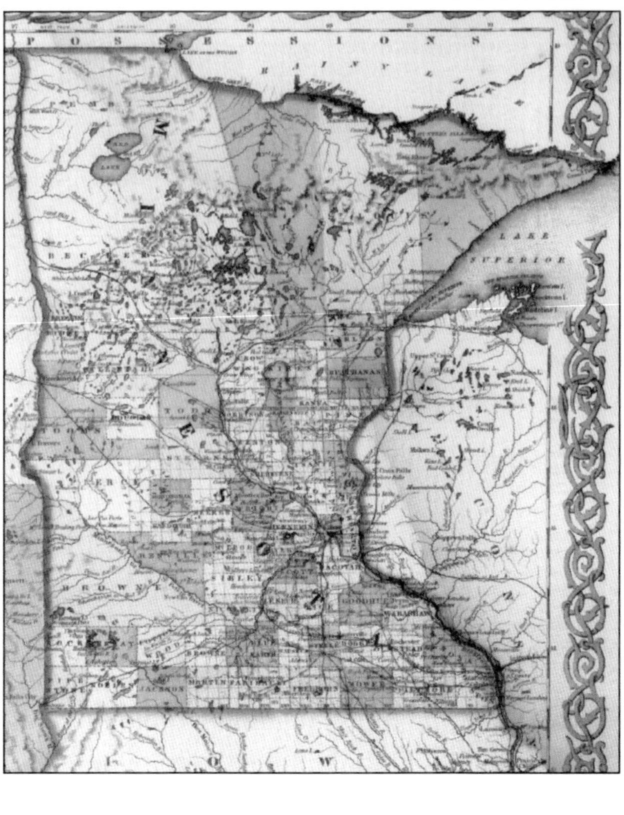

For a brief period in the 1850s, Northern Pine County was actually Buchanan County. The southern border of the new county ran just north of Hinckley, which was not incorporated until 1874. The town of Fortuna was platted in 1857 as the Buchanan County seat, but it was never settled. Buchanan County, population 12, was dissolved in 1860 and reunited with Pine County.

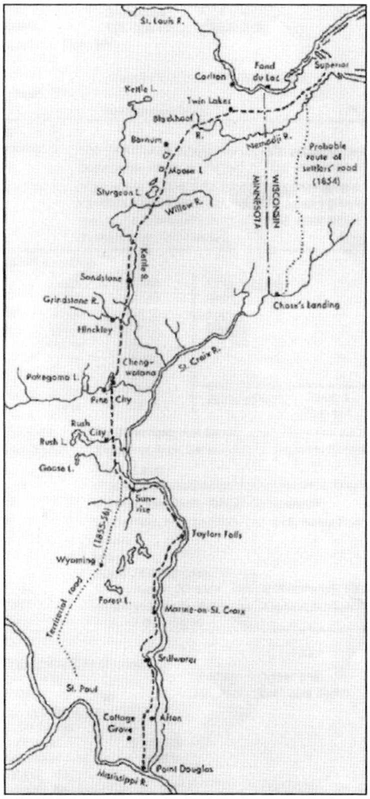

In 1850, the Minnesota Territorial Government approved the building of five military roads intended to ease travel for the settlers who had begun to spread throughout the territory. The Point Douglas to Superior Military Road passed through Pine County to connect the Mississippi with the Great Lakes. Surveying and construction for the Military Road lasted seven years (1851–1857), and the road was never completed.

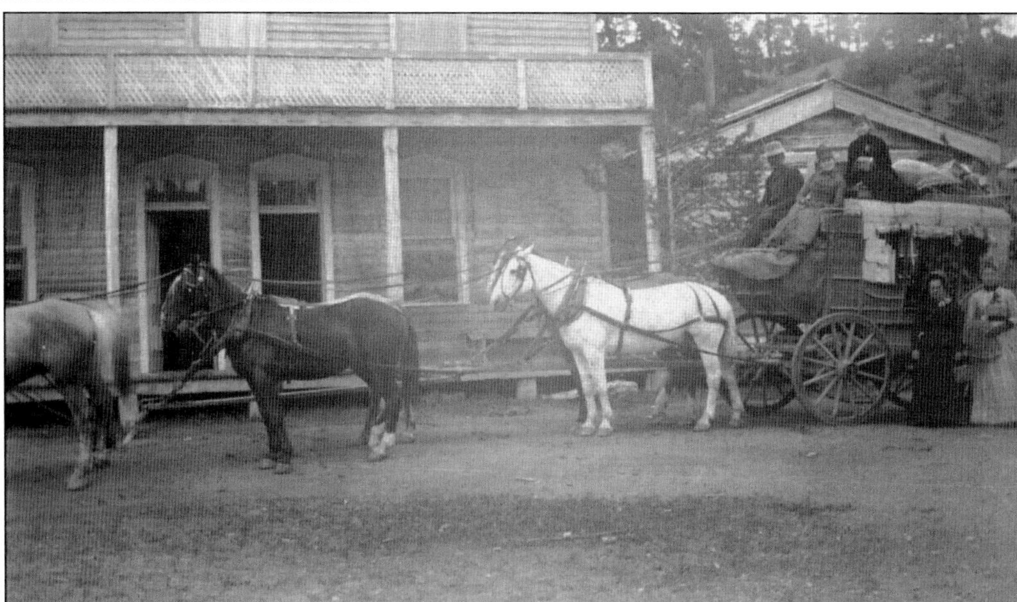

A stagecoach ran along the Military Road from 1861 to 1870, carrying passengers and mail. The stages, which were pulled by four to six horses, were usually known as "Concord coaches" because they were built in Concord, New Hampshire. The route was operated by the St. Paul firm Burbank, Merrian, and Company.

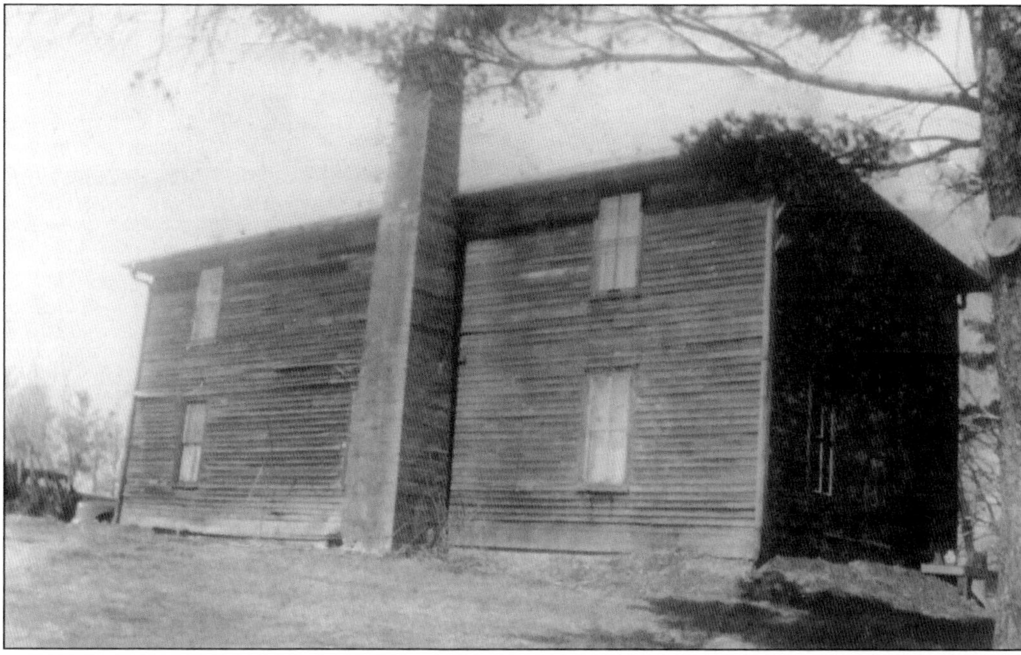

Stage stops, like this one at Twin Lakes, lined the road, providing horses and passengers with necessary breaks during the rough, muddy journey. A usual stage trip took six days, and it was not recommended for women and children. The heyday of the Military Road ended in 1870 when the railroad became the primary way to travel between St. Paul and Duluth, but portions of the road are still used today.

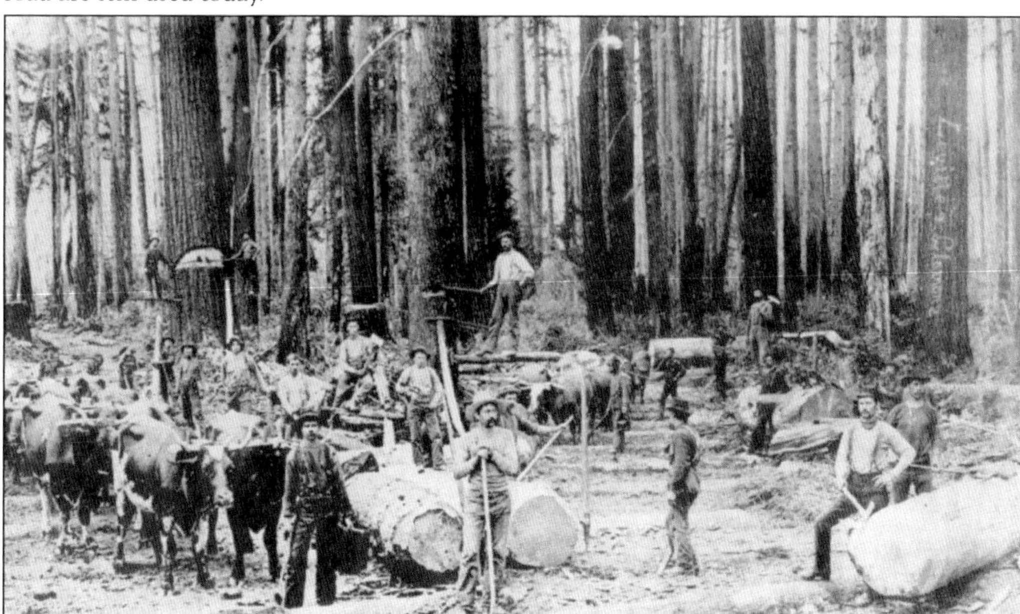

Northern Pine County was once covered by majestic forests of white, Norway, and jack pine. In fact, 665,000 of the county's 906,366 acres were forested and provided prime timber for enterprising lumber companies that began their logging operations in the 1860s. Hundreds of lumberjacks soon converged on the forests, and trees fell by the thousands.

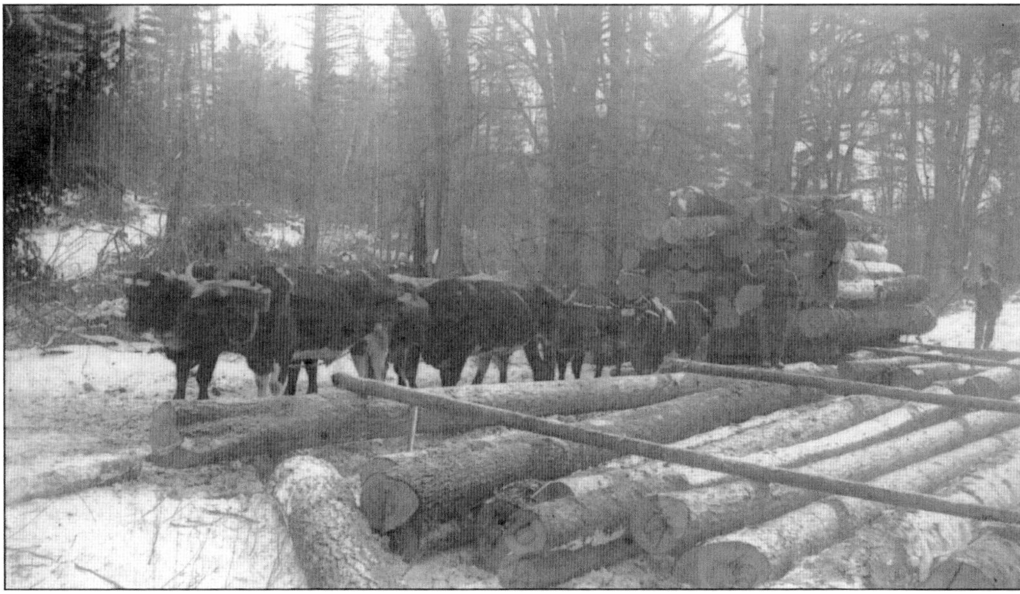

Cruisers were the first lumberjacks to reach a new stand of pine. They platted each stand and prepared for the undercutters, who marked the trees, and the sawyers, who felled them. Swampers cut off the trees' limbs and created trails on which to skid the logs out to the main road. Loggers, called "road monkeys," kept the trails and roads well iced so logs would skid smoothly.

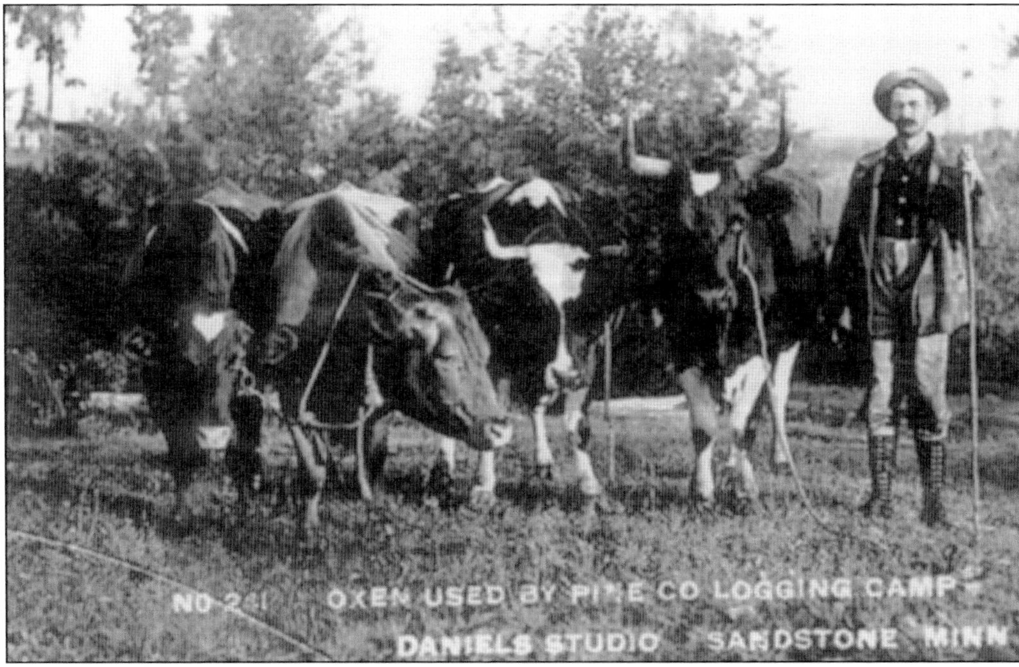

Oxen were used to skid logs to the main road. These animals were sturdy and steady but also stubborn. One lumberjack remarked that while he had seen many teams of oxen pull heavy loads out of the woods, he had never seen one go back into the woods without been driven. Perhaps they were smart enough to realize that if they went back, they would soon be skidding more logs.

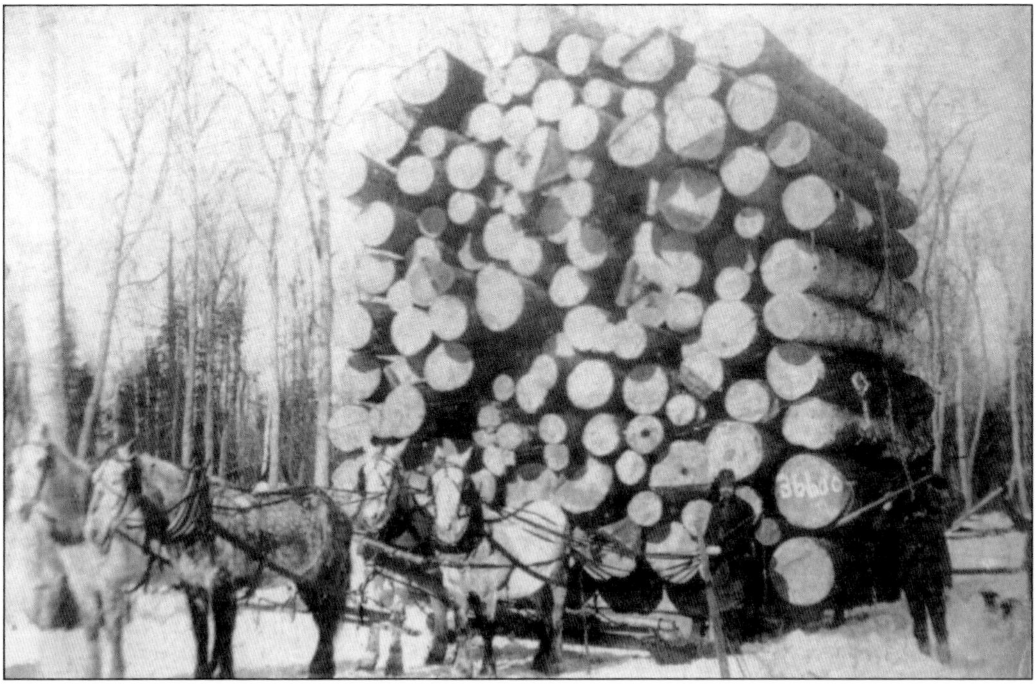

When the logs arrived at the main road, the teamster and loaders rolled the logs on to sleds. As the stack grew higher, they lifted them with ropes and pulleys. Most loads were six to eight tiers high, but some, like the one pictured here, were stacked merely for show. Lumberjacks enjoyed finding out how many logs they could pile up without the whole stack crashing down.

This show load was created by the Rutledge Lumber Company's camp. Fifty-six logs were stacked to a height of 26 feet and a top width of 20.5 feet. With the sled and chains, the load weighed about 4 tons. This show load was actually hauled about 4 miles by two teams of horses on February 22, 1895, making it the largest load ever pulled by horses.

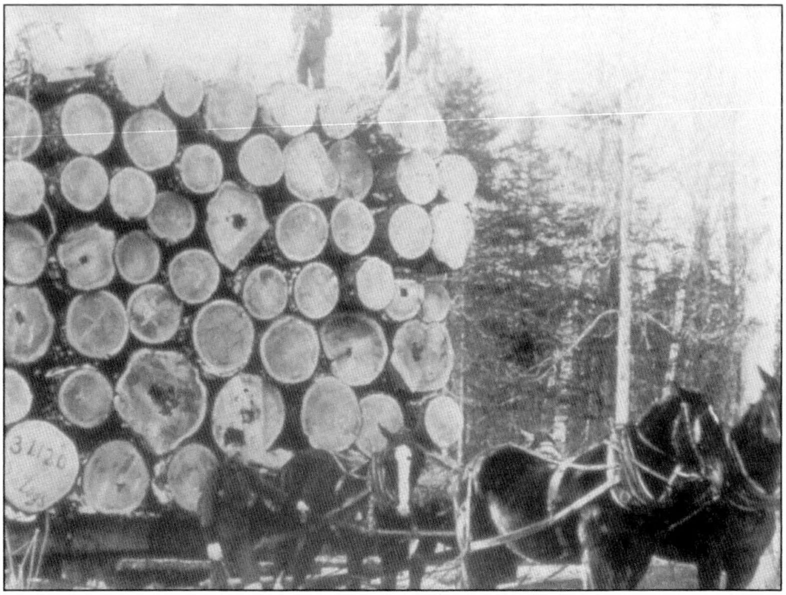

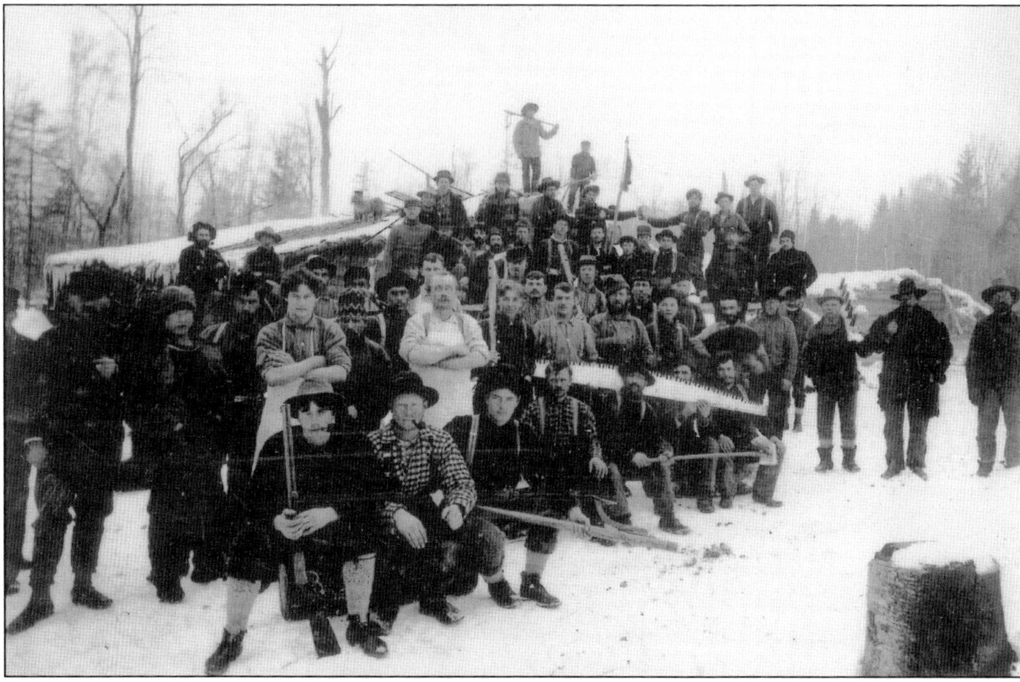

Lumberjack life was not easy. The work was hard, the weather was cold (most logging was done in the winter when logs could be slid along the ice), the camp was crowded, and privacy was nonexistent. At least the food was plentiful and usually at least satisfying if not even quite good, unless, of course, the "hashslinger" (cook) was a "stomach robber" (bad cook).

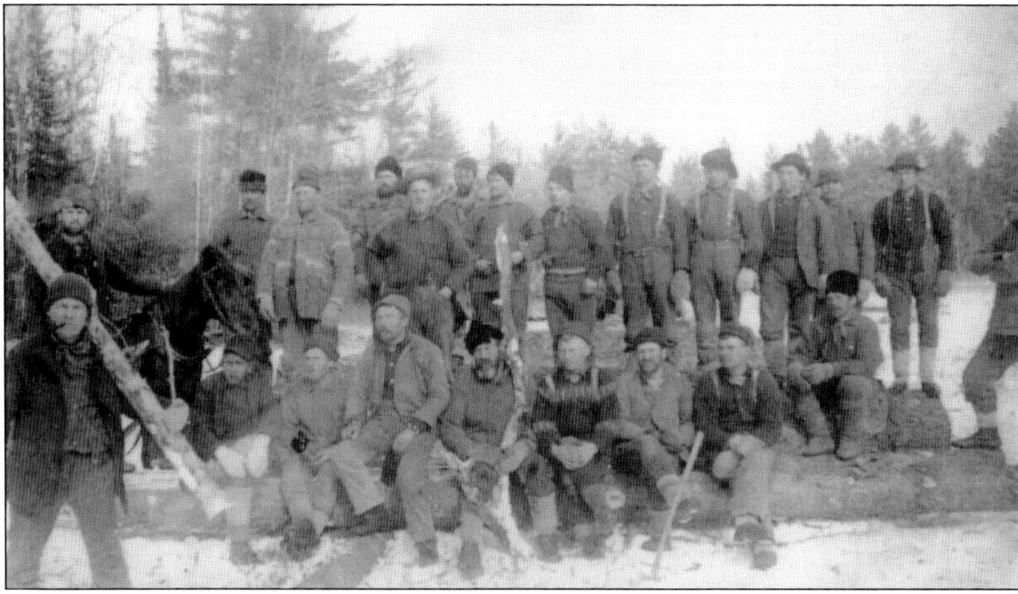

Men of all nationalities worked together in the lumber camps. Germans, Swedes, Norwegians, and Irishmen, many of whom were new immigrants, found jobs in the pineries, often making more money than they ever had before and probably working at least twice as hard. Language differences made for communication problems, but lumberjacks soon learned camp slang such as "swamp water" (tea), "hayburner" (horse), and "India silks" (overalls).

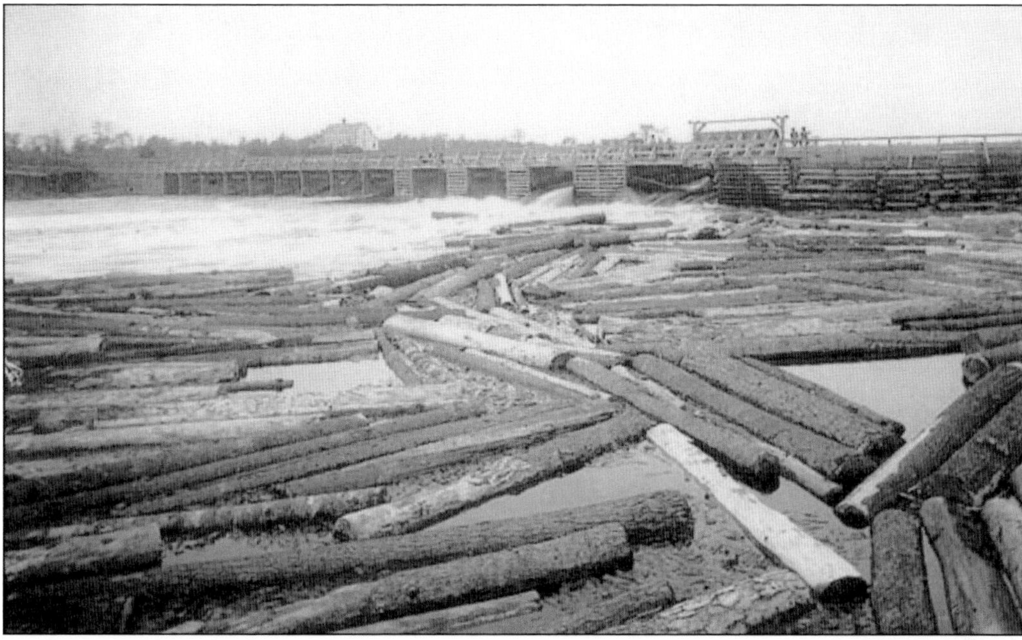

Loads of logs were hauled to the nearest river or stream and stacked on the banks to await the spring thaw. When spring came, the logs were rolled into the river to begin their trip south to the sawmills. Northern Pine County's elaborate system of waterways aided in the efficiency of the log drives as "river pigs" (log drivers) attempted to guide thousands of logs through the water.

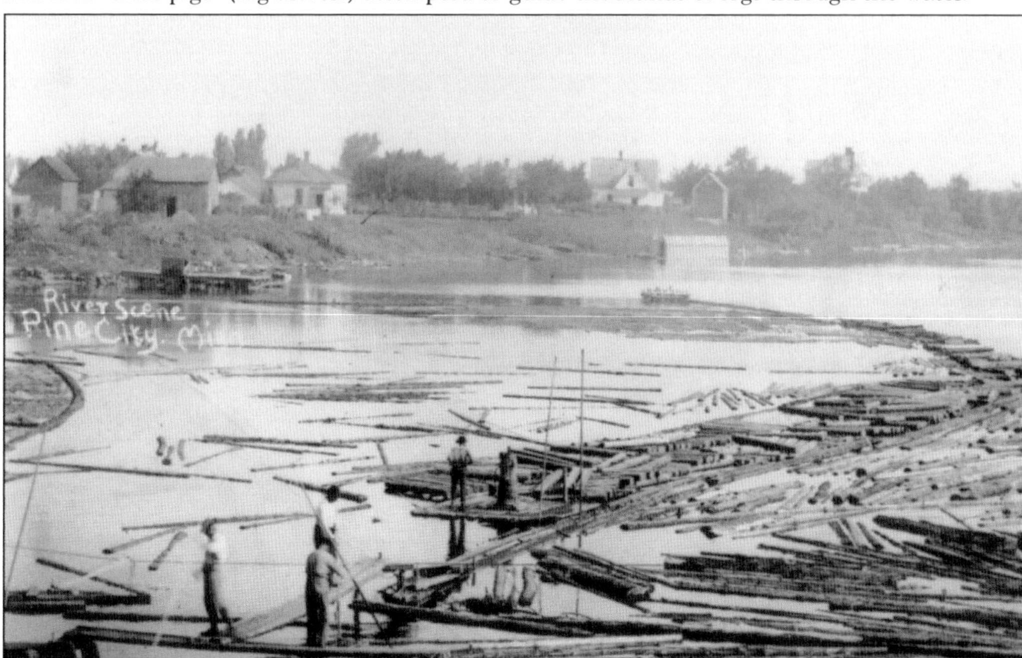

Lumber companies built dams along the waterways to control the flow of logs and try to avoid log jams, which occurred frequently. The log drivers in this picture were probably glad they did not have to deal with such an overflow of logs, but they still had plenty of work to do as they used peaveys, which are long, pointed poles, to keep the logs on the move.

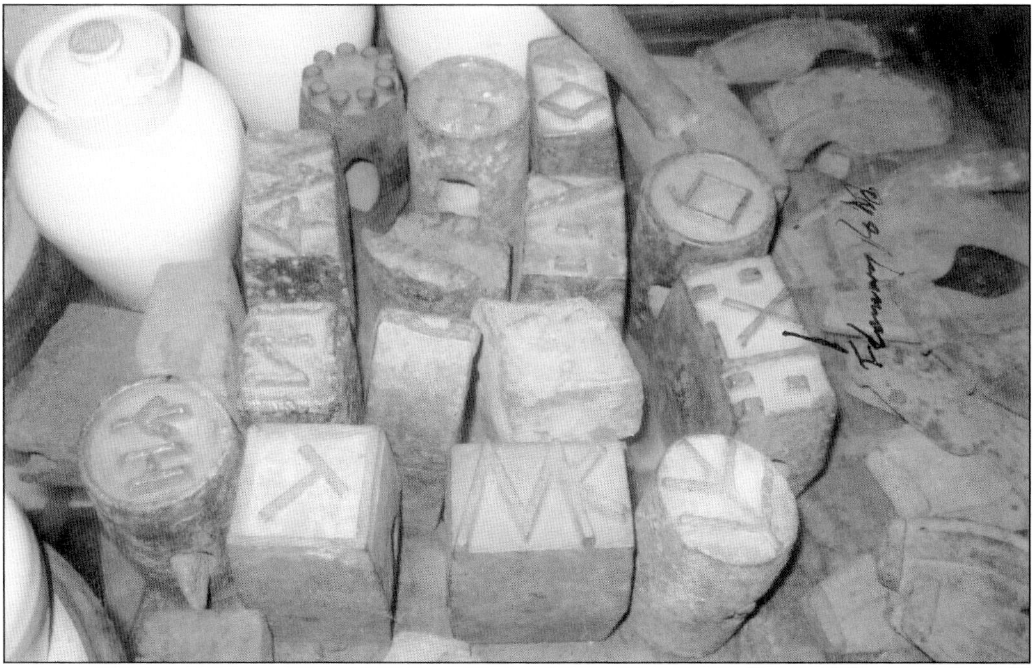

Before each log began its journey downstream, loggers used hammers like these to brand it with a unique symbol so sawmill workers could identify its owner. This system did not keep all lumberjacks honest. Less scrupulous companies cut logs on other people's lands, claiming, if they were caught, that they misjudged boundary lines. Notice the snuff jars on the left of the brands and the oxen shoes on the right. The collection shown here belongs to Richard Berglund.

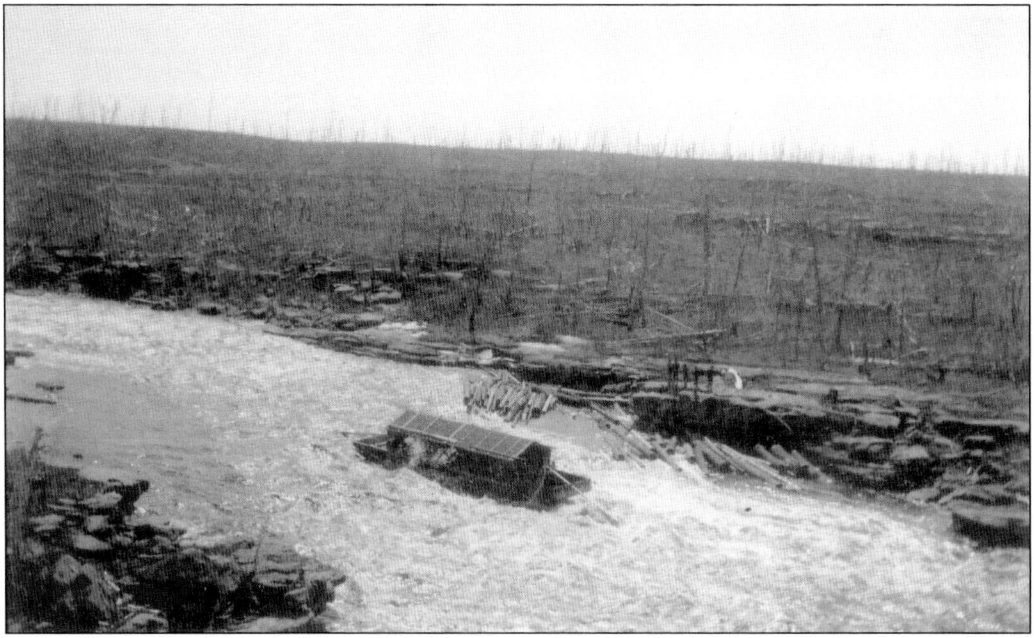

Wanagans, like this one on the Kettle River, floated after the logs. Cooks used these covered rafts to store supplies and prepare meals for the log drivers. This picture was taken after the 1894 fire. Notice the sparse, blackened landscape in the background.

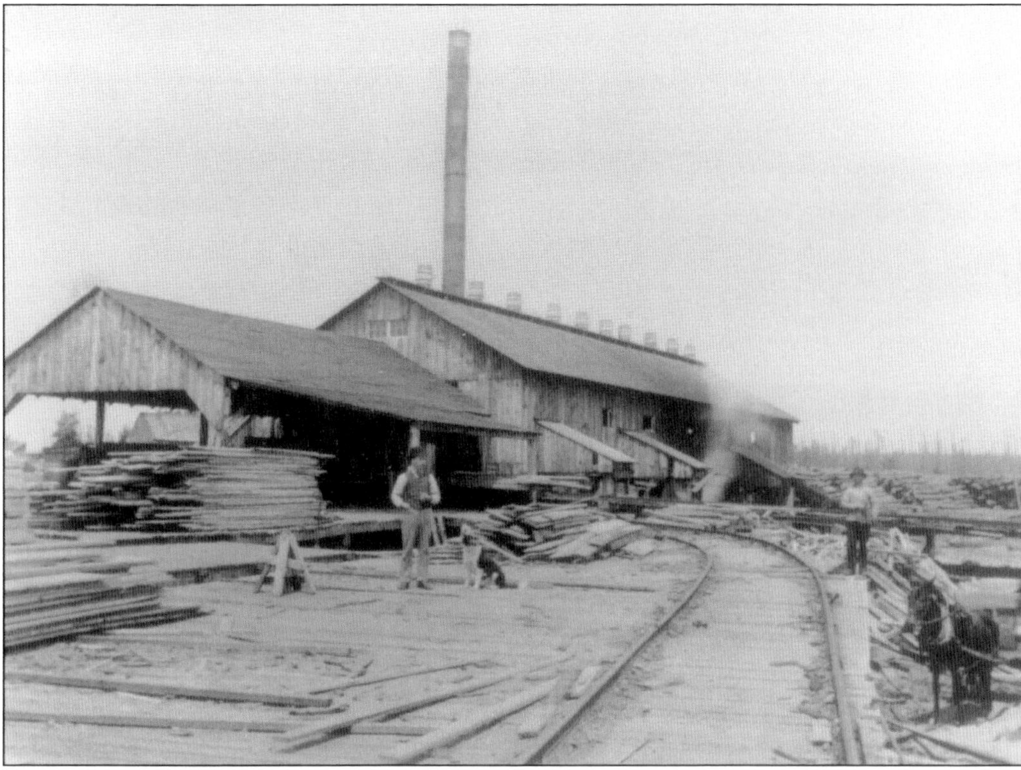

The Mission Creek lumber mill a few miles south of Hinckley was built, owned, and operated by the John B. Martin Lumber Company. Mill power was supplied by 100 teams of oxen. The company constructed the entire town of Mission Creek to house its employees and their families. The village was completely destroyed in the 1894 fire, but residents saved themselves by huddling together in a potato patch.

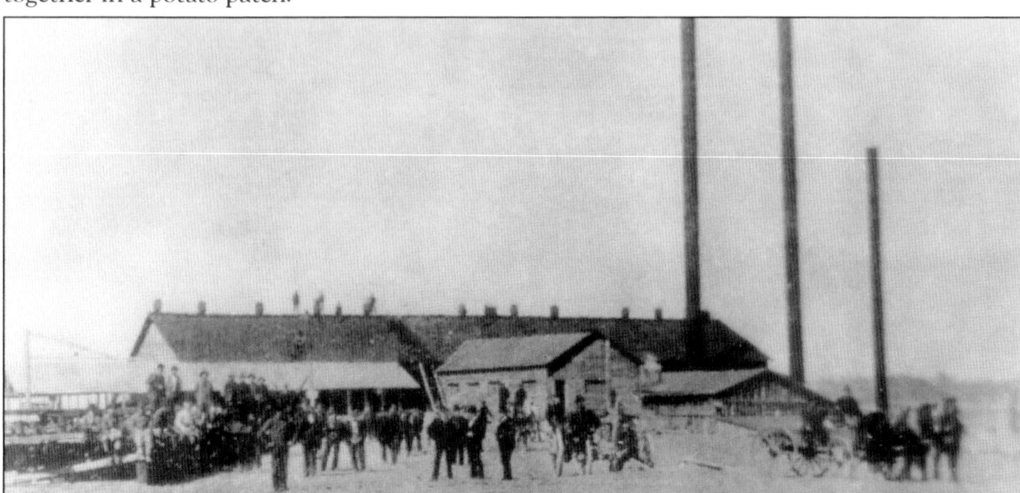

Willow River's Atwood Lumber Company was first called the Fox-Wisdom Lumber Company after its founders, Warren D. Fox and John Wisdom. At its peak, the sawmill employed 125 men and cut 125,000 feet of lumber daily. Logs were pulled into the mill on a steam-engine-powered ramp and cut to order. Barrels of water lined the mill's roof in case of fire.

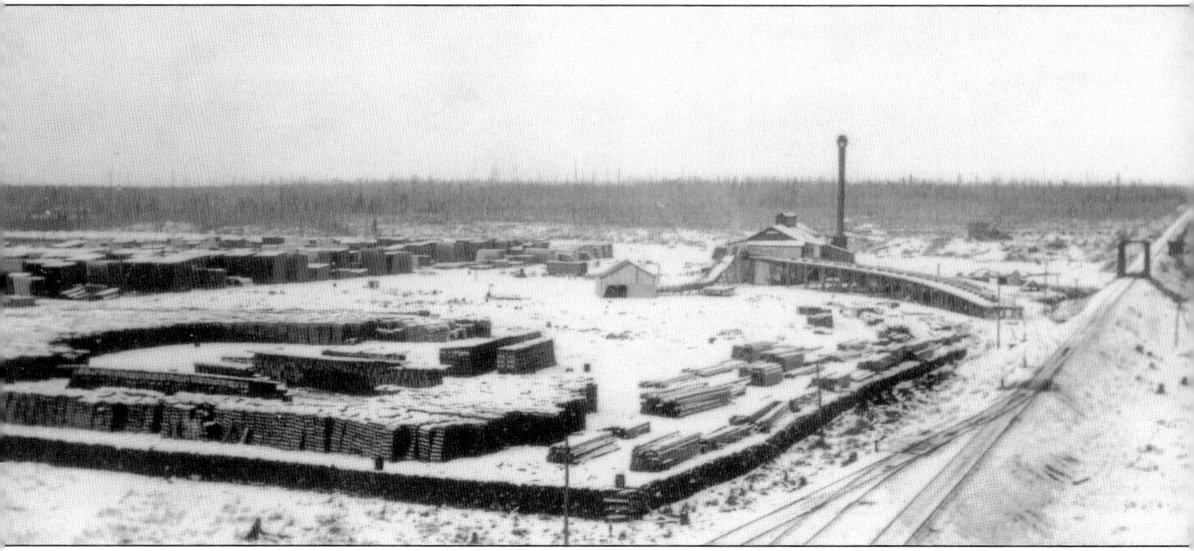

The Brennan Lumber Company sawmill in Hinckley was a highly successful operation until 1894. The mill crew was certain they could save the complex from fire. Barrels of water were strategically positioned along the roof so that workers could release several thousand gallons of water almost instantly. The Brennan mill was also protected by water mains and hydrants throughout the 36-acre complex on Hinckley's northern edge. In the end, the fire-prevention system failed. On September 1, 1894, about 28 million board feet of lumber was stacked in the open lumberyard. Around 4:15 p.m., the mill and yards literally exploded with the force of a nuclear bomb. The fire continued to burn for days. The mill was never rebuilt.

Two

Northern Pine County's Towns

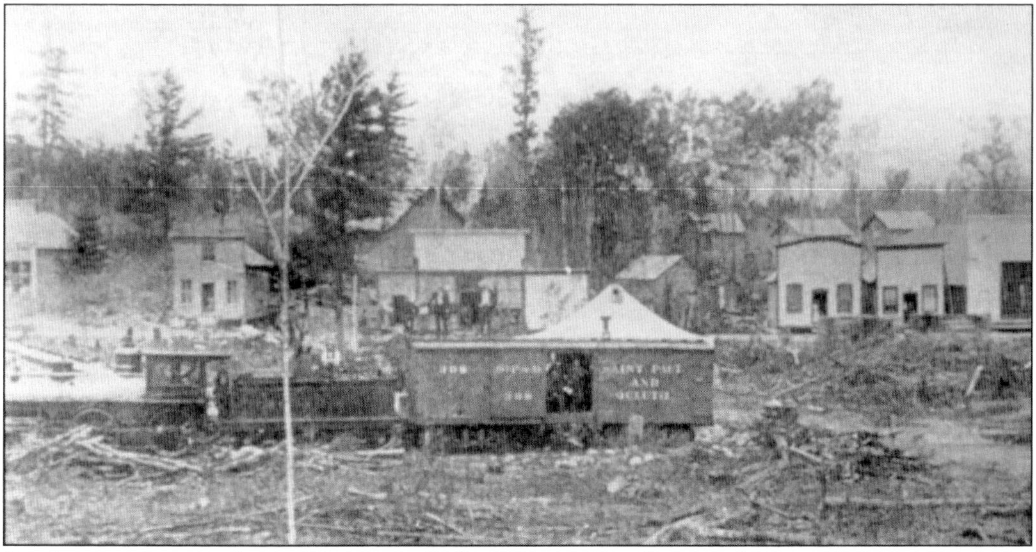

Sandstone was a small, unincorporated village when this photograph was taken in 1888. A few stores, several hotels, and two saloons made up the business district and served the workers who labored in the sandstone quarry founded in 1885. Sandstone was officially incorporated in 1889, the same year the Eastern Minnesota Railway connected the village to the Twin Cities.

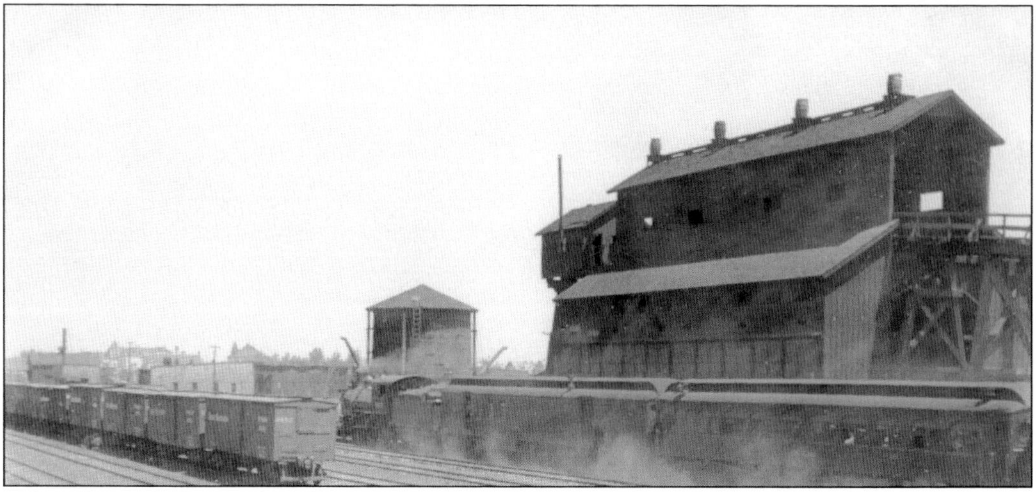

After the 1894 fire, railroad magnate James J. Hill decided to move the Eastern Minnesota Railway's division point from Hinckley to Sandstone. Construction on the new railroad yards began immediately. By 1895, a 20-stall roundhouse (the stone building visible in the background) was completed. A coal shed, water tank, depot, and several other buildings were soon added. At one point, 11 tracks stretched across the rail yard.

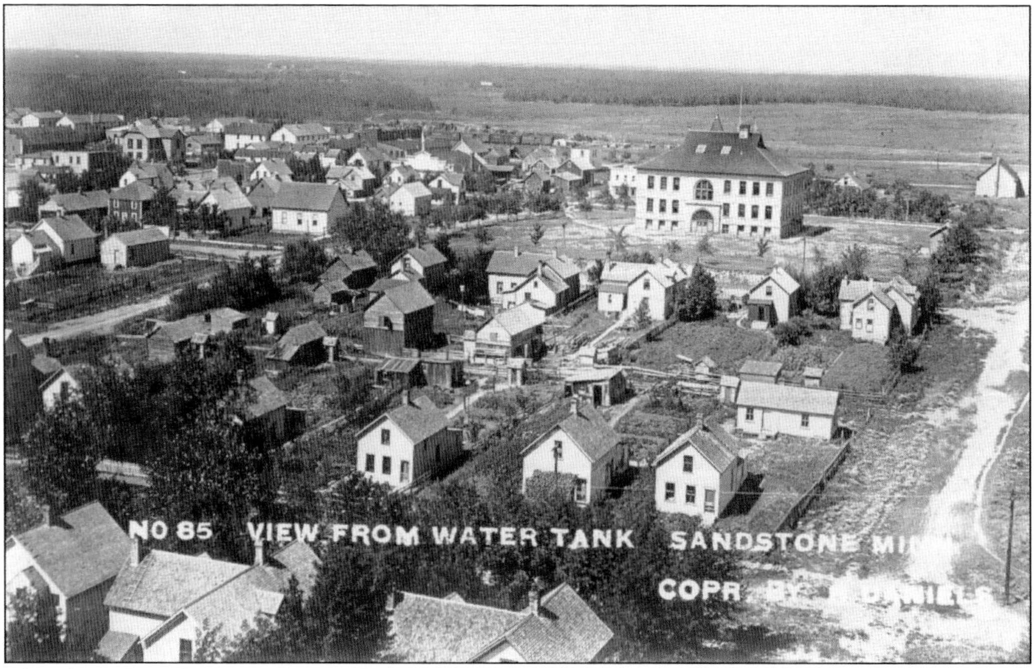

This shot of Sandstone was taken from the top of the water tower and looks west toward the town's center and 1901 schoolhouse. The three small houses in the foreground were "fire relief houses," built as part of the recovery effort after the 1894 forest fire had destroyed the village. The Fire Relief Commission helped many families build small, simple homes for between $125 and $190.

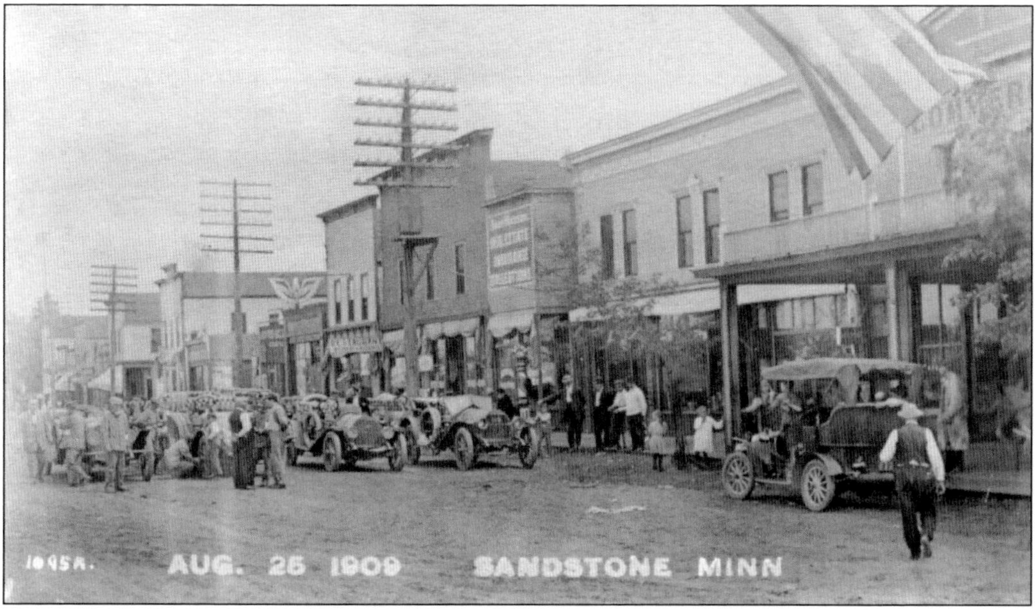

Automobile races were an exciting novelty in 1909. Drivers lined up on Sandstone's main street on August 26 to prepare for their race while spectators gathered along the board sidewalks. The Commercial Hotel, on the far right, was considered fancy for its day with 40 rooms and steam heat. It was destroyed by fire in 1926.

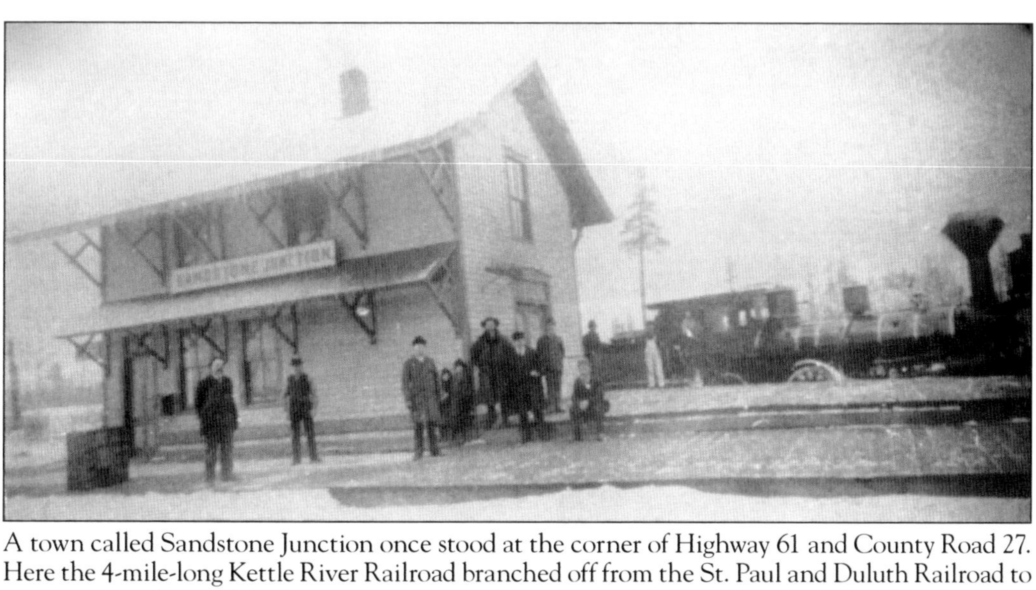

A town called Sandstone Junction once stood at the corner of Highway 61 and County Road 27. Here the 4-mile-long Kettle River Railroad branched off from the St. Paul and Duluth Railroad to transport supplies and sandstone to and from the quarry to the east. This picture of the Sandstone Junction depot was taken in the winter of 1888. The train was fondly called "Old Skally."

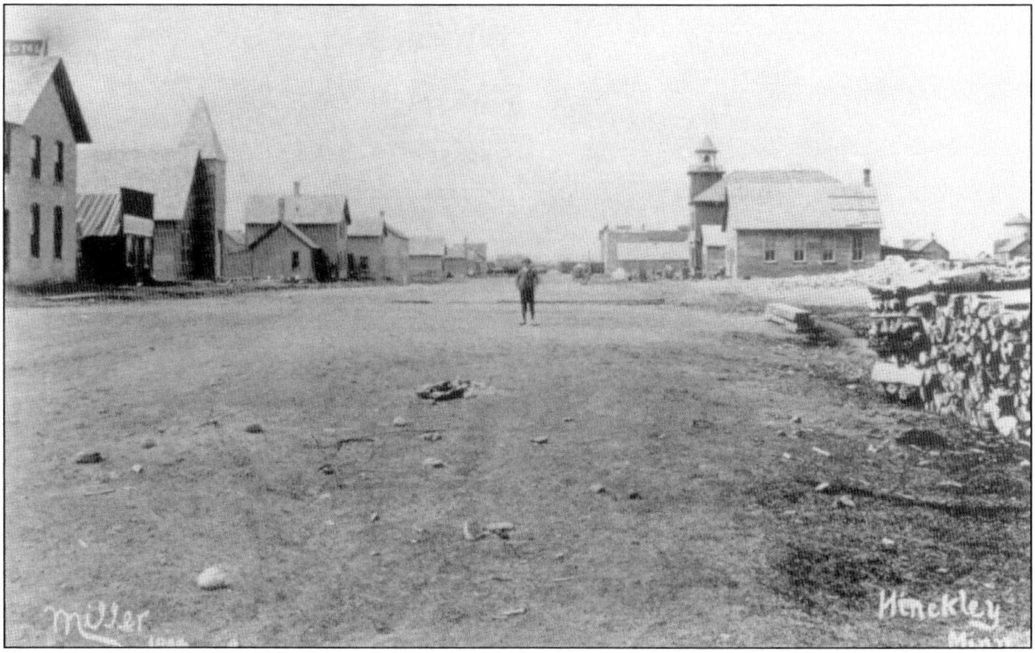

Hinckley was completely destroyed in the 1894 forest fire, but residents began to rebuild almost immediately. They constructed simple structures for their homes and businesses with help from the State Fire Relief Commission and donations from caring citizens. This photograph, taken shortly after the fire, shows new stores, churches, and a hotel.

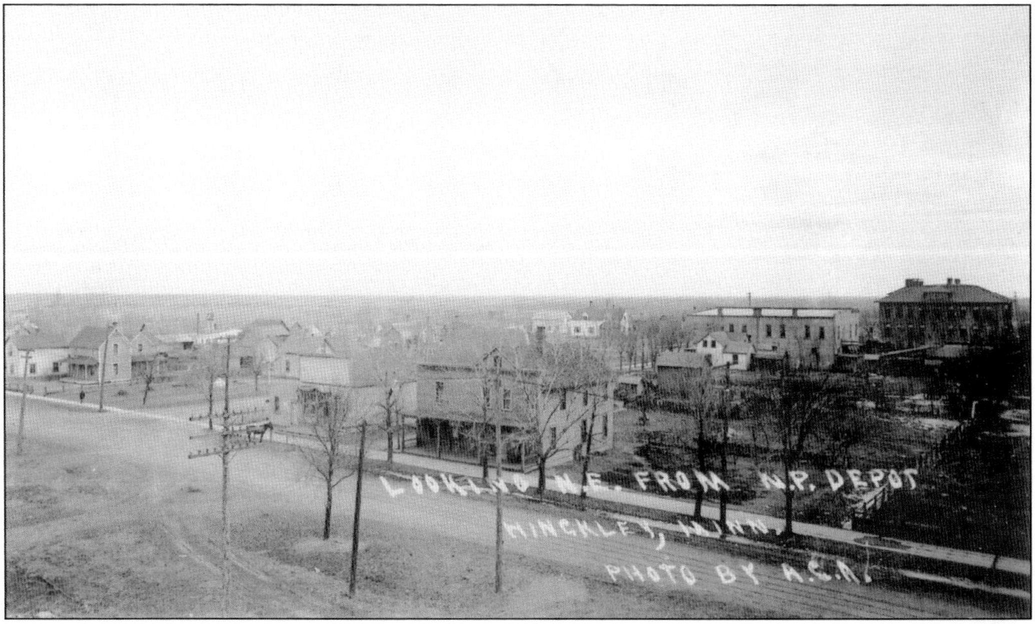

Hinckley was named for Isaac Hinckley, a Massachusetts man who held stock in the St. Paul and Duluth Railroad. It was originally incorporated as Central Station. This picture, taken from the Northern Pacific depot, captures the northeast part of town, including the 1911 brick schoolhouse. Notice the absence of trees on the horizon. The 1894 fire's effects were still visible even after over a decade.

Friesland was settled by Dutch immigrants who named their new community for their home province in the Netherlands. The Theodore Koch Land Company, which owned most of the land around Friesland, advertised heavily in Holland, hoping to attract settlers and assuring them of excellent soil quality. These advertisements conveniently neglected to mention the proliferation of rocks covering the area.

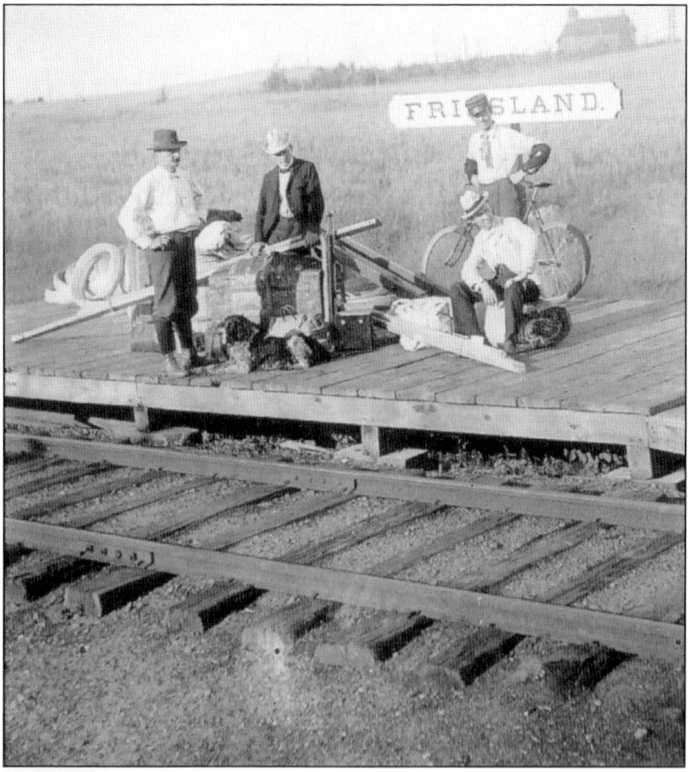

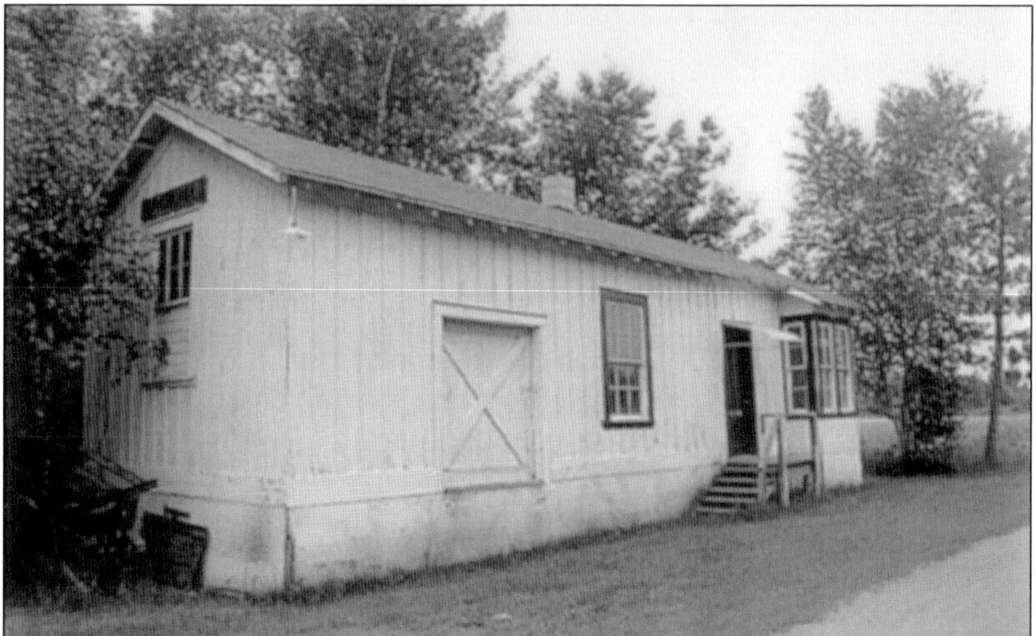

Miller Station was located northwest of Sandstone along the St. Paul and Duluth Railroad. Dutch settlers changed the village's name to Groningen after the 1894 fire. By 1918, Groningen was a flourishing little town with two general stores, a school, a garage, a barbershop, several blacksmiths, a bank, three cream buyers, and a potato warehouse.

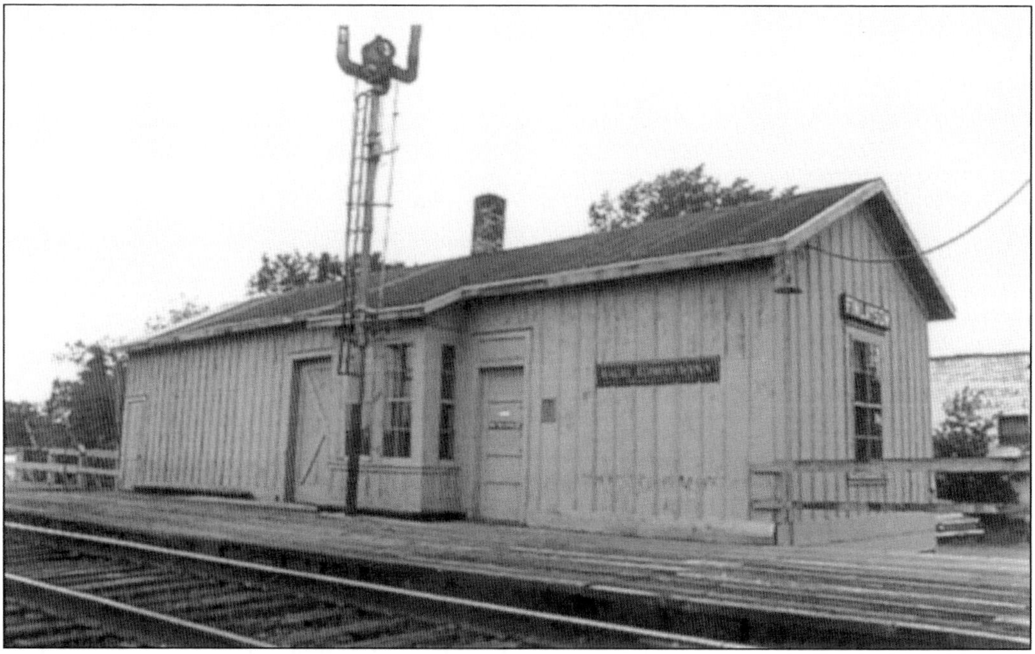

Finlayson, incorporated in 1905, is located northwest of Sandstone along the St. Paul and Duluth Railroad. The Finlayson area was largely settled by people of Finnish extraction, including John A. Oldenburg, who built a large house, the Villa Blanca, on the future town site in 1892. Although its name seems to reflect this Finnish heritage, the village was actually named for Scottish lumberman and sawmill owner David Finlayson.

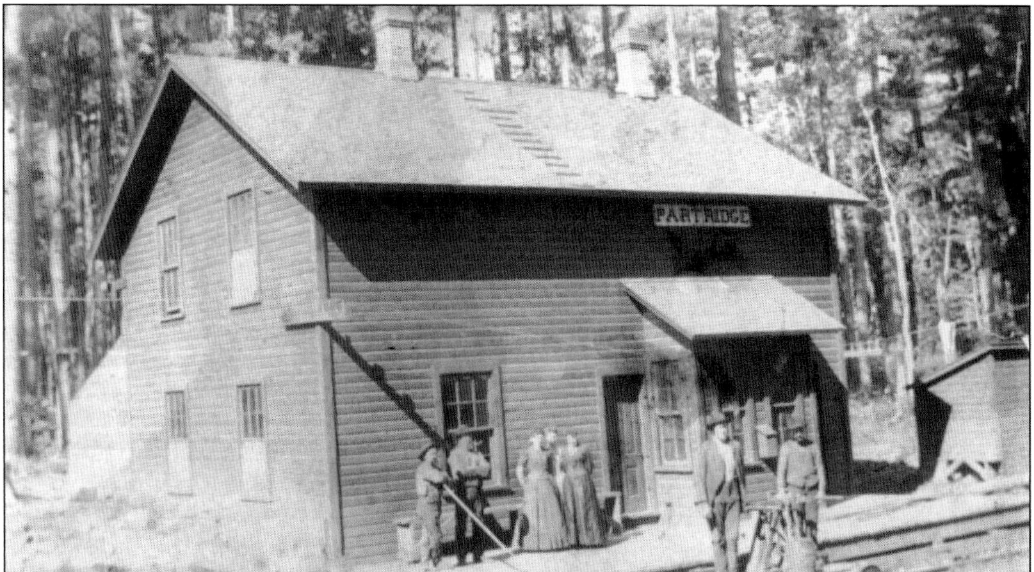

The town of Partridge, today called Askov, was settled in the late 1880s. In 1888, the Eastern Minnesota Railway built a depot there. By the mid-1890s, the village, population 50, boasted several houses, a hotel, the depot, a section house, a telegraph station, and a water tank. Everything except the water tank was destroyed in the 1894 forest fire.

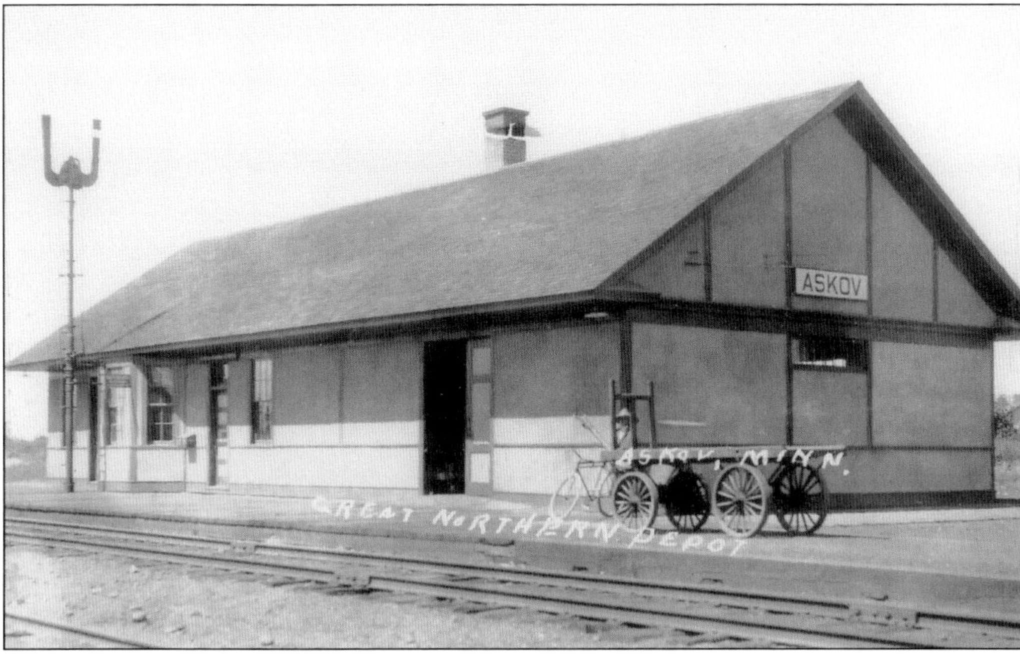

In 1905, the Dansk Folkesamfund Society purchased 20,000 acres in and around Partridge and sold lots to Danish settlers in hopes that Danish culture would flourish. It did. Partridge was renamed Askov in 1909 after one of Denmark's folk high schools. By 1920, there were 520 Danish immigrants living in Pine County, mostly in Askov and the surrounding areas. The Askov depot, along the Eastern Minnesota Railway, is pictured here.

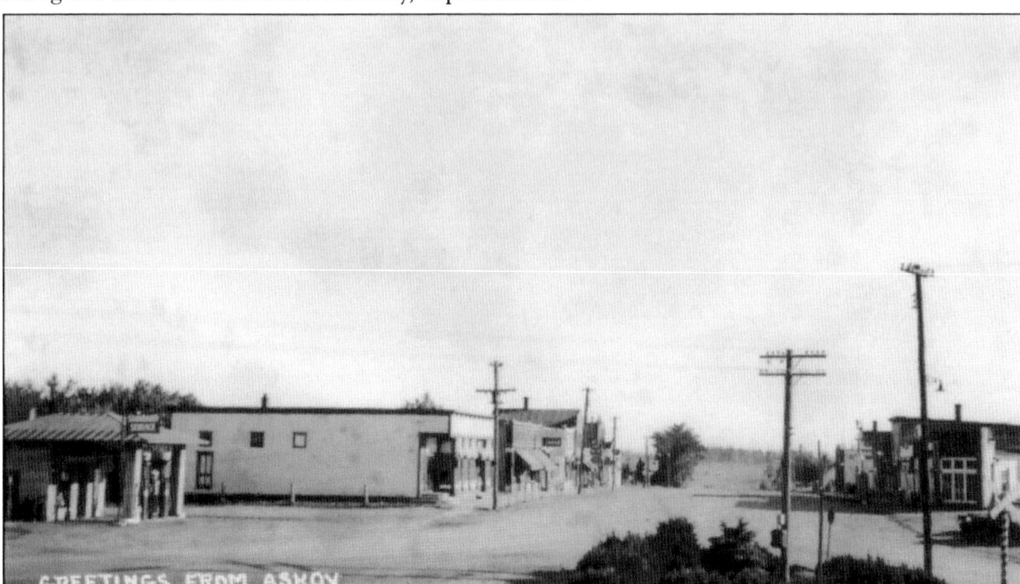

Askov's main street was similar to the business districts of other American small towns with its stores, offices, and gas station. Askov's streets, however, have Danish as well as English names. Danish was the primary language of businesses and churches for many years. It was also taught in Askov's schools. Danish customs continued to thrive, too, including the community Christmas celebration, Klippegilde.

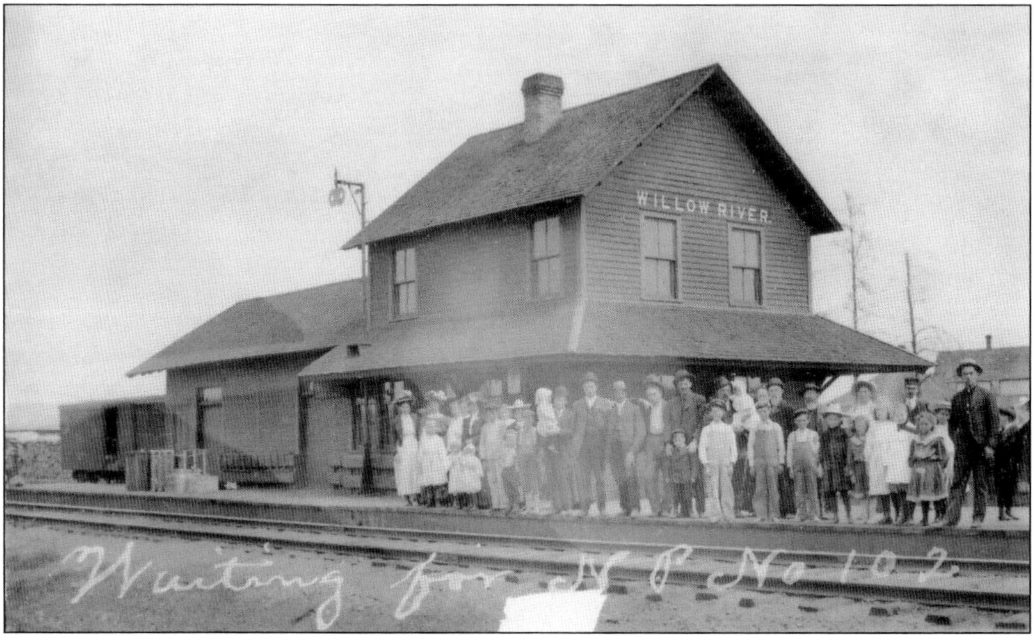

Willow River was platted in 1889 as a lumber town for the employees of the Fox-Wisdom Lumber Company. The company constructed a sawmill in 1890, and the village was incorporated the following year. The St. Paul and Duluth Railroad built the Willow River depot shortly afterward. Apparently, speeding trains were problematic, so the village council set a railroad speed limit of 6 miles per hour in 1894.

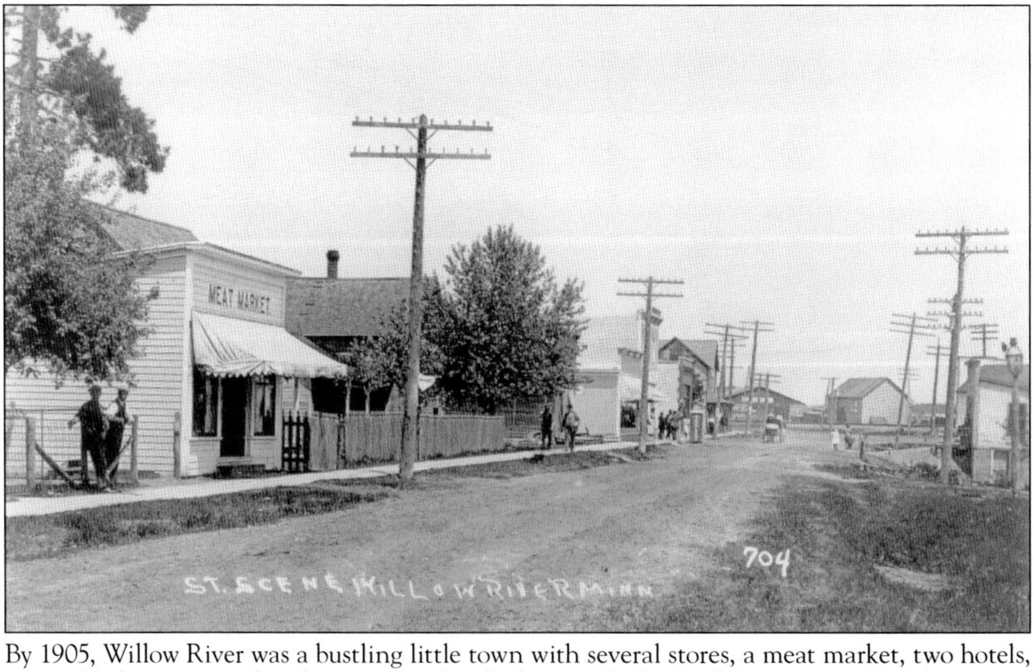

By 1905, Willow River was a bustling little town with several stores, a meat market, two hotels, a boardinghouse, two churches, and a school, along with the lumber company. Residents were arriving from countries throughout Europe, including Poland, Czechoslovakia, and Russia. Willow River was soon a diverse community and home to people of many nationalities.

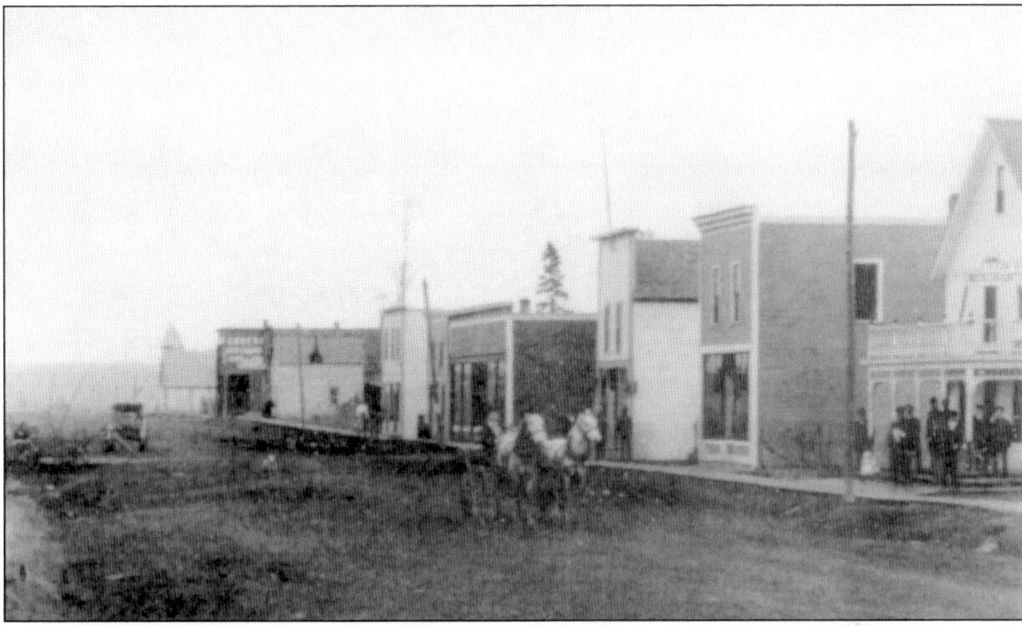

The railroad loading station Mansfield was renamed Bruno in 1898. No one knows how the village, shown here in 1908, got its new name. It might have been borrowed from hotel owner Bruno Vinette, or it may have been a corruption of the German word for "bear." A local saloon kept live bears for the amusement of its customers, which included German loggers.

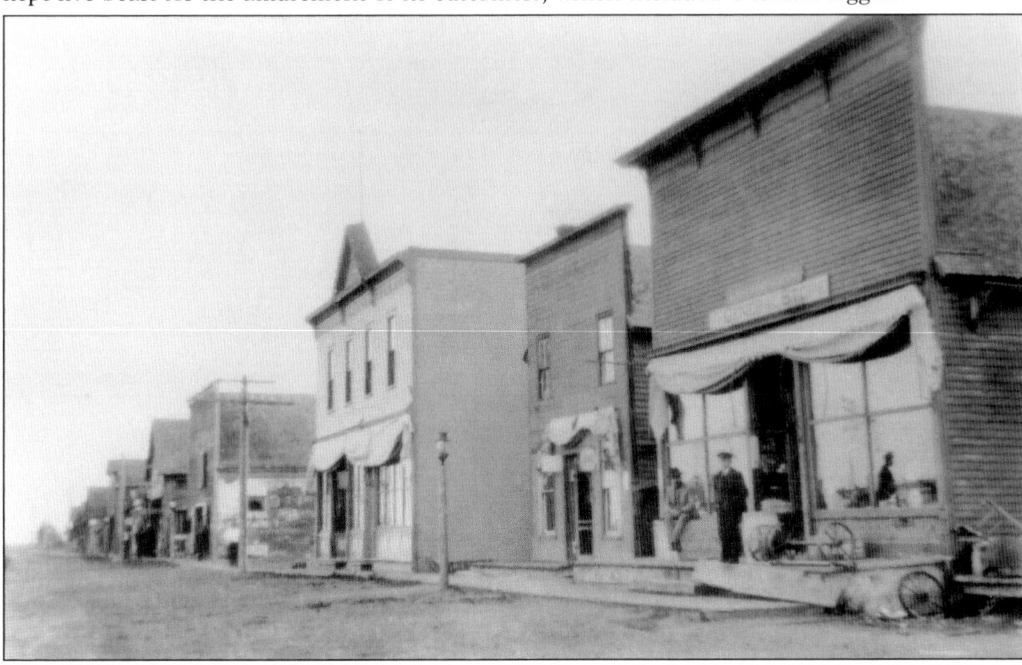

Sturgeon Lake started as a small group of buildings huddled around the St. Paul and Duluth Railroad depot. It was formally platted in 1899 and incorporated in 1901, taking its name from a nearby lake. This picture, which shows the Cunningham General Store, the Hotel Sturgeon, and Ernie Newbloom's barbershop, was taken shortly before the whole block was destroyed by fire in 1933.

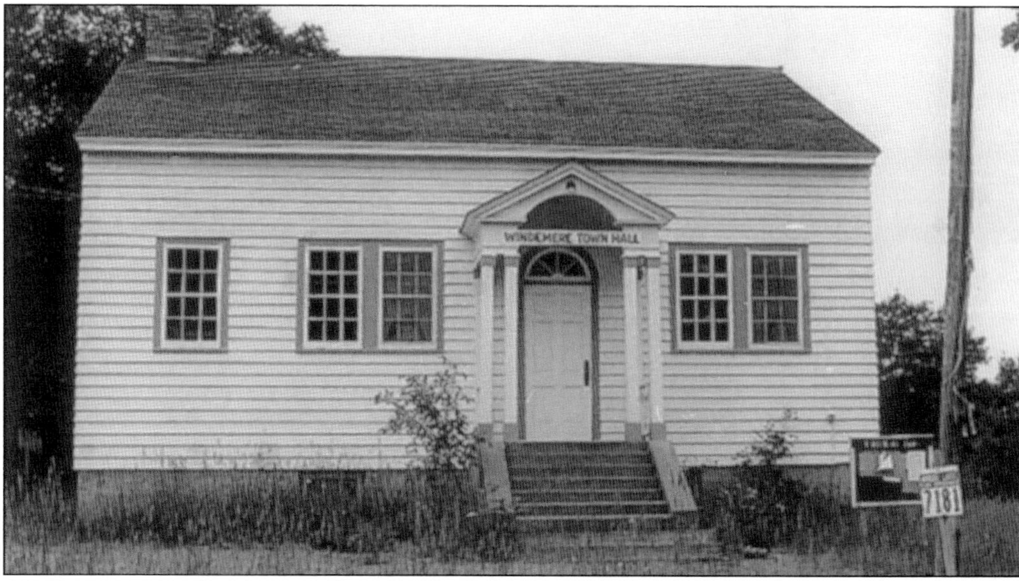

Windemere Township, organized in 1882, was named for Windermere Lake in Lancashire, England, the home of early settler William Pitt. Windemere residents participated in two rather unique industries. Early settlers supplemented their meager incomes by making charcoal out of plentiful hardwoods like maple. Windemere's citizens also picked blueberries in such abundance that they could ship them to markets all over the state as a cash crop.

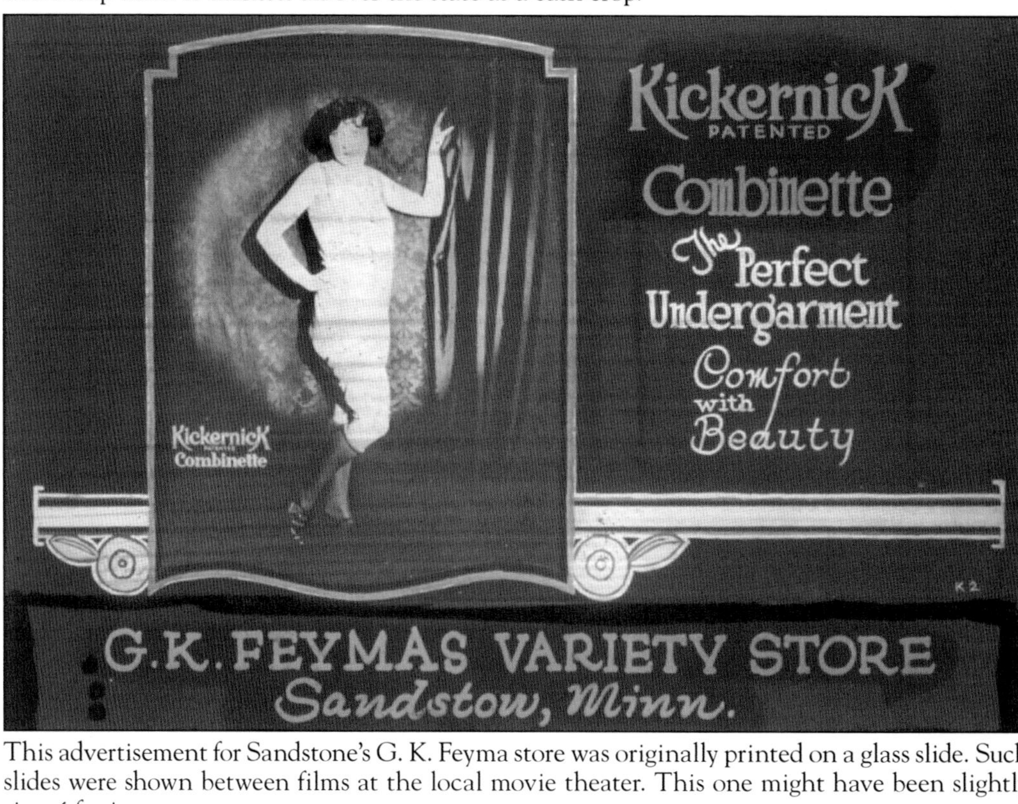

This advertisement for Sandstone's G. K. Feyma store was originally printed on a glass slide. Such slides were shown between films at the local movie theater. This one might have been slightly risqué for its era.

Three

Building an Economy

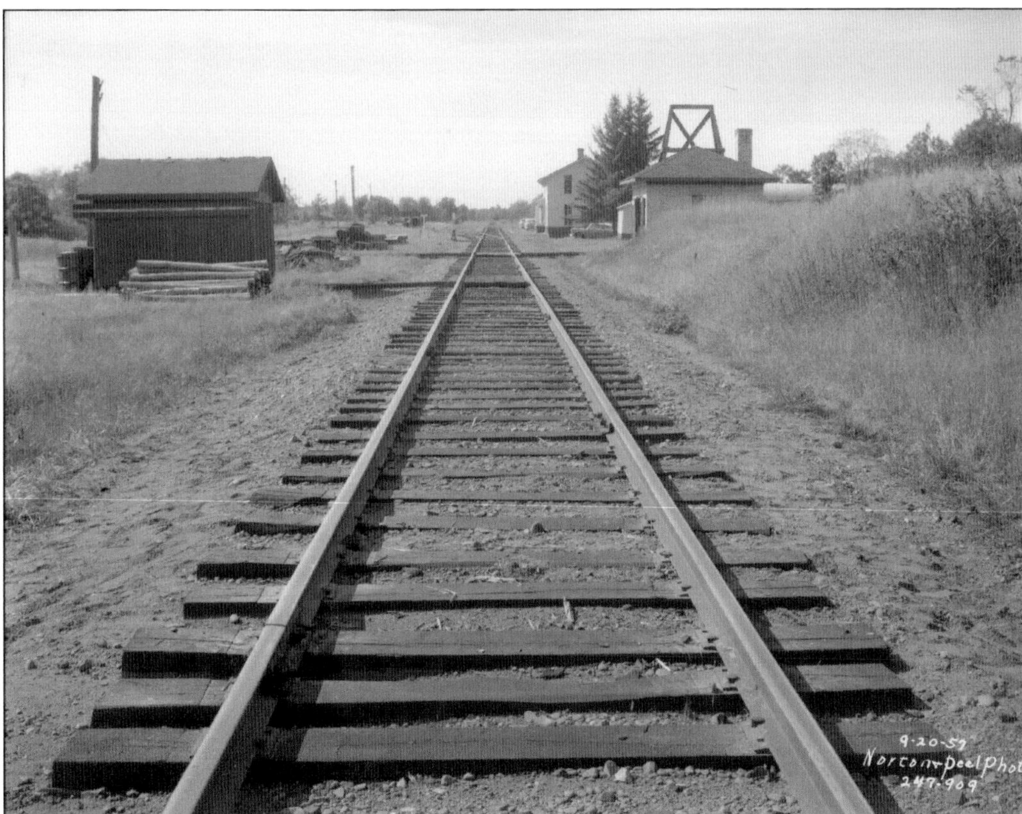

The railroad was critical to Northern Pine County's economic growth. The first railroad, the Lake Superior and Mississippi, was laid in 1870. It became the St. Paul and Duluth in 1877. In 1888–1889, James J. Hill's Eastern Minnesota Railway crossed the territory and connected the Twin Cities with West Superior, Wisconsin. This photograph shows a typical railroad scene in Beroun, about 7 miles south of Hinckley.

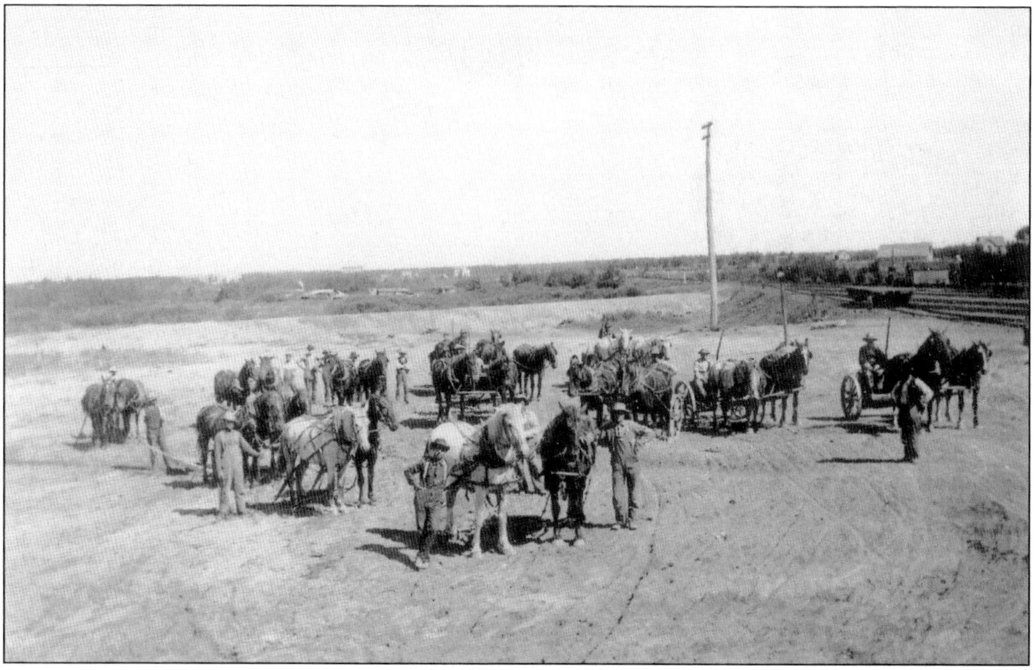

This railroad crew was levelling land for the Eastern Minnesota's Hinckley depot in 1888. Railroads revolutionized small town life, offering easier travel, faster mail service, telegraph communications, and greater access to the goods and services of larger cities. Trains and their passengers were also entertaining to small town folk, who frequently gathered at the local depot to chat and watch for daily trains.

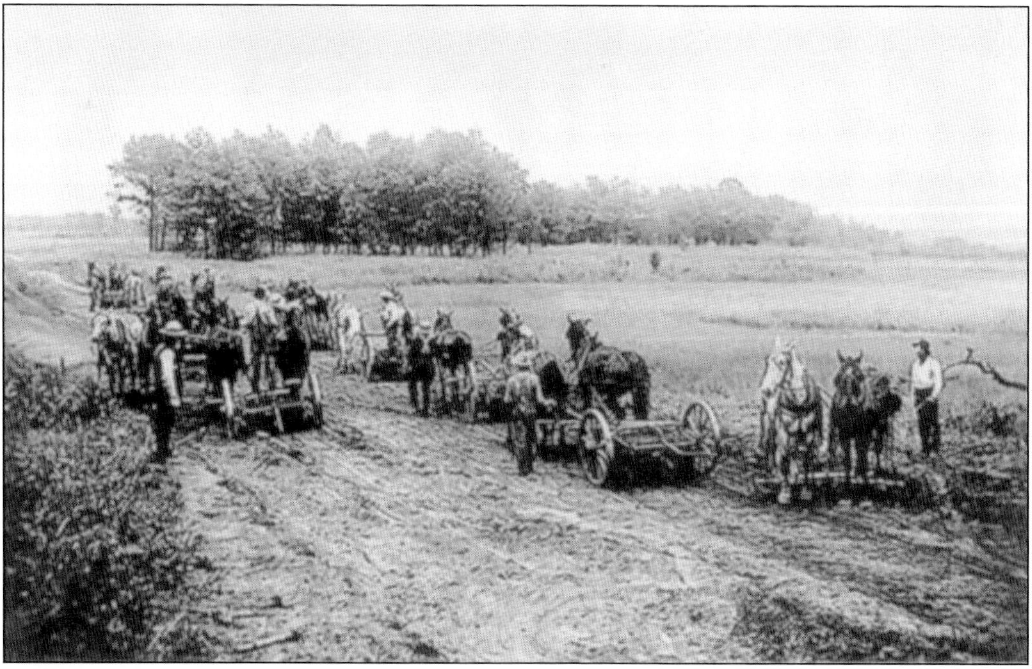

Railroad crews worked hard grading land before railroad tracks could be laid. This crew was preparing for the Eastern Minnesota Railway to pass between Pine City and Hinckley about 1888.

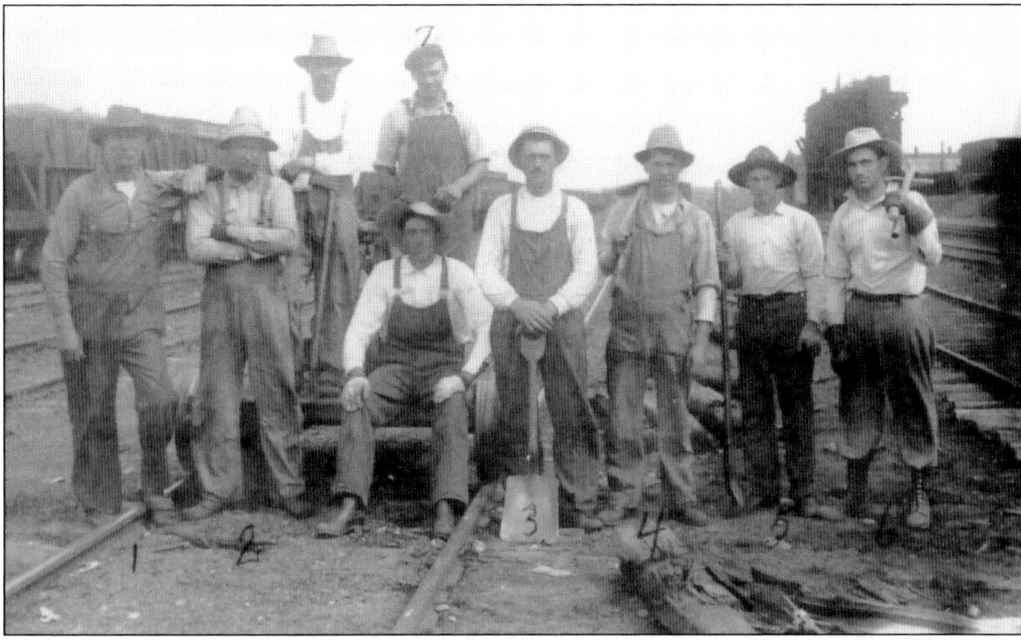

A railroad crew paused for their photograph in Hinckley. From left to right are "Big" John Anderson, Mr. Boyer, John White, Delbert Palmer, Charles Spry, Harold Bassett, and Tom Metchel. Note the coal chute in the background on the right. Coal was a key ingredient to make steam engines run.

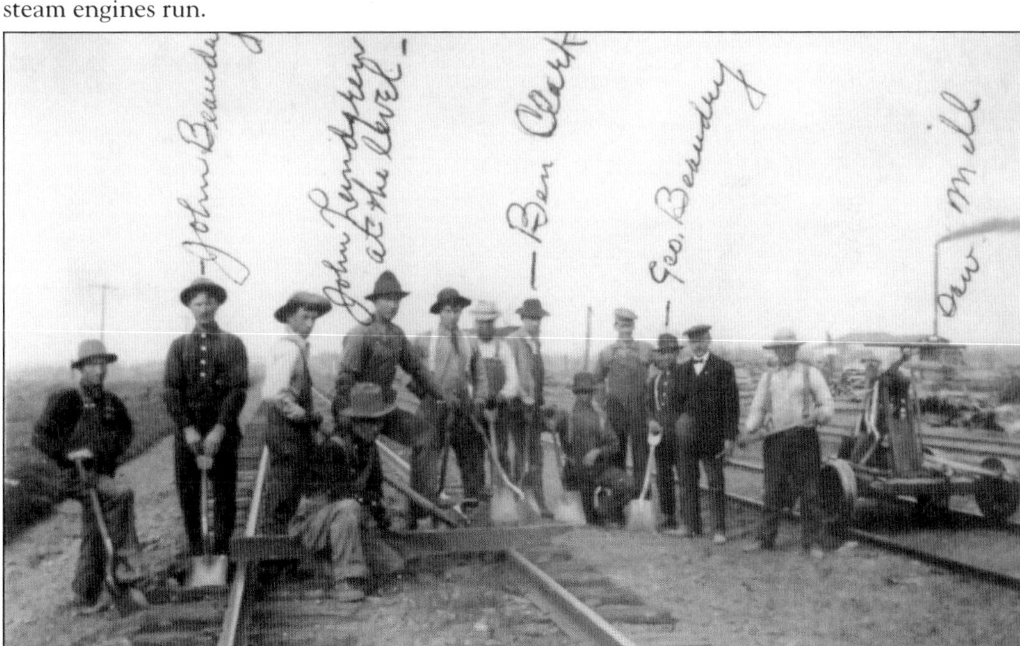

Railroad workers, including John Beaudry, John Lundgren, Ben Clark, and George Beaudry, took a break from their work in Sturgeon Lake to pose for this picture. Railroad work could be dangerous. John Lungren's father, Eric, was killed in a handcar accident in 1912 when he could not get out of the way of an approaching train fast enough. John died five years later after being struck by an engine.

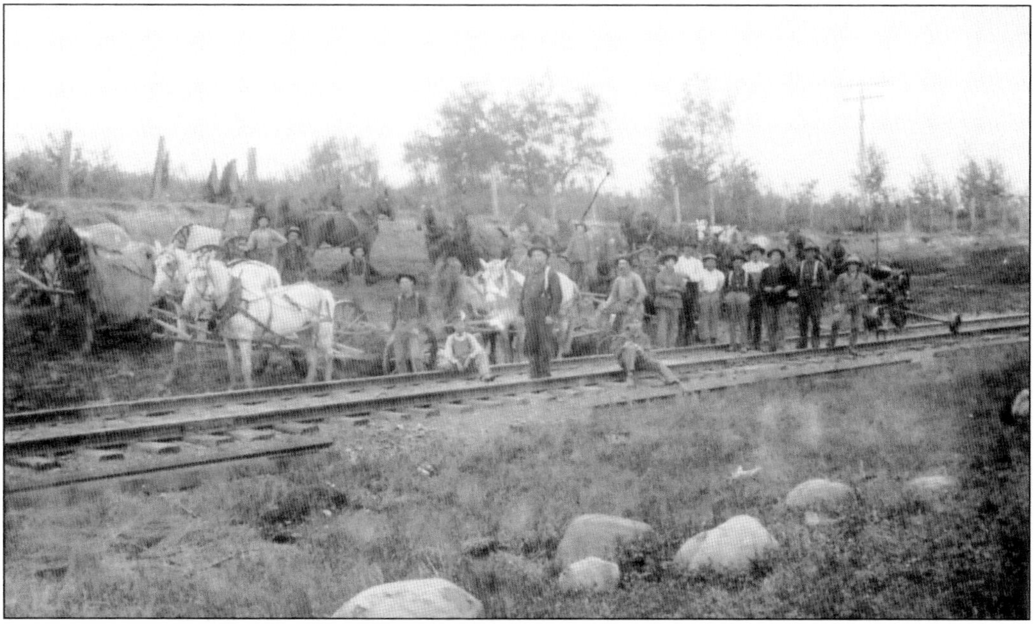

This crew was side-grading near Hinckley to help prevent fires caused by sparks. The machine on the far right is a velocipede. This three-wheeled handcar was often used by railroad inspectors and road masters in the 1880s to check rail lines and travel to railroad crews' work sites. Velocipedes were pedaled by one rider but had seating space for two.

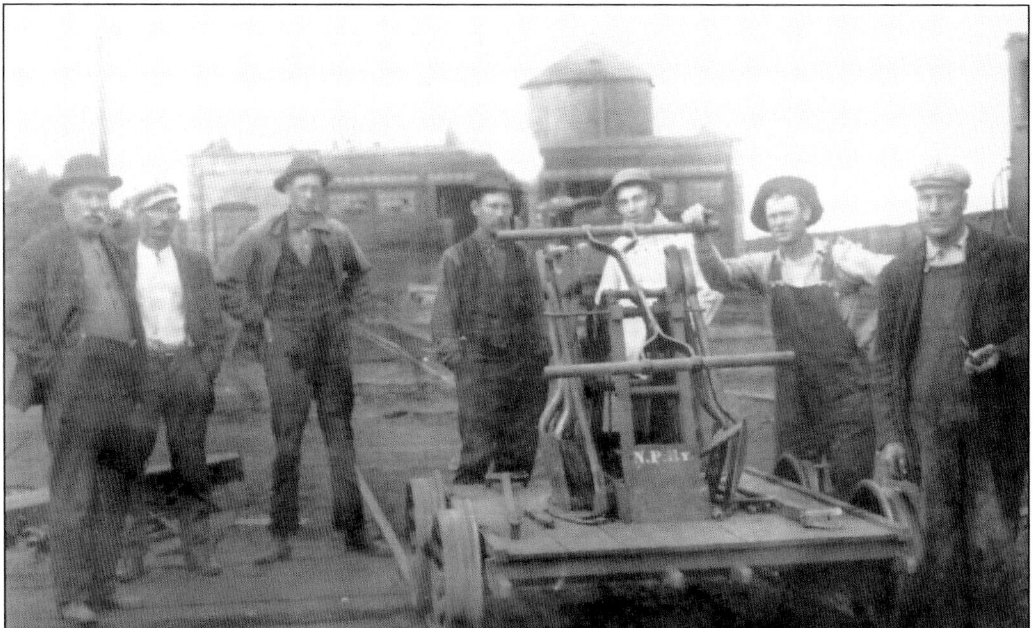

Railroad men and their families were prominent residents in Northern Pine County towns. Tracks and rail yards required constant maintenance, so workers settled in villages along the rail lines and became involved in local government, commerce, and organizations. This group appears to be ready to head out on a handcar to check the track or perform necessary repairs.

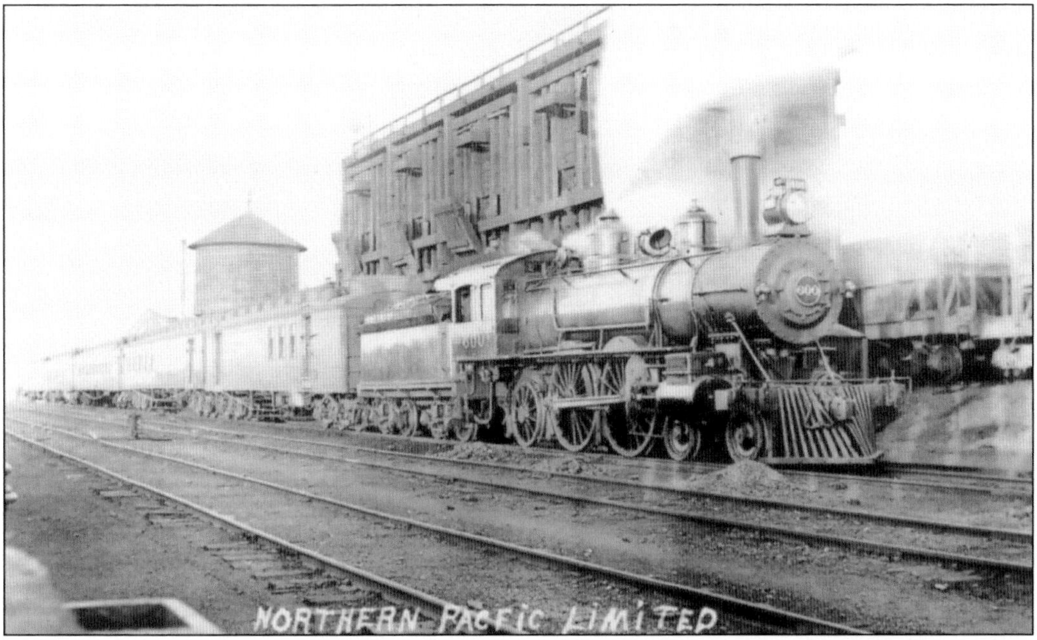

The Northern Pacific Limited, engine No. 600, arrived at the coal chute at Hinckley to take on more coal and water for its journey. The engine pulled several passenger cars. While railroad travel in the early 1900s was uncomfortable by modern standards, it was faster and easier than travel by horse and wagon. The Northern Pacific Railway Company absorbed the St. Paul and Duluth Railroad in 1900.

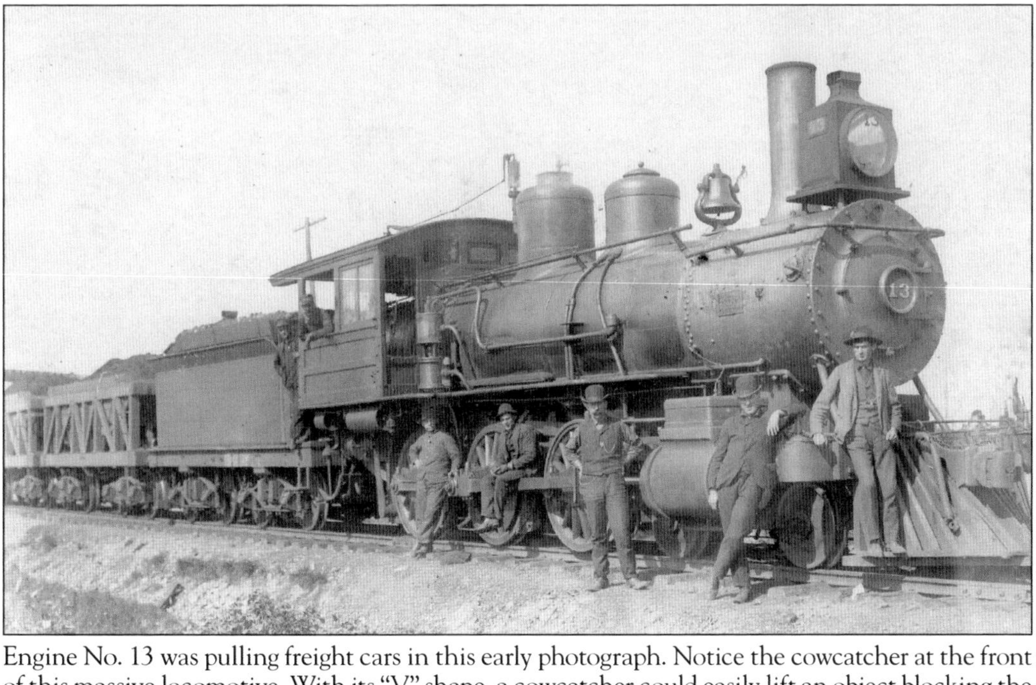

Engine No. 13 was pulling freight cars in this early photograph. Notice the cowcatcher at the front of this massive locomotive. With its "V" shape, a cowcatcher could easily lift an object blocking the track and deflect it to one side without the engine slowing down. Objects pushed out of the way did not fair too well, however, and railroads were often sued over injured or killed livestock.

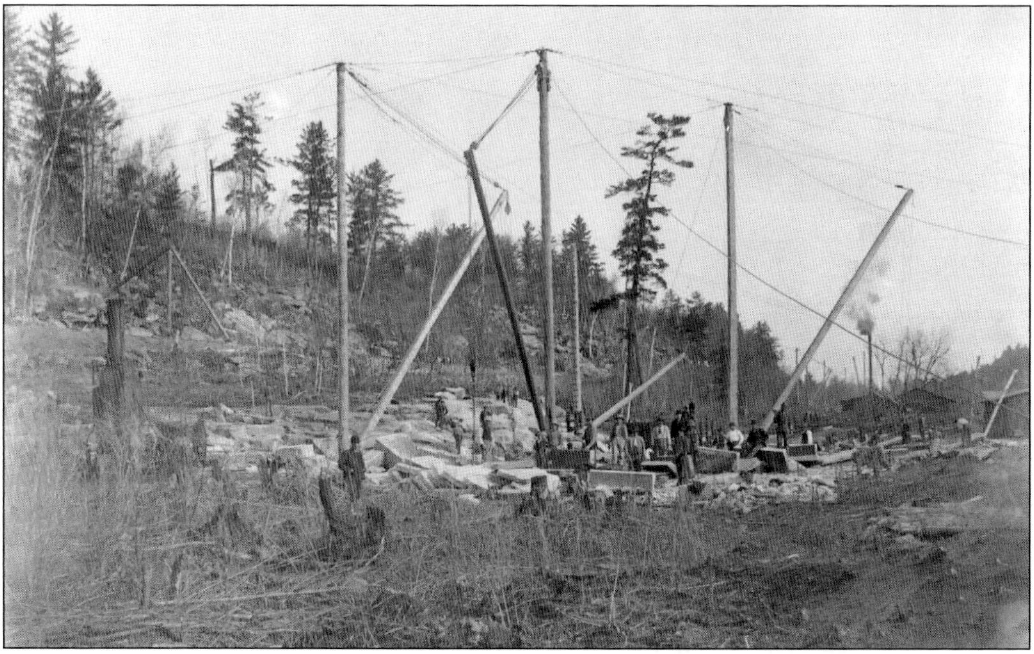

William H. Grant founded the Sandstone quarry along the Kettle River in 1885. The strong, durable, uniformly colored, and relatively easy-to-cut sandstone was soon being used for buildings all over the United States and Canada. Quarry workers used derricks, like the ones shown in this 1888 photograph, to lift heavy blocks of sandstone onto ox-drawn wagons and, later, railroad cars.

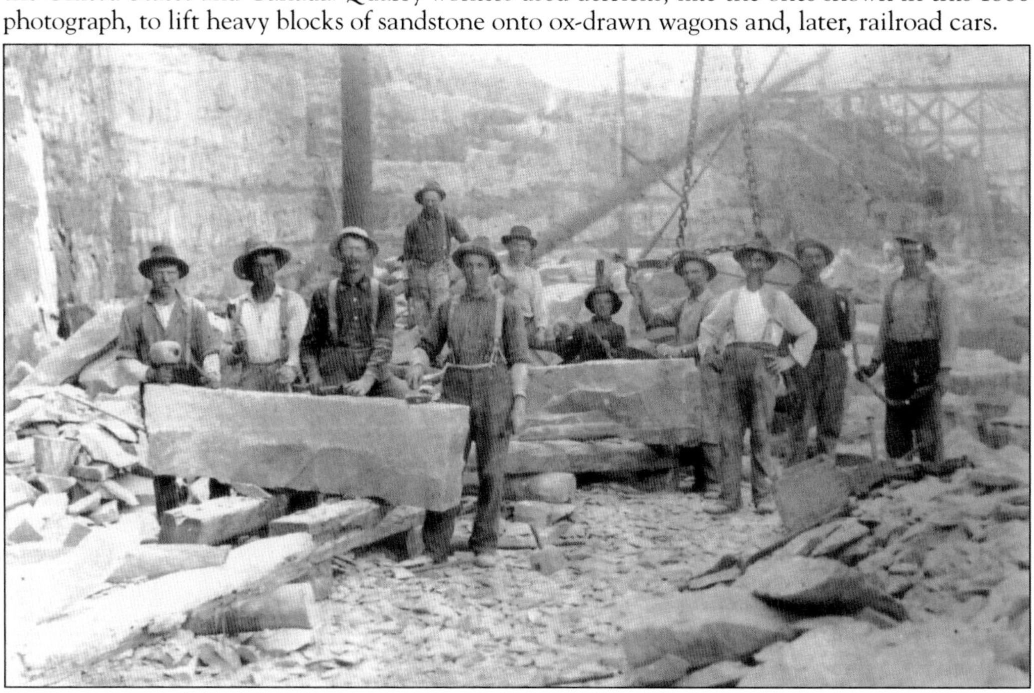

Quarry workers drilled deep holes into the sandstone, filled them with black powder, and blasted large chunks of stone free from the cliff walls. Stones were cut to order with a variety of chisels and mallets. In the mid-1890s, there were 100 to 125 men employed in the quarry, earning $1.35 a day for laborers and $1.50 a day for skilled drillers. A typical workday lasted 10 hours.

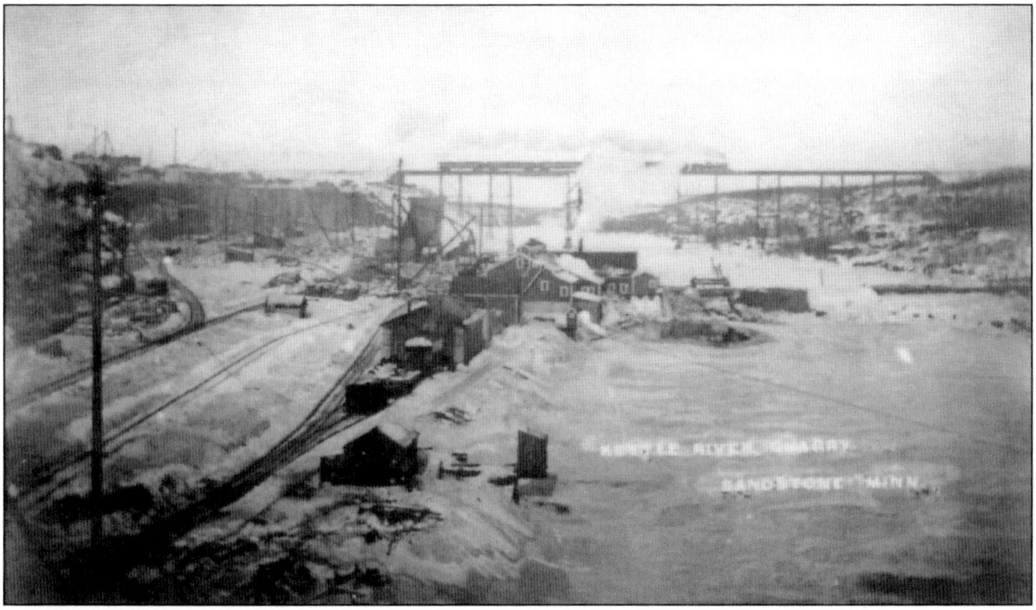

At its high point, the quarry was a complex operation complete with a dam to generate electric power. Buildings housed a toolshed, a quarry office, an engine house, a sawmill, a powerhouse, a blacksmith shop, a rock crusher, and storage bins. Railroad tracks that lined the bottom of the quarry could be moved to accommodate new drilling areas. Note the Kettle River high bridge in the background.

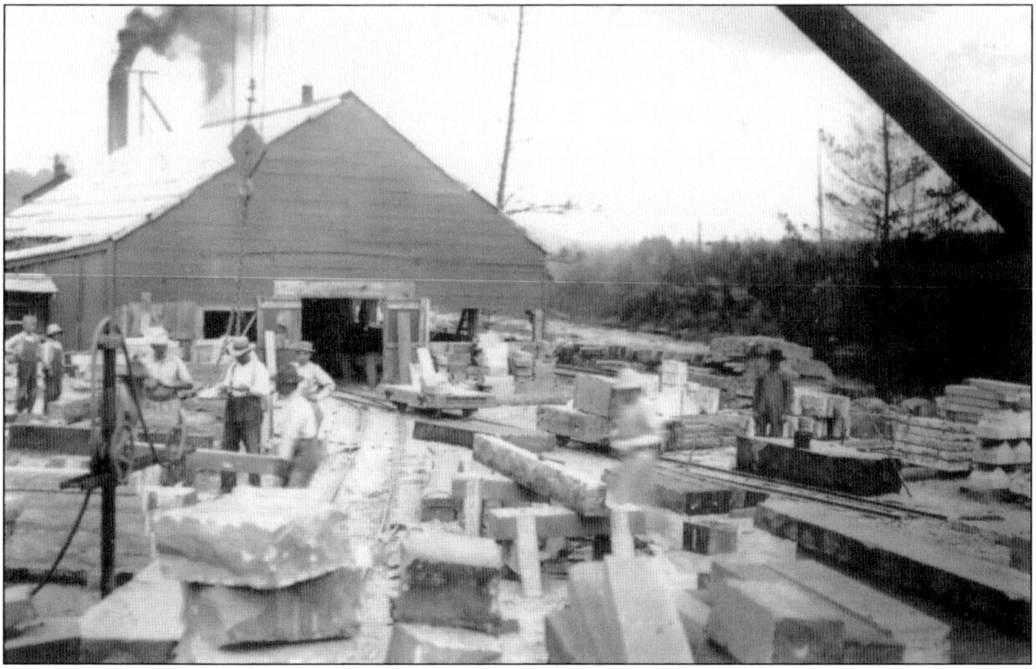

At the stonecutting shed, sandstone was carved into everything from paving blocks to specialized works of art. Stonecutters were among the highest paid quarry workers. Many of them came from England and proudly contributed their talents to Sandstone village choirs and soccer teams.

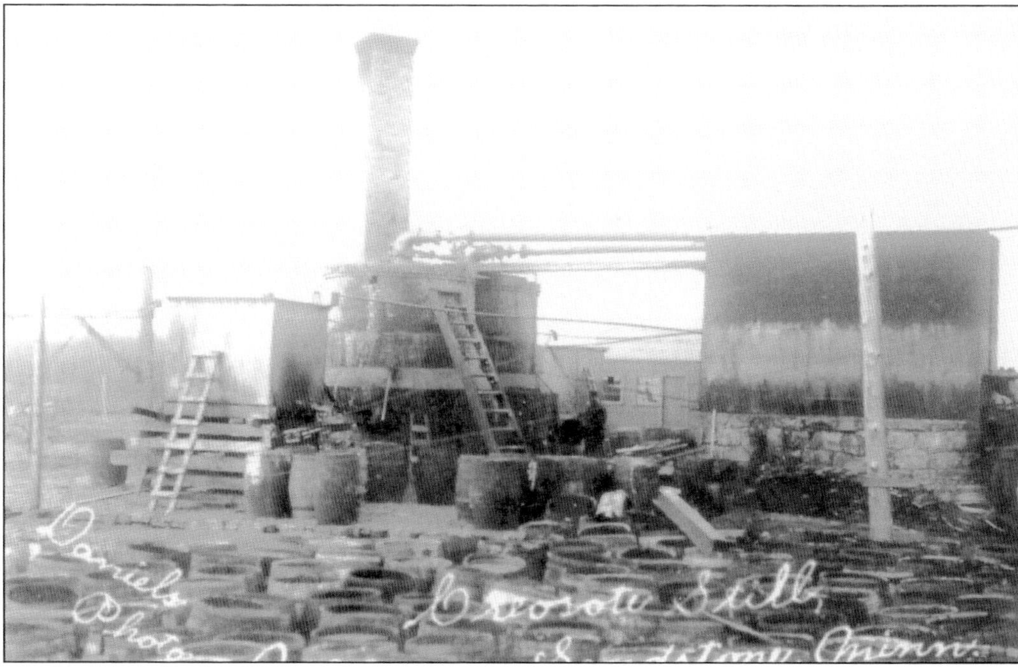

In 1905, the Kettle River Quarries Company opened a creosote plant in Sandstone. Creosote is a smelly, black liquid made by distilling oil or wood tar and used to preserve wood for poles, railroad ties, and paving blocks. During its peak production in 1910, Sandstone's creosote plant reached a gross income of $2 million and employed 600 men.

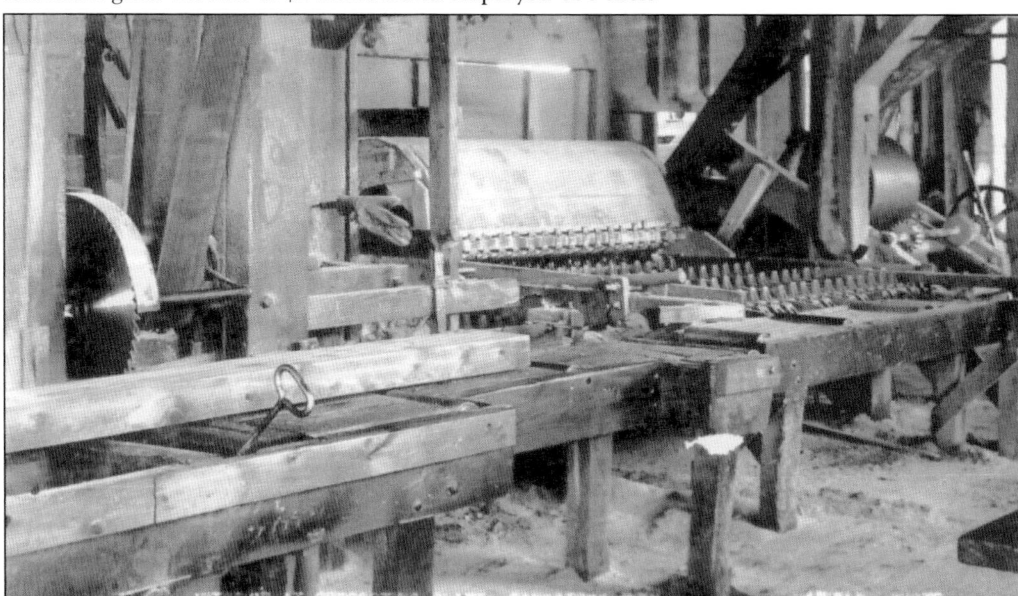

Sandstone's creosote plant was the largest in the world, but it survived fewer than 15 years. Demand for paving blocks made from local pine and tamarack dropped off sharply when folks discovered that streets paved with them tended to buckle and become impassible in the spring. Southern pine proved more effective, and a new creosote plant was built in Missouri. The obsolete Sandstone plant closed in 1918.

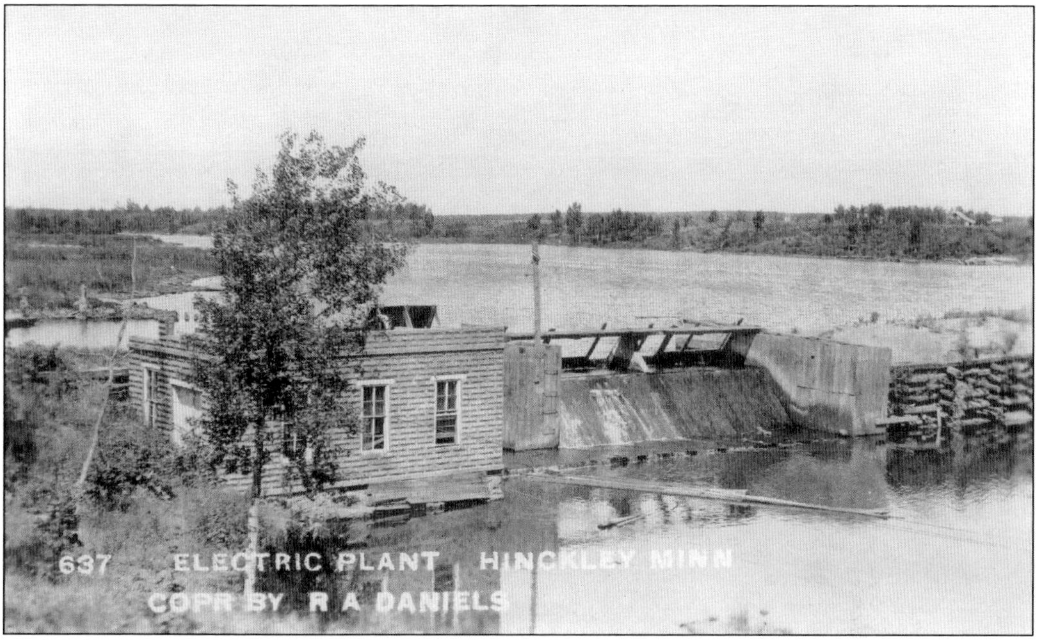

Hydroelectric power generated by dams supplied much of Northern Pine County's electricity in the first decades of the 1900s. Hinckley's dam and electric plant is shown in this photograph taken by Ross Daniels.

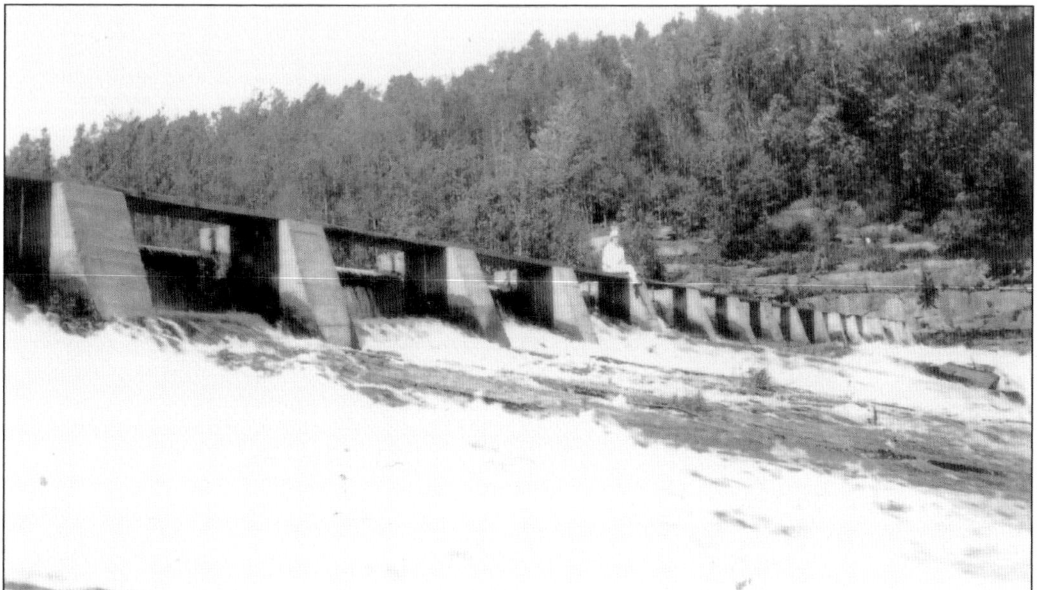

Sandstone's new dam on the Kettle River was built in 1905 about a mile downstream from the old dam that had generated power only for the quarry. The new dam provided electricity for Sandstone and its vicinity for nearly 60 years. The dam was removed in the early 1990s. This photograph was snapped by Bill Bantleon in 1930.

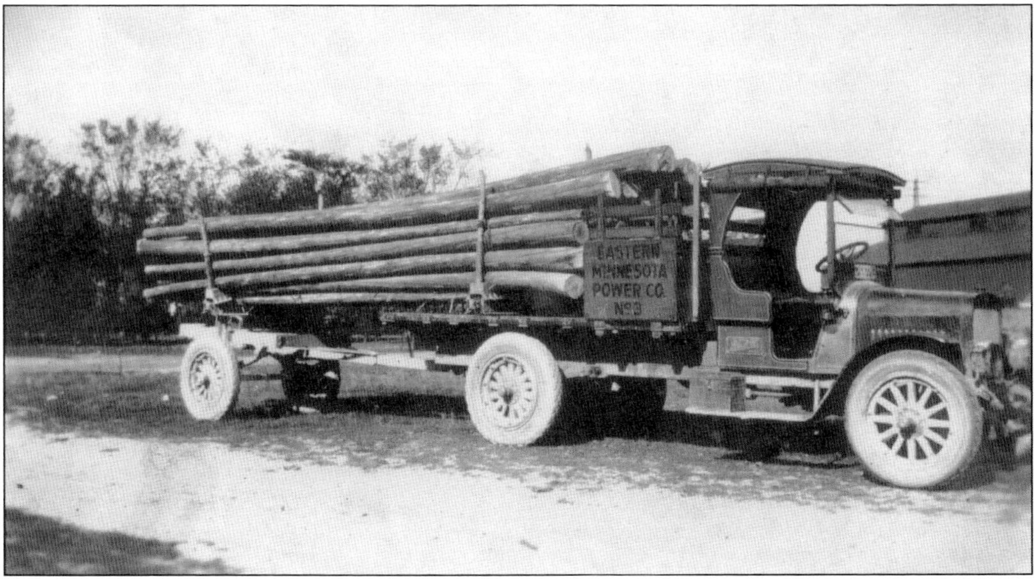

This truck carried a load of power poles. Although electricity was generated by hydroelectric dams, it remained inaccessible to many residents until the 1920s or 1930s. Some people preferred living without electricity. One Sandstone man accidentally stuck his finger in an outlet shortly after his house was hooked up to the power grid. He quickly returned to kerosene lamps.

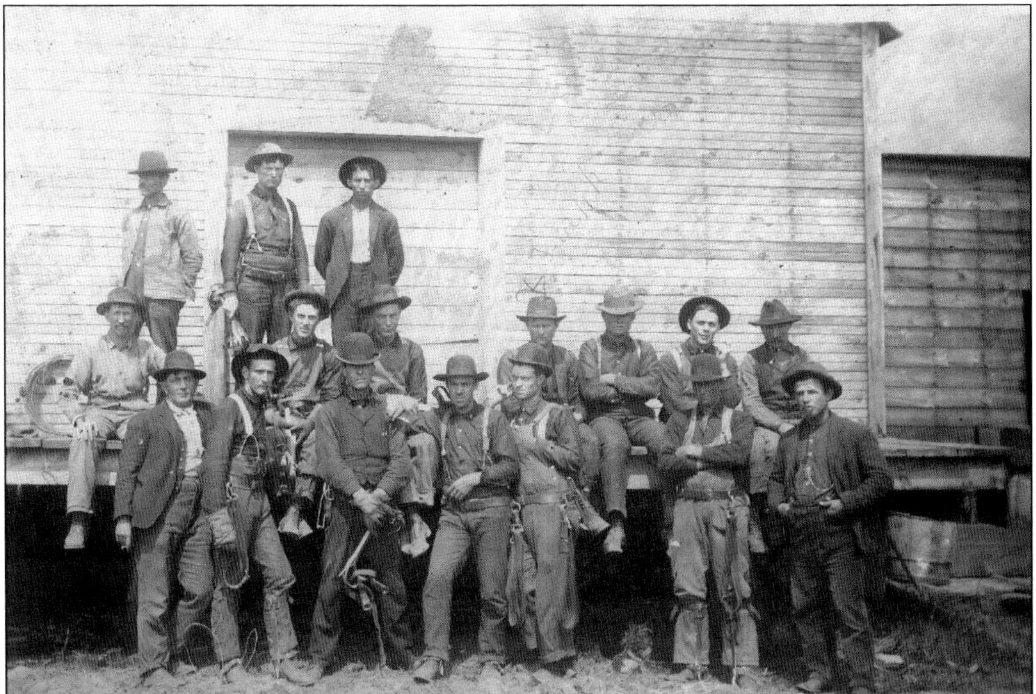

This construction crew was ready to head out for a day of raising and stringing power and/or telegraph lines. Railroads depended heavily upon telegraph communications to dispatch trains and keep them on schedule. Every depot had a telegraph operator to tap out messages up and down the lines.

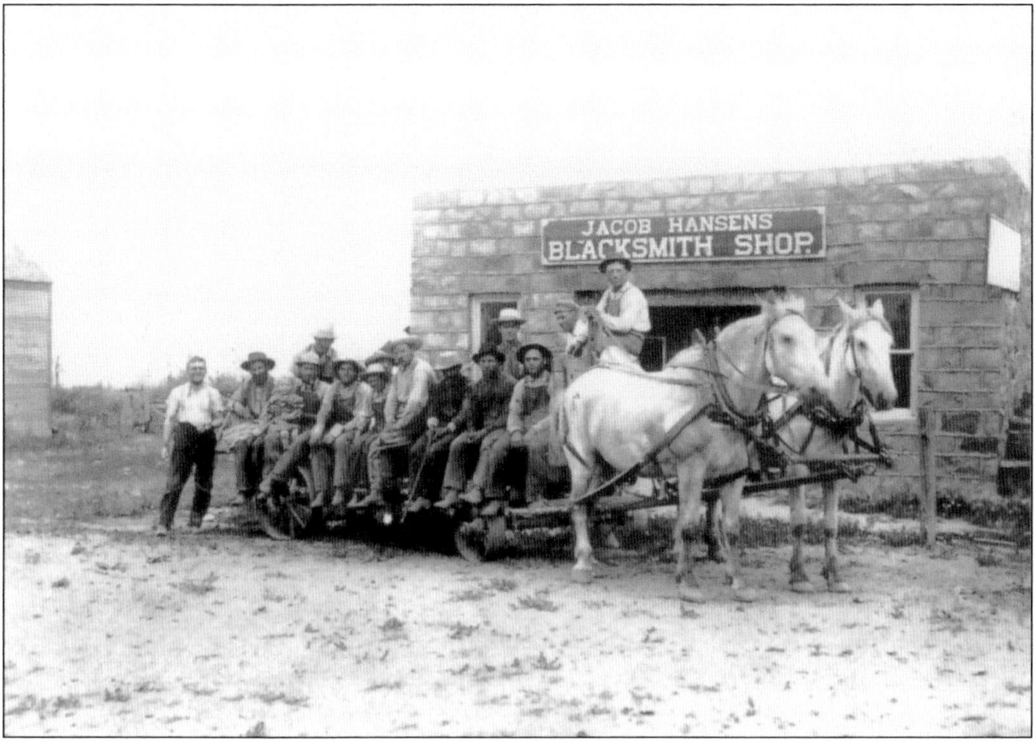

In the days of horse-and-buggy (or wagon) transportation, blacksmiths were important members of the community. Along with forging horseshoes and wagon parts, they made and repaired a wide variety of iron tools, hardware, farm implements, and household necessities. Jacob Hansen's Blacksmith Shop in Askov is shown here. The Askov fire department rested in front of the shop after a practice run.

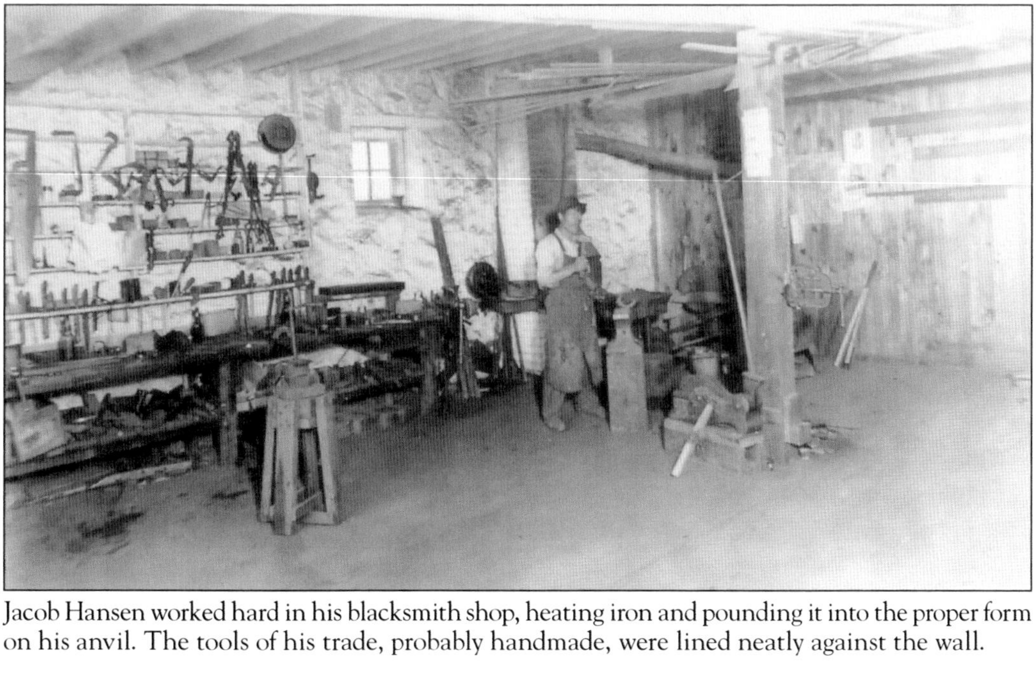

Jacob Hansen worked hard in his blacksmith shop, heating iron and pounding it into the proper form on his anvil. The tools of his trade, probably handmade, were lined neatly against the wall.

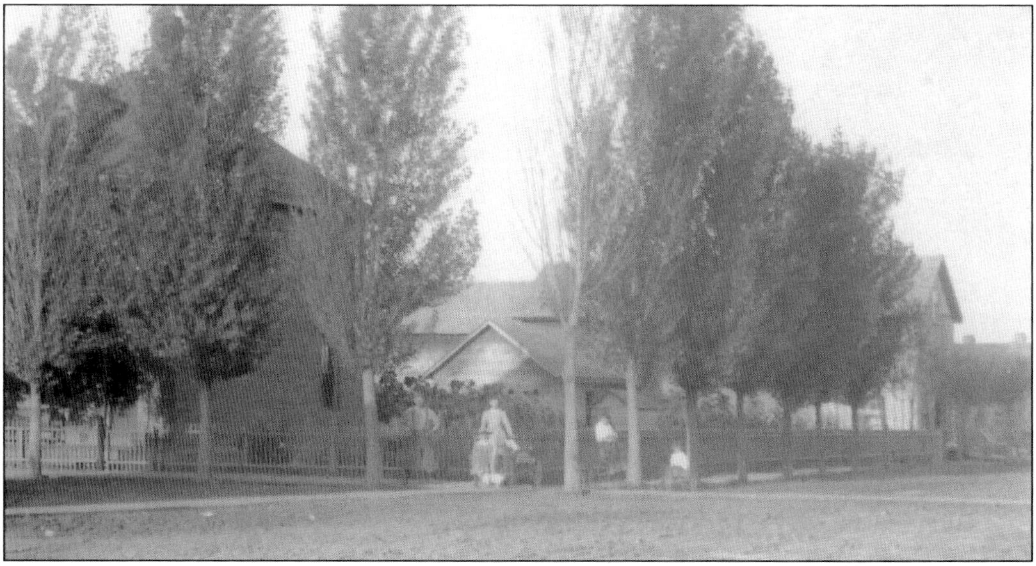

To keep up with changing times, blacksmiths like Pine City's Julius Newbauer expanded their businesses to provide a wider range of services. Newbauer's blacksmithing complex took up a whole city block and consisted of his family home (on the left), a two-story warehouse with a full basement, the blacksmith shop, a wagon shop, and a stable. Newbauer, his wife, and their children posed in front of their home and business.

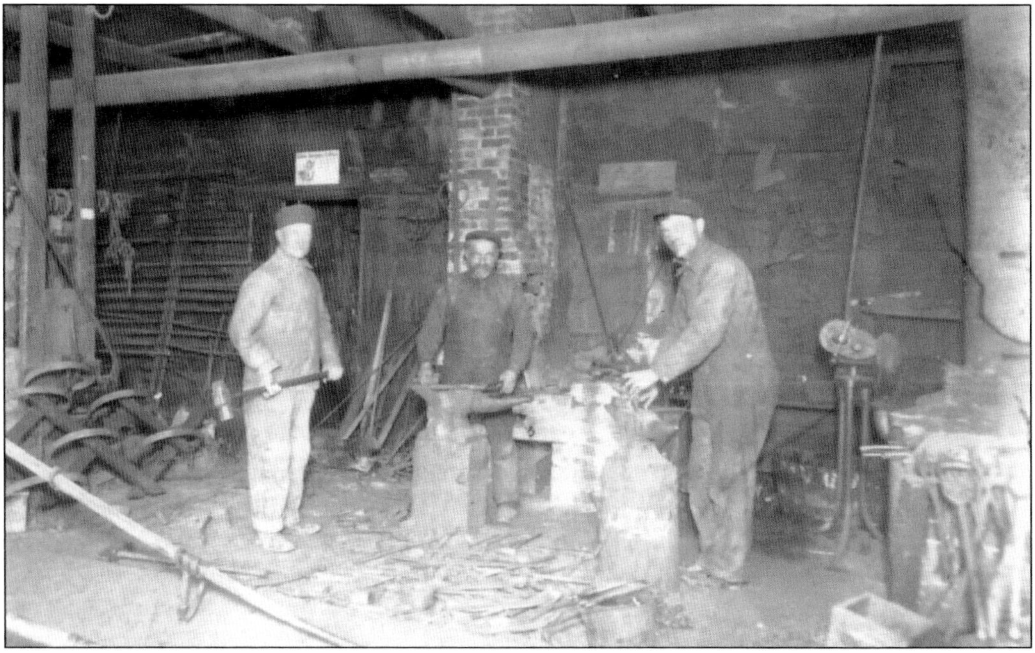

Newbauer (center), his son Albert (right), and their colleague used two forges, two anvils, and many tools in their work. Blacksmithing as a profession began to dwindle with the rise of the automobile, but since early cars and trucks broke down frequently, blacksmiths learned to fix them. As the world continued to change, however, many blacksmiths turned to other professions.

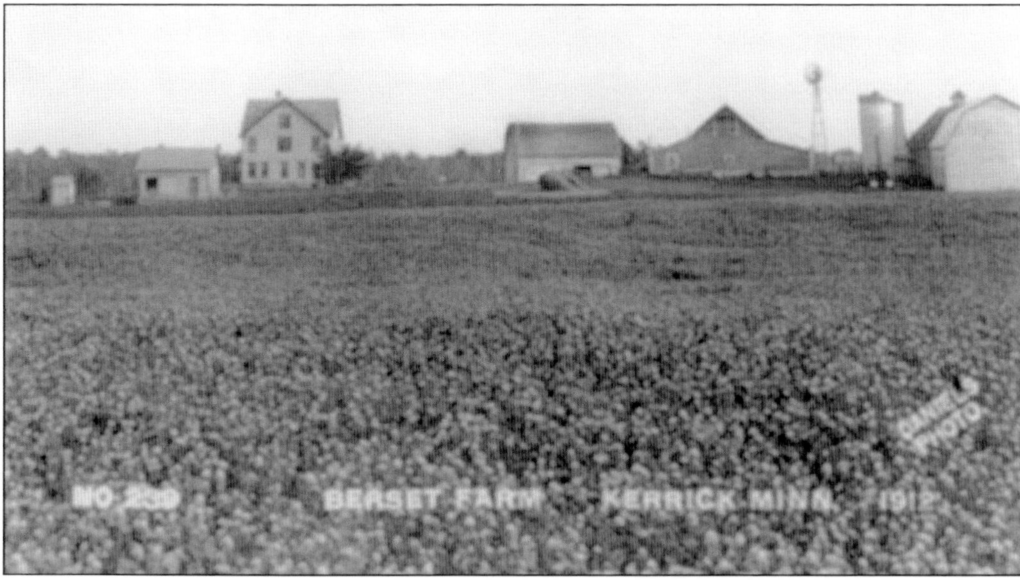

Farming was a major business in Northern Pine County after loggers had cleared the land. The Berset Farm near Kerrick is shown here in 1912. The towns of Kerrick, Duquette, and Nickerson in the northernmost part of Pine County sprang up along the Eastern Minnesota Railway in the late 1890s.

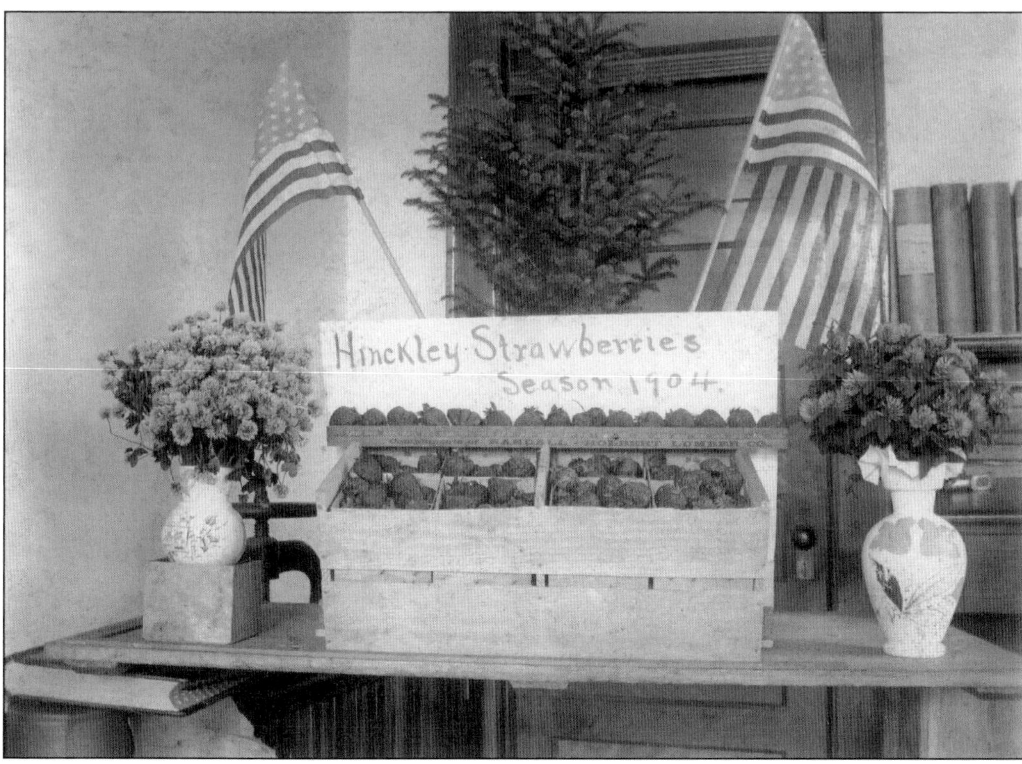

Strawberries and raspberries were the first crops in the areas of Northern Pine County affected by the 1894 fire. Since berries grow well in ashy soil, they were a perfect fit for burned-over lands. This 1904 exhibit of Hinckley strawberries looks delicious.

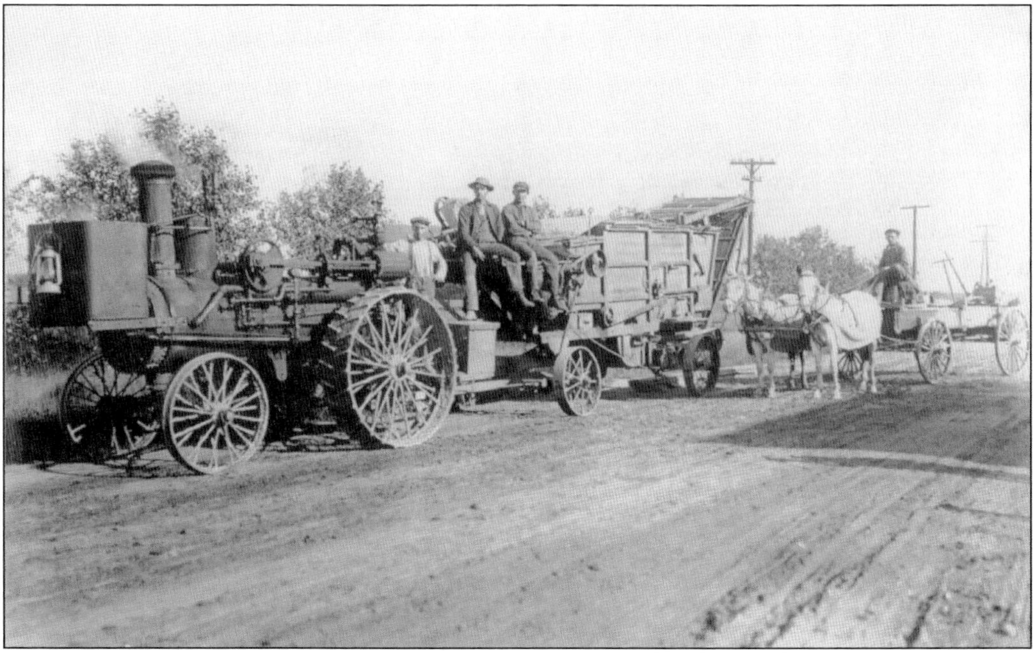

Threshing crews like this one traveled from farm to farm during the post-harvest threshing season. Neighbors worked together: the men running the threshing machine that separated the grain from husks and stalks and the women preparing large meals to feed the hungry crews. This machine was run by steam, but earlier ones depended on horses or oxen for power.

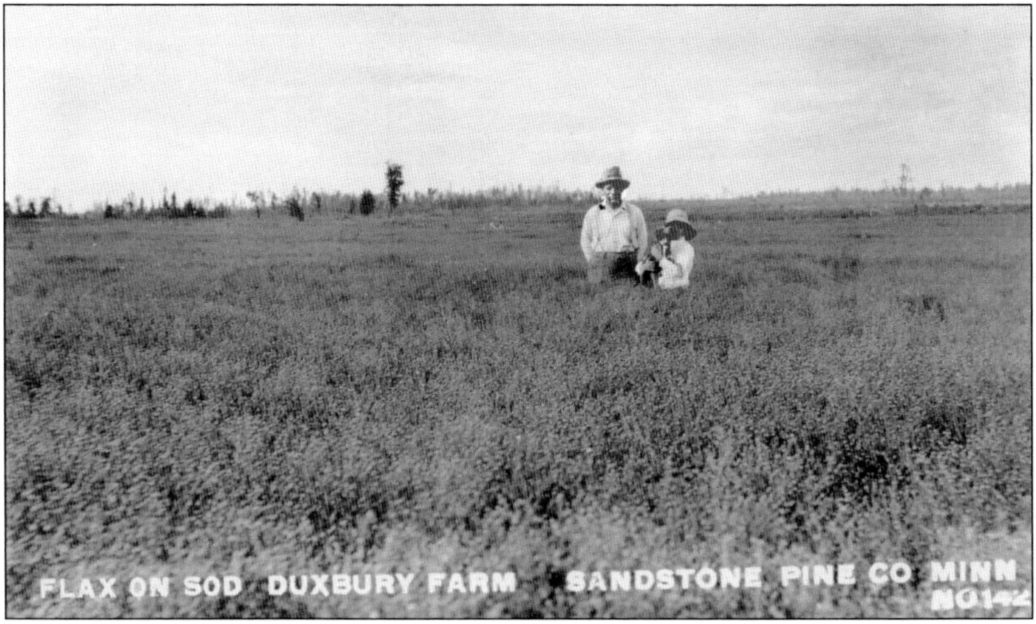

Duxbury farmers worked hard to grow oats, wheat, and flax. If the Arrow Line, an electric railroad proposed in 1907, had been built in eastern Pine County, the farmers' lives might have been quite different. The Western Land and Improvement Company, which sponsored the railroad, sold stock and land and platted towns, including Duxbury. Unfortunately, the entire plan fell through in 1911.

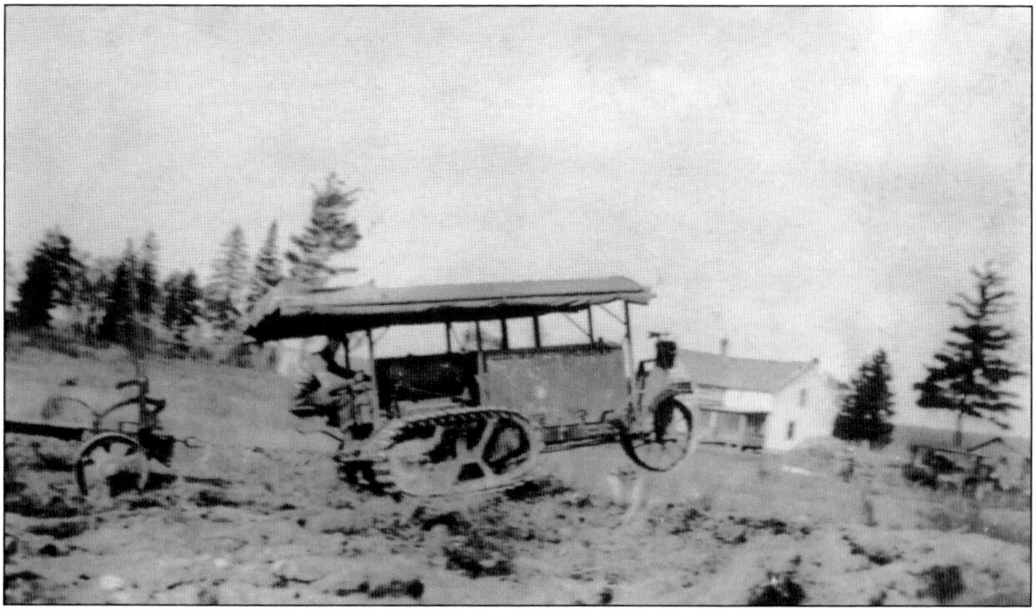

This steam tractor had a hard time maneuvering through the hard soil on the Red Clover Land Company's showplace farm near Cloverton. The company purchased 28,000 acres in eastern Pine County in 1910 and advertised for homesteaders. Settlers flocked to the area, establishing towns like Cloverton and Markville. They soon realized that promises of fertile farmland were deceptive. Many moved on after only a few difficult years.

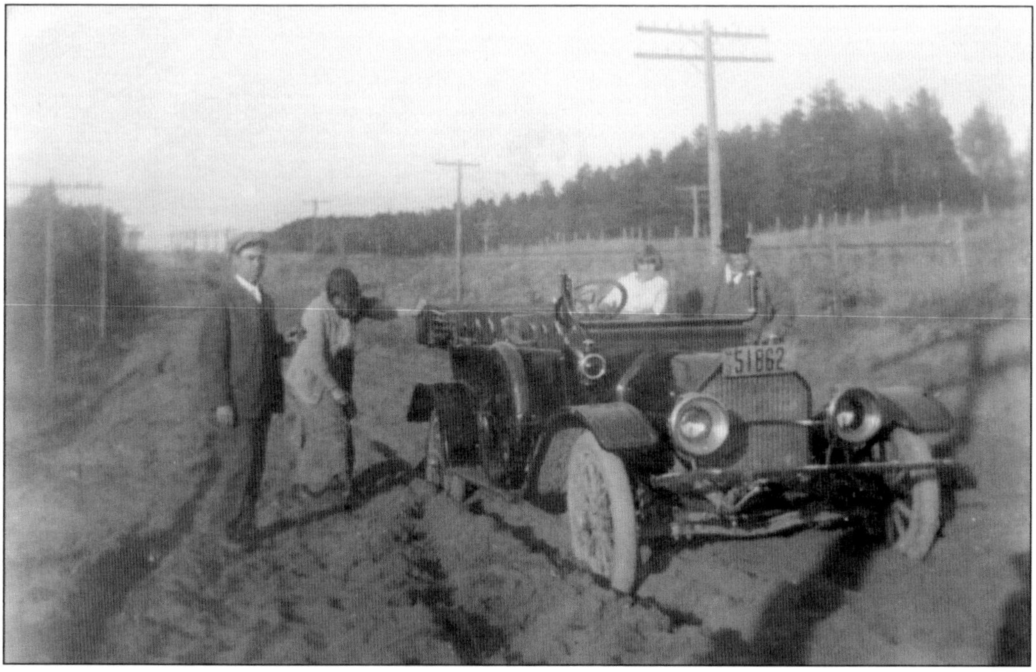

Travel was not easy in Northern Pine County, even after the arrival of the automobile. This car was firmly stuck in the mud when this picture was taken in the early 1910s. Local residents banded together to try to improve the roads. Bruno men had to commit to two days of roadwork per year or pay a $3 fine. Even so, roads remained notoriously poor for many years.

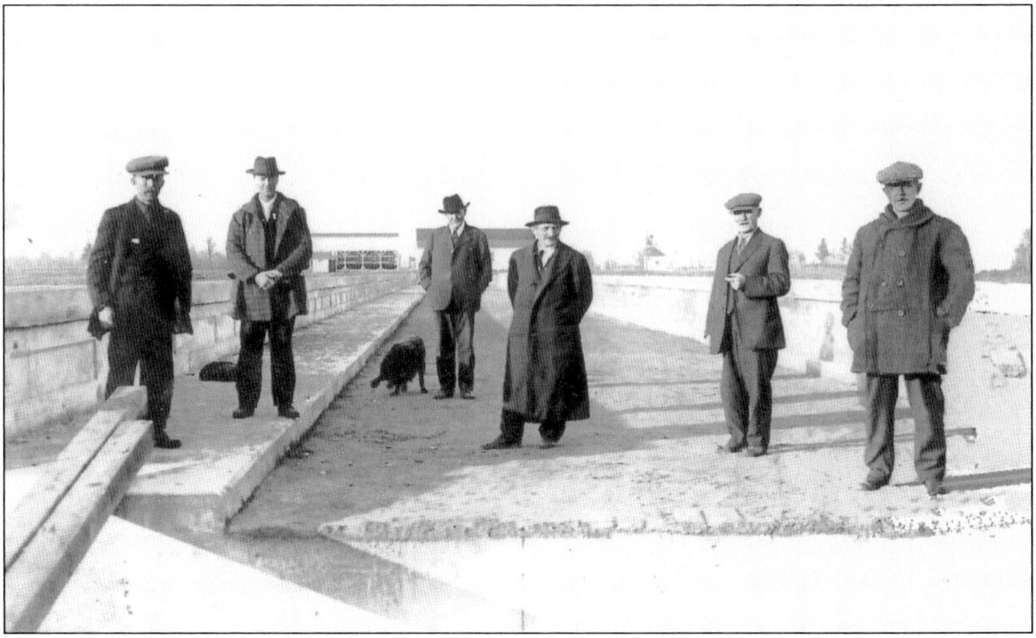

Pine County's commissioners posed for this 1914 photograph on the newly dedicated concrete bridge across the Snake River. The commissioners, (from left to right) Mr. Johnson, Fred Degerstrom, W. H. Hamlin, George Studt, Bob Dirr, and Andrew Edin, were especially proud of this bridge, which was the first of its kind in the county.

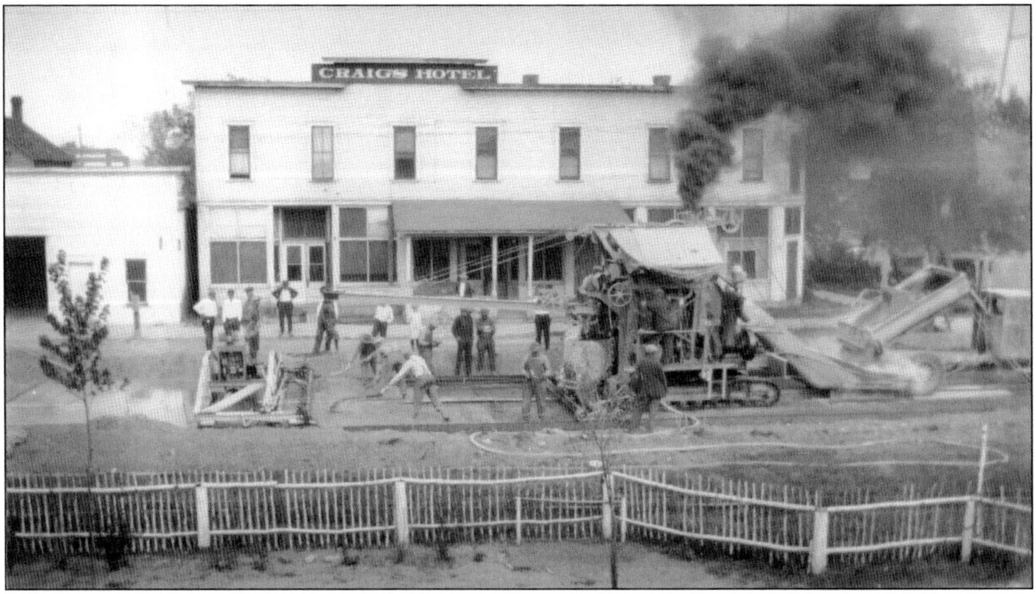

Around 1927, Highway 1 through Hinckley was paved. Running from St. Paul to Duluth, Highway 1 was the longest concrete highway in the world at that time. Craig's Hotel in the background was formerly the Phoenix Hotel and later became Tobie's Eat Shop and Bus Stop.

Four

Opportunities for Entrepreneurs

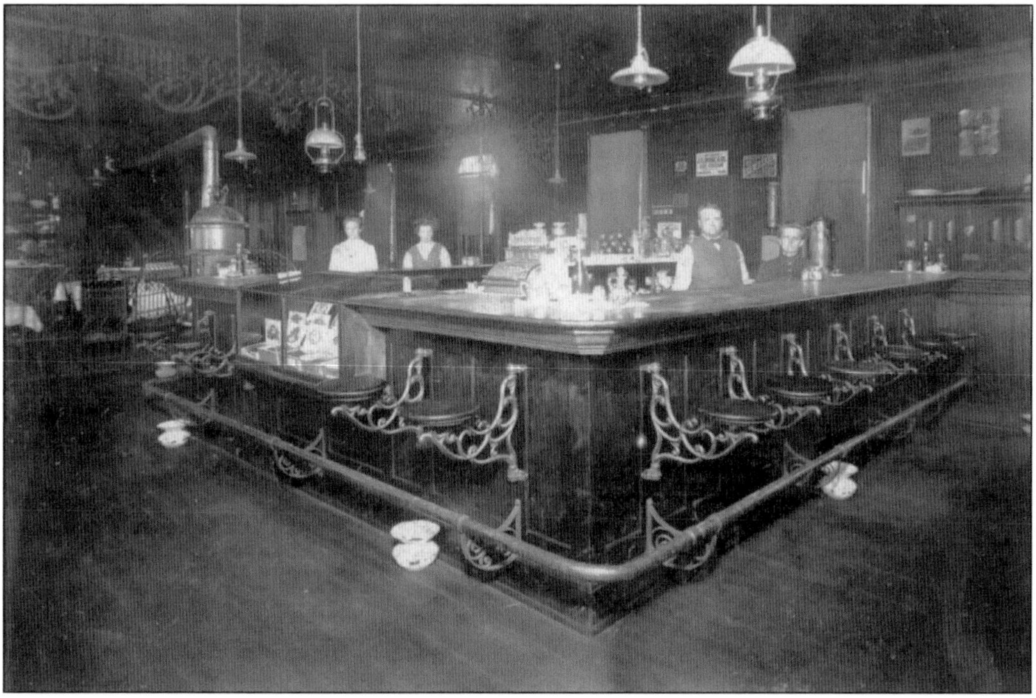

Built as part of Hinckley's new St. Paul and Duluth depot after the 1894 fire, the Beanery was the perfect place to have lunch or refreshments while waiting to catch the next train. The Beanery featured all the amenities of its day, at least for Hinckley, including 24-hours-a-day service, woodstove heat, intricately designed bar stools, and strategically placed spittoons. Proprietor O. H. Ingram and workers Florence Fix and Martha Maxwell are pictured here.

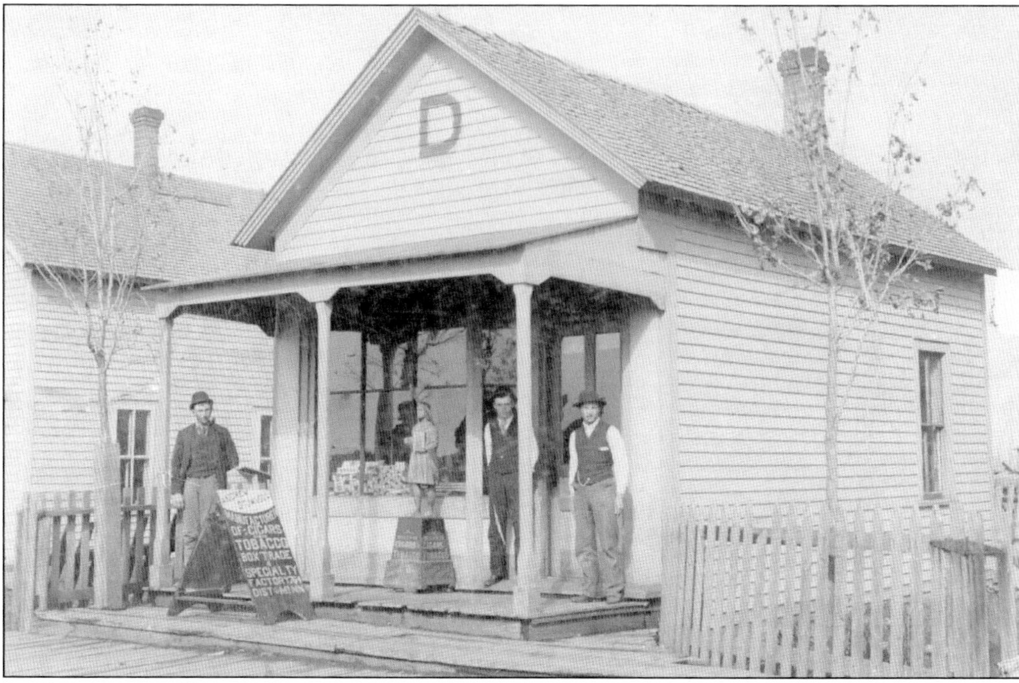

Andrew Stumvoll owned a cigar store on Main Street in Hinckley prior to the 1894 fire. Local men and visitors alike enjoyed Stumvoll's hand-rolled cigars, including the ever-popular "Belle of Hinckley." Customers savored fine tobacco and conversation on the store's front porch. A typical cigar store Indian stood by the front door.

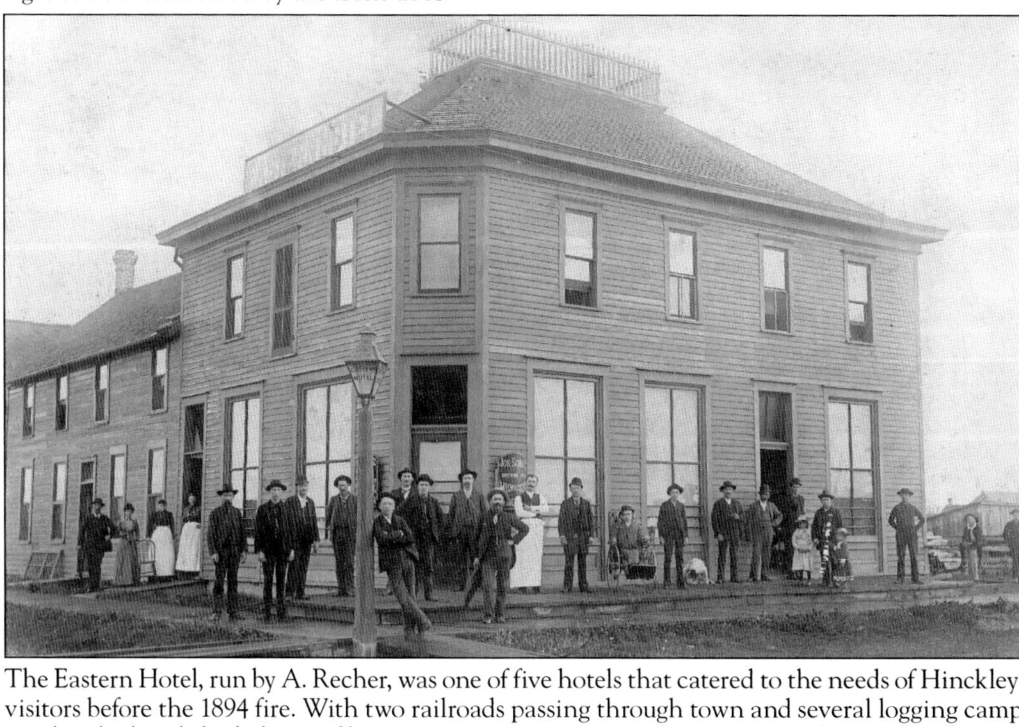

The Eastern Hotel, run by A. Recher, was one of five hotels that catered to the needs of Hinckley's visitors before the 1894 fire. With two railroads passing through town and several logging camps nearby, the hotels had plenty of business.

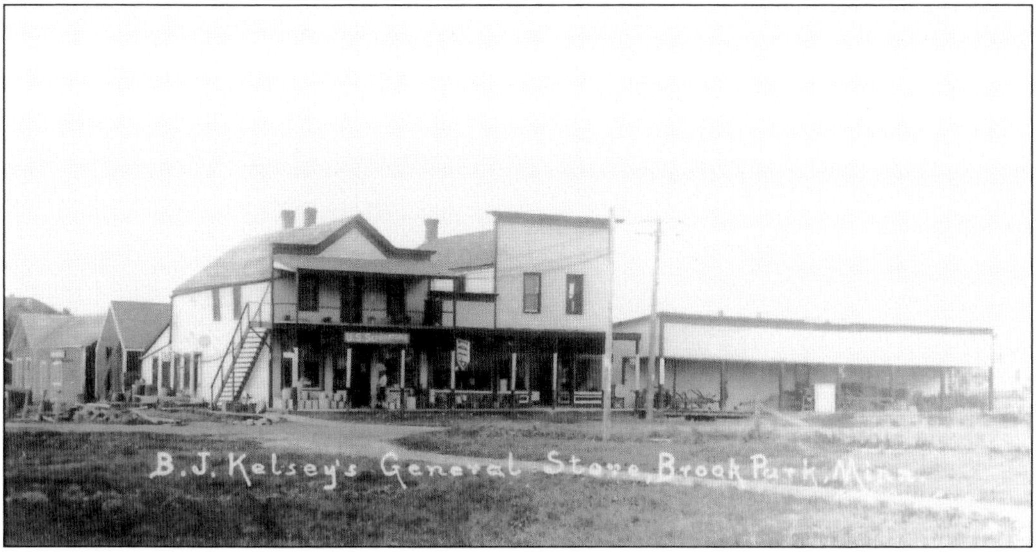

Brook Park, originally named Pokegama, was founded by Dr. C. A. Kelsey shortly before the 1894 fire, which subsequently completely destroyed it. Residents like B. J. Kelsey, brother of Dr. Kelsey, quickly returned to rebuild their homes and lives. B. J. Kelsey owned and operated this general store and helped many new settlers get their farms off to a good start.

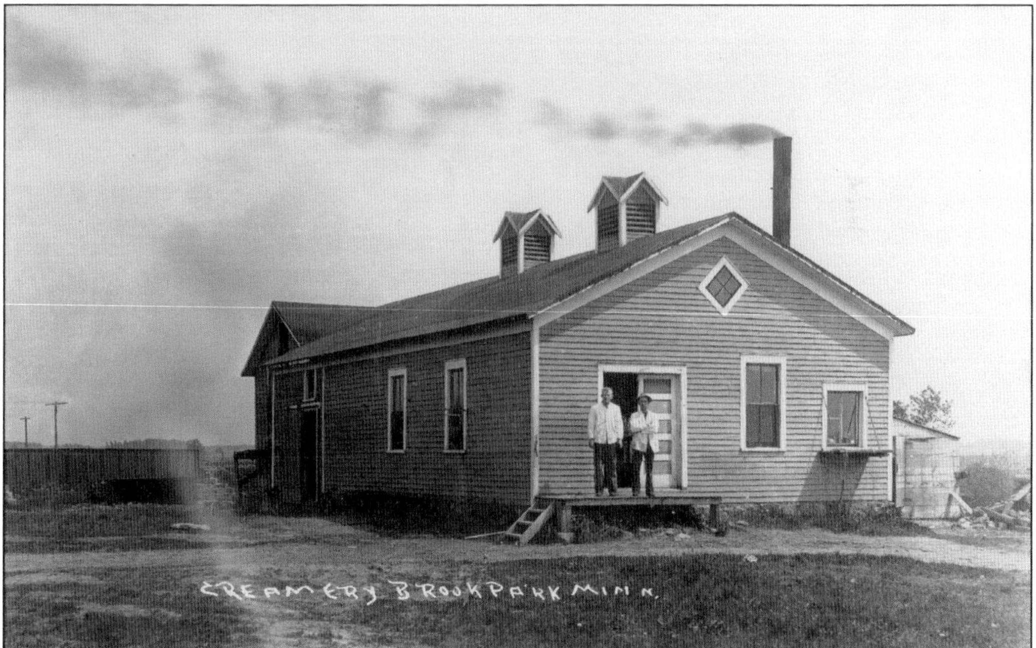

Brook Park's creamery is shown here about 1919. The first village creamery was founded in 1905 as a private establishment. The Brook Park Farmers Cooperative Creamery, one of the earliest of its kind in the country, began operations in 1913. By 1918, it was paying out nearly $75,000 a year to its patrons.

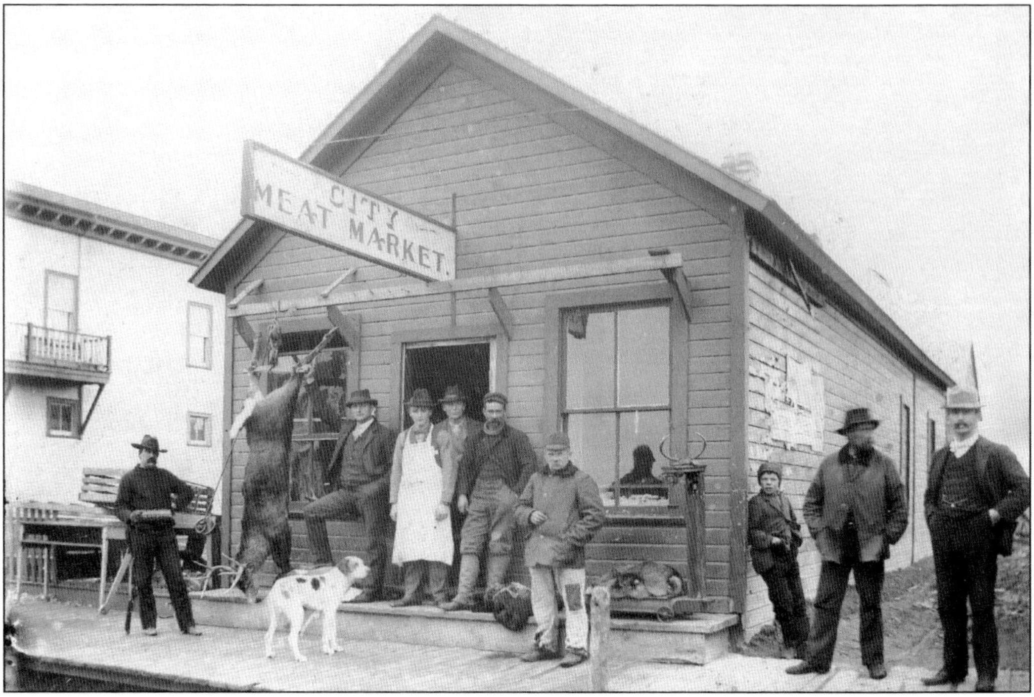

Hinckley's City Meat Market was a popular place to pose for a photograph in the late 1800s. The store, owned by Wilfred H. Carrier (in the white apron), sold both domestic meats and wild game. Notice the deer hanging upside down on the left.

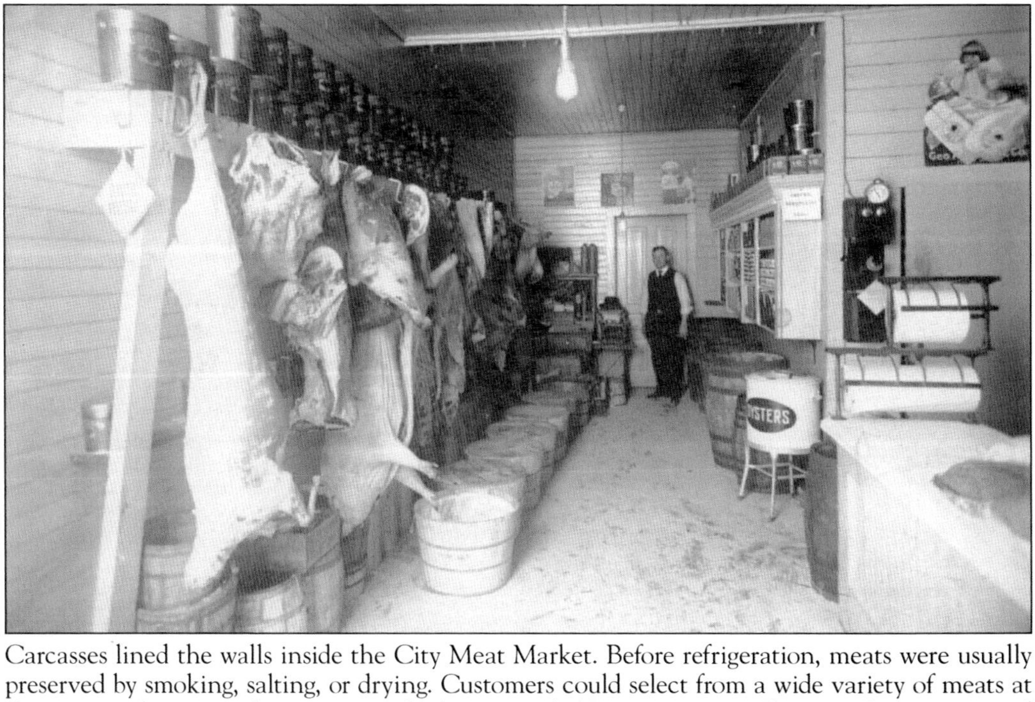

Carcasses lined the walls inside the City Meat Market. Before refrigeration, meats were usually preserved by smoking, salting, or drying. Customers could select from a wide variety of meats at this store and even purchase oysters, which were probably quite a treat. Their purchases were paid for and wrapped in white paper at the counter on the far right.

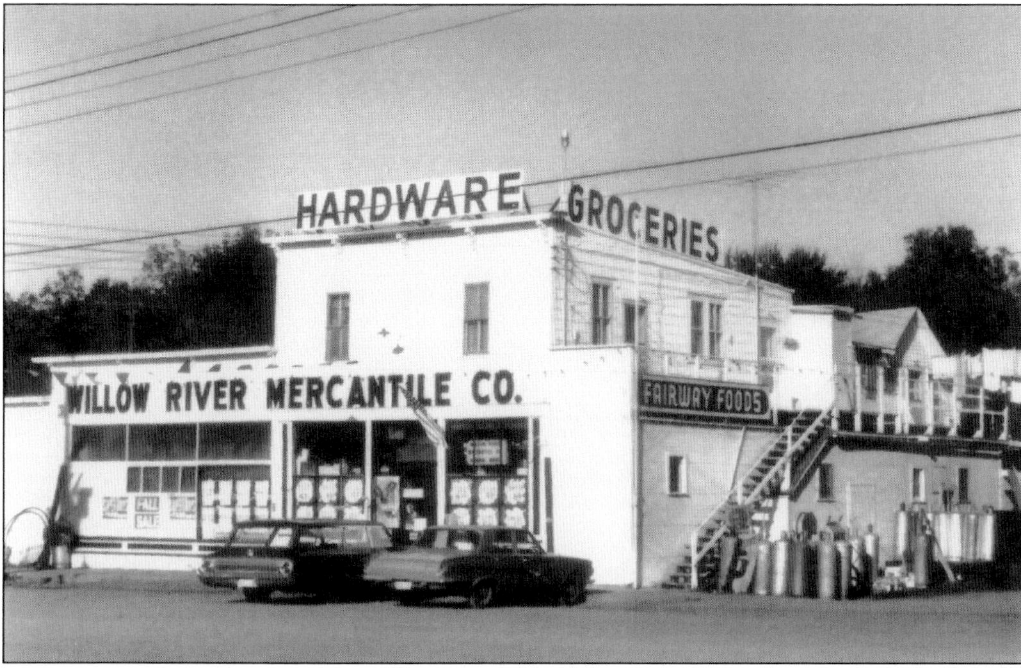

The Willow River Mercantile began as the Stekl confectionery and general merchandise store in 1901. In 1902, Edward Halva and Joseph and Josephine Bocheck purchased the business, renamed it, and decided to focus exclusively on general merchandise. The Atwood Lumber Company's store offered some stiff competition at first, but the mercantile survived and is still operating today. It is one of Pine County's oldest businesses.

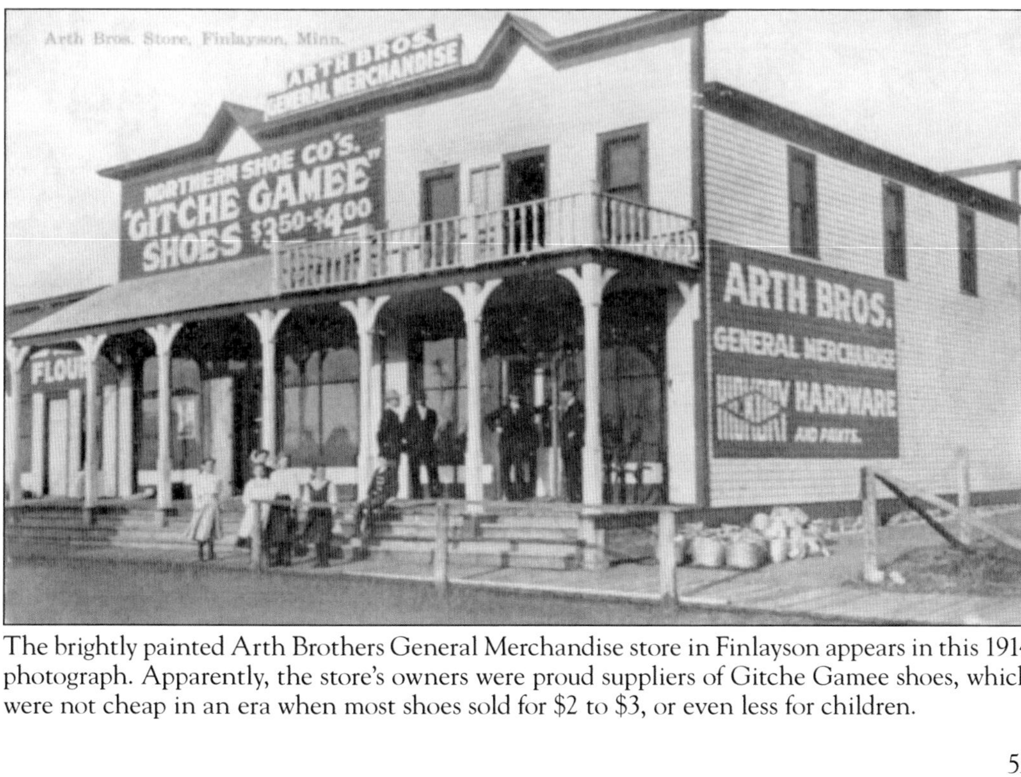

The brightly painted Arth Brothers General Merchandise store in Finlayson appears in this 1914 photograph. Apparently, the store's owners were proud suppliers of Gitche Gamee shoes, which were not cheap in an era when most shoes sold for $2 to $3, or even less for children.

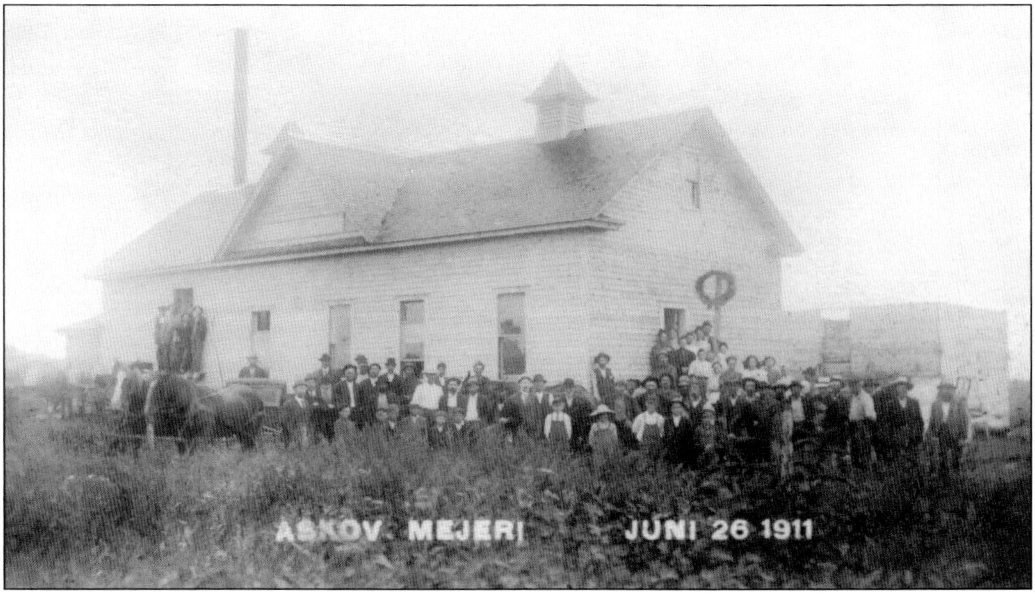

The Askov creamery was built in 1911. Opening day, June 26, was festive. People gathered to sing, listen to speeches, partake of coffee and lunch, and dedicate the new building with a traditional Danish wreath. The creamery's machinery was ready for business, but the first cream brought in by local farmers smelled horrible. Cows allowed to forage in the woods and eat wildflowers and weeds do not produce good cream.

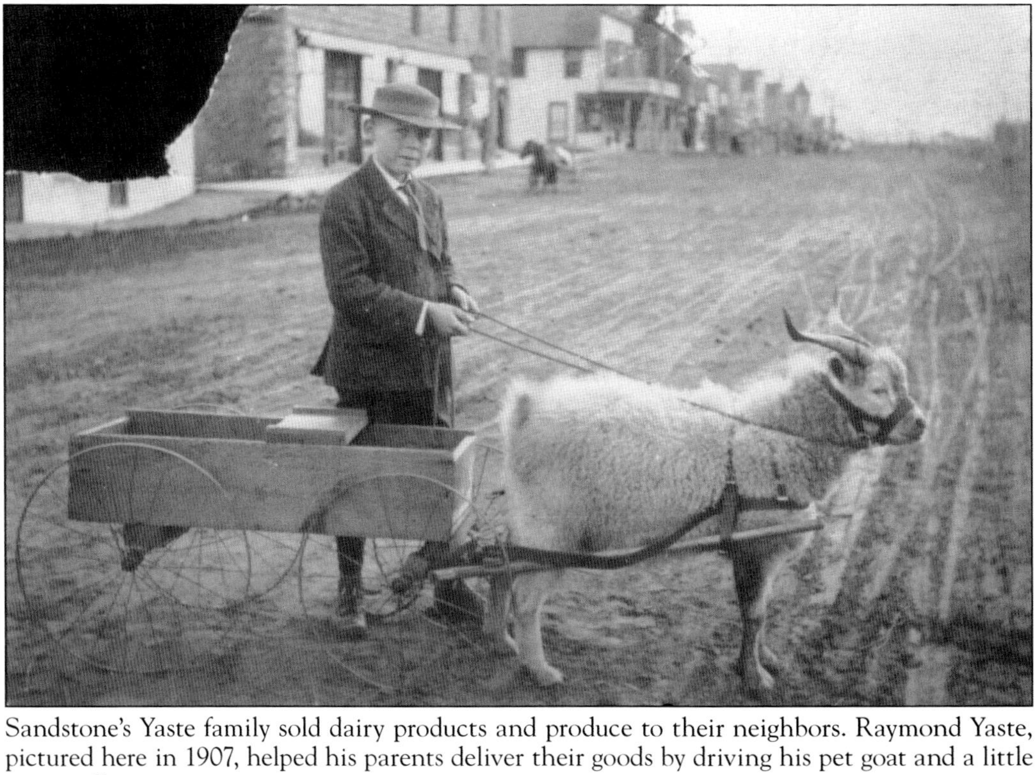

Sandstone's Yaste family sold dairy products and produce to their neighbors. Raymond Yaste, pictured here in 1907, helped his parents deliver their goods by driving his pet goat and a little wagon all over town.

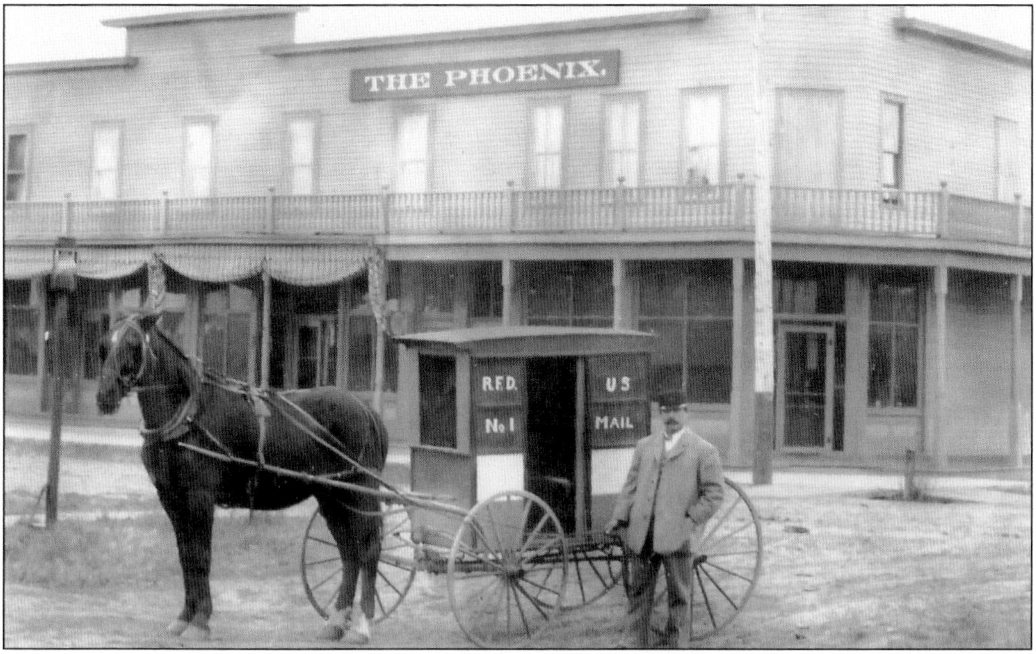

Hinckley's Phoenix hotel, located on the northwest corner of Main Street, literally rose from the ashes of the 1894 fire as the town struggled to recover. Baptiste Rolle posed with U.S. Mail Rural Free Delivery wagon No. 1 in the foreground. Rural mail delivery officially began in 1896 and became a permanent part of the U.S. Postal Service in 1904.

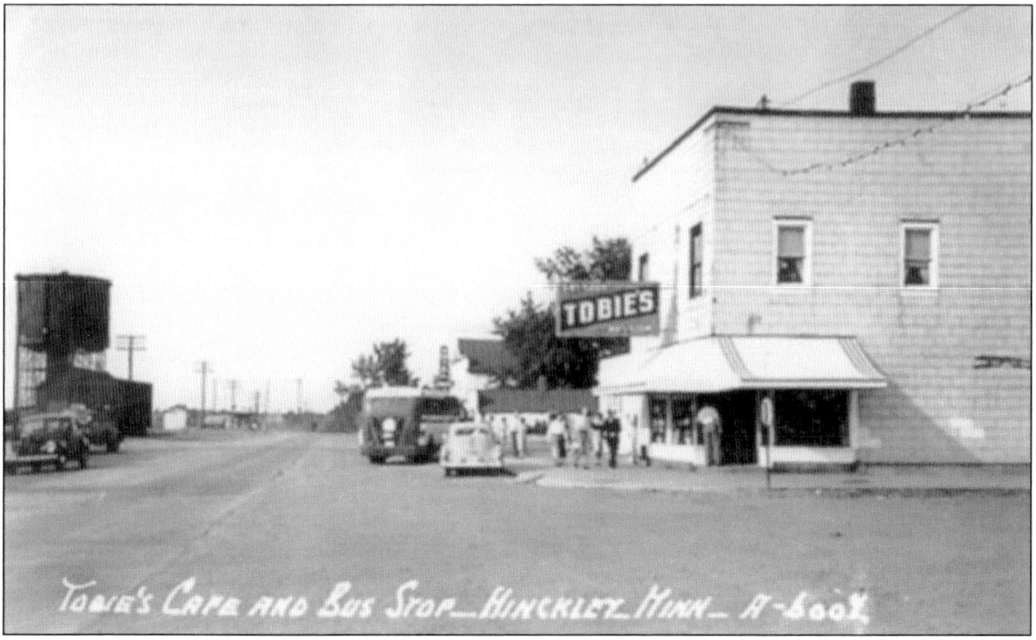

In 1920, Mr. and Mrs. Isadore Wendt opened a cafe and bus stop on the northwest corner of Hinckley's main street. Twenty-seven years later, they sold their business to Mr. and Mrs. Tobie Lackner, who renamed their new venture Tobie's Eat Shop and Bus Stop and began selling an average of 200 to 300 doughnuts, 100 rolls, and 50 to 60 pies daily. Tobie's is still famous for its baked goods.

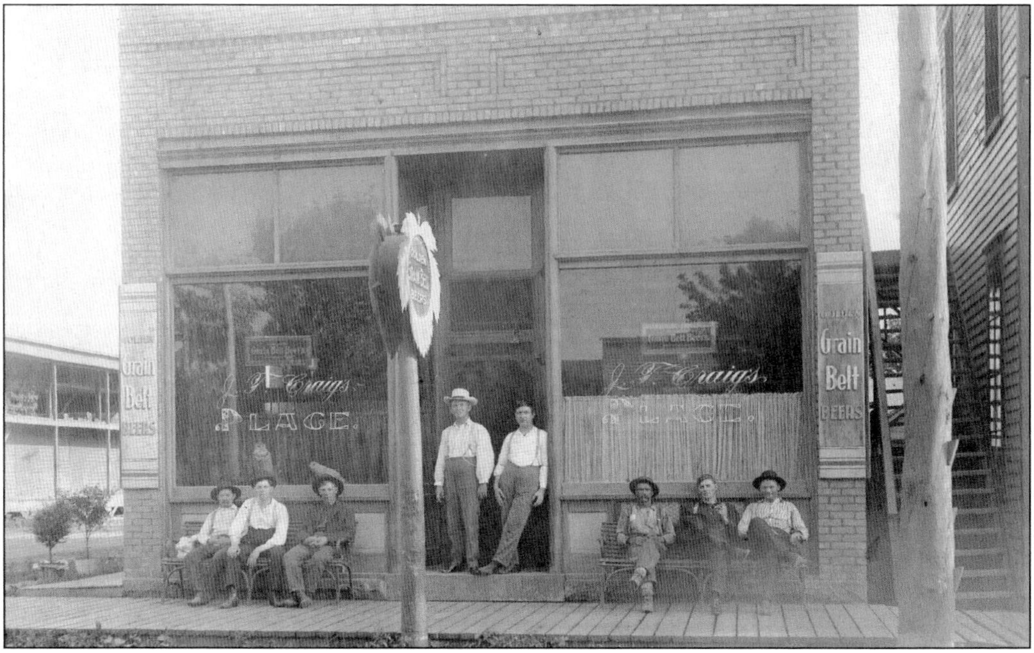

Craig's Place, on the south side of Hinckley's main street, was a popular gathering spot for locals and visitors, at least those who felt the need for something stronger than water, coffee, or tea.

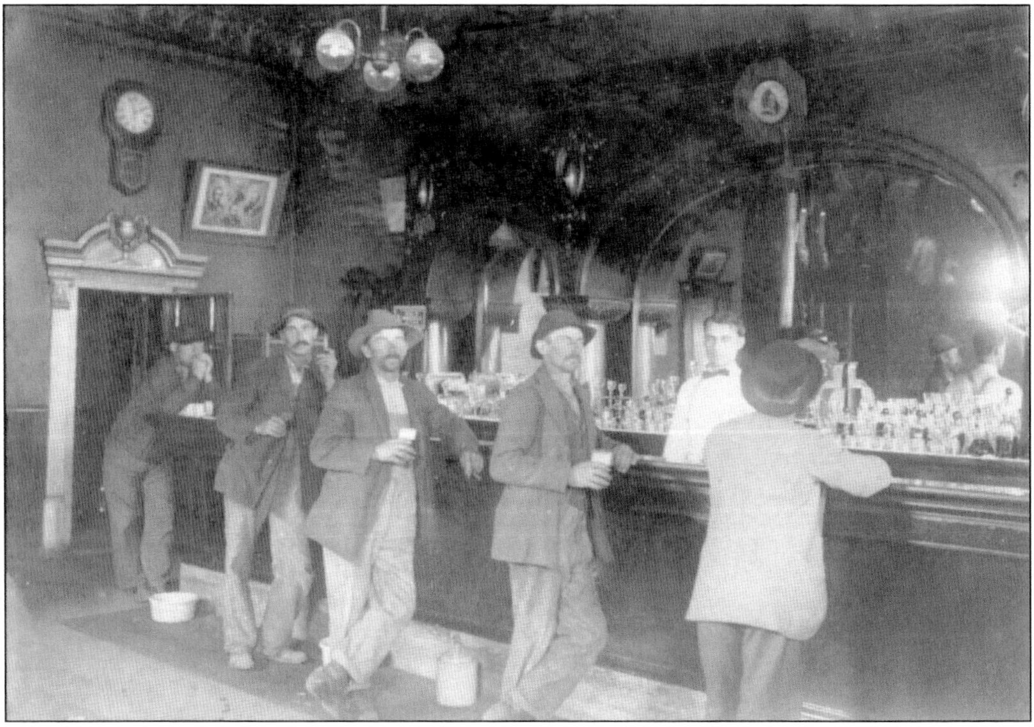

Customers lined up along the bar at Craig's Place with their drinks and cigars. These men may have been railroad workers, farmers in town to do some shopping, or travelers waiting for the next train.

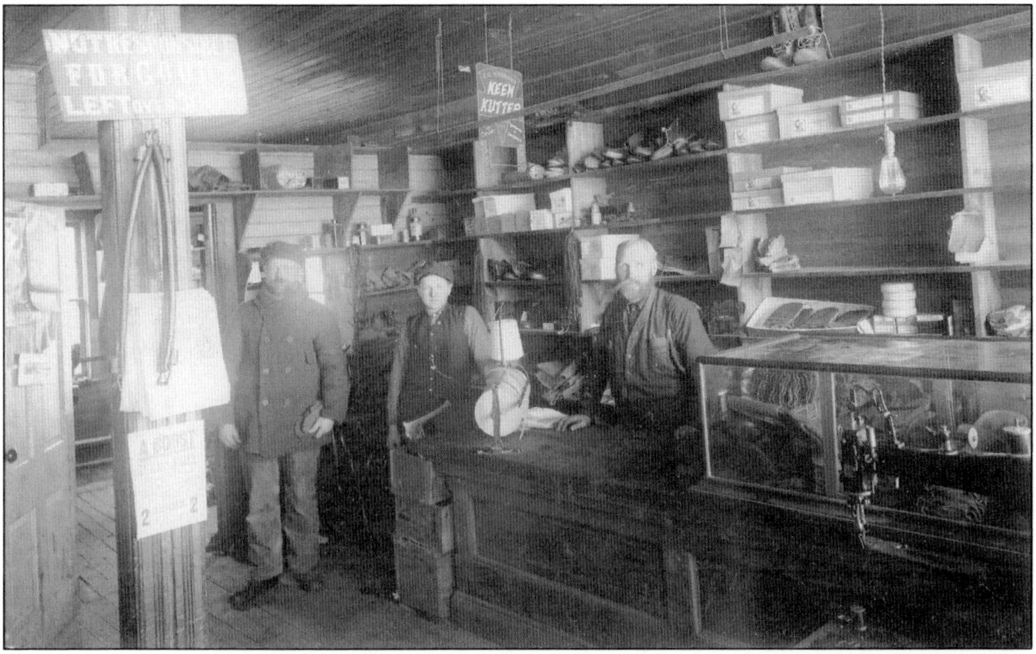

John Lundquist's Shoe Service and Harness Shop was a successful Sandstone business in the early years of the 20th century.

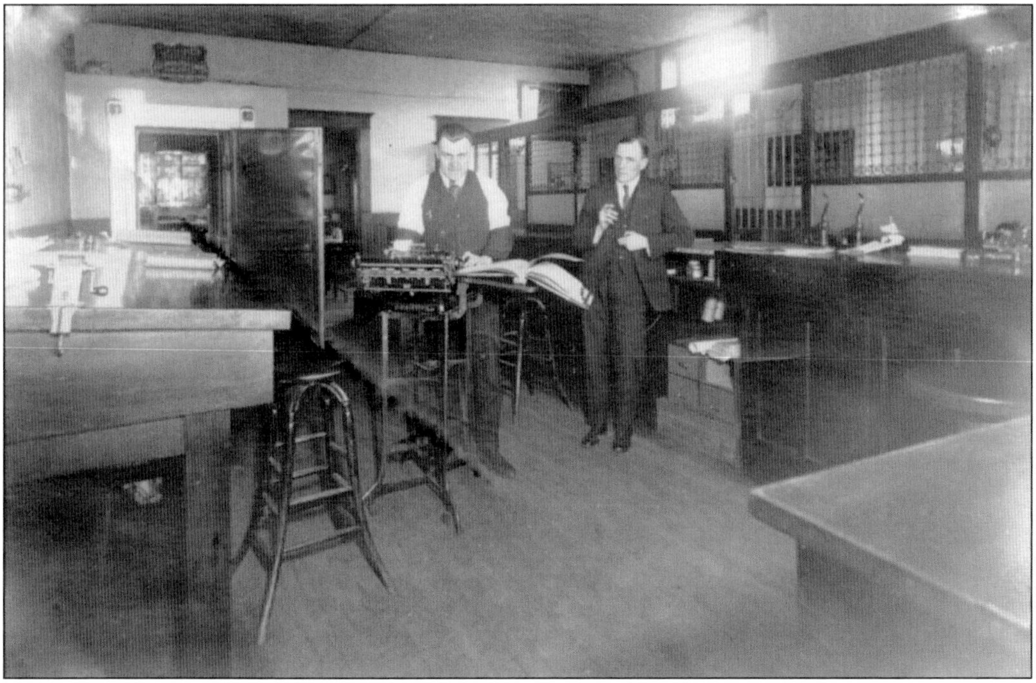

Sandstone State Bank was organized on May 25, 1906, and began operations in the former Webb Hardware building at the corner of Fourth Street and Main Avenue. In 1909, it converted to the First National Bank of Sandstone and, by 1922, claimed resources amounting to $241,012.94. The establishment reconverted to a state bank in 1940 but remained at the same location until it moved into a new building in 1969.

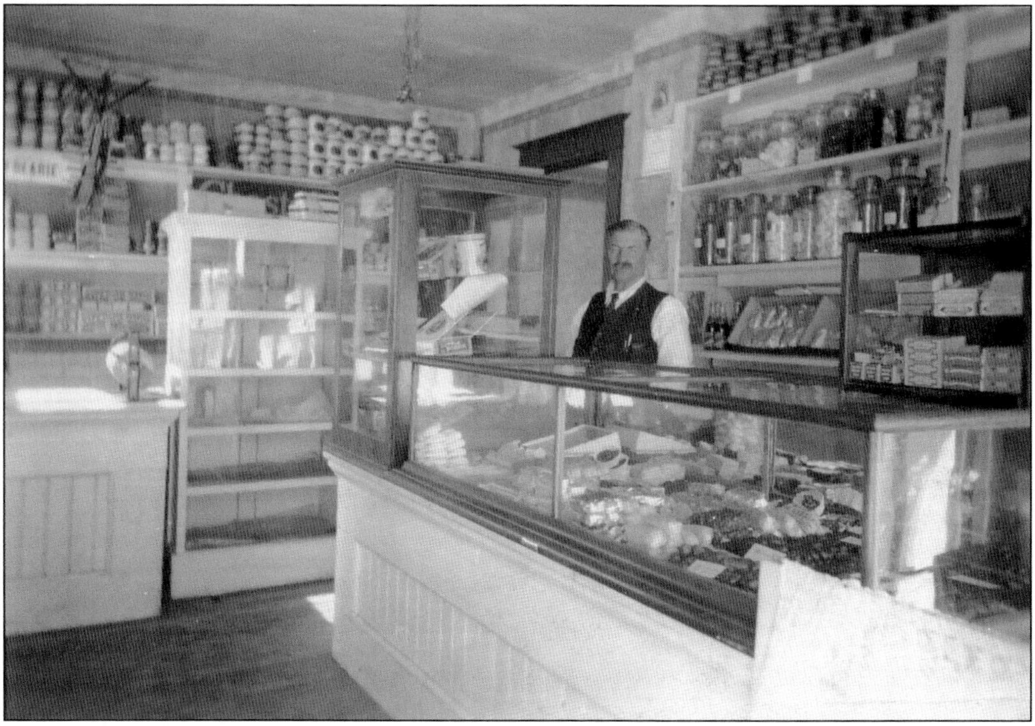

In 1917, Einer Lund posed behind the counter of his new bakery on Commercial Avenue in Sandstone. The front display case was packed with freshly made treats, while the back display cases featured candy and chewing gum. Lund was conveniently located across the street from the local school and certainly did brisk business with hungry schoolchildren.

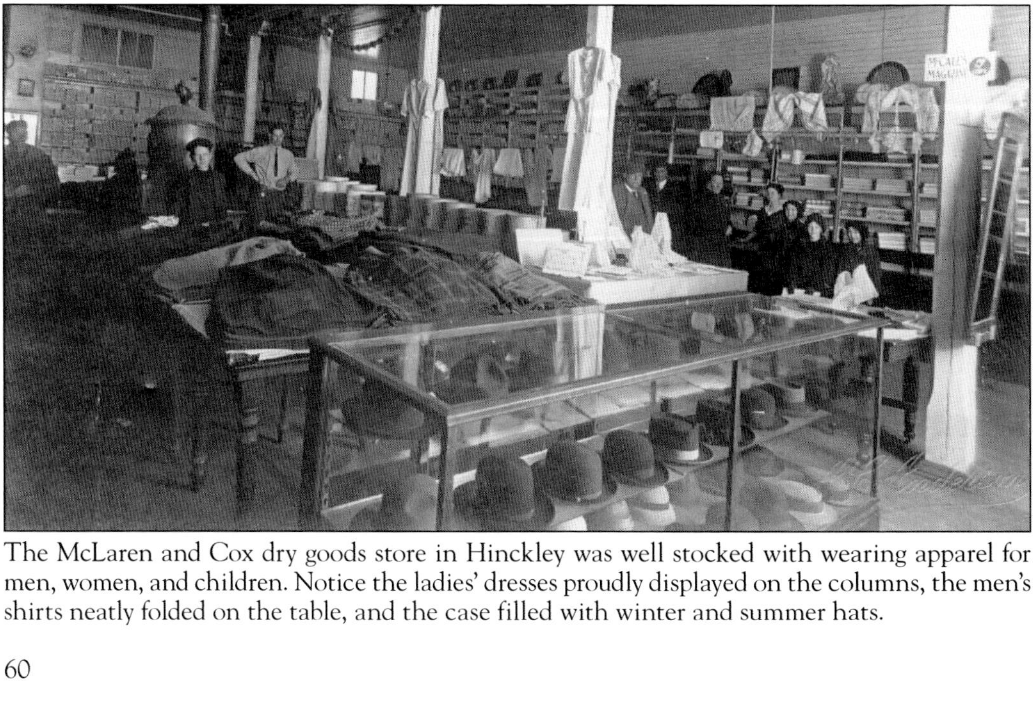

The McLaren and Cox dry goods store in Hinckley was well stocked with wearing apparel for men, women, and children. Notice the ladies' dresses proudly displayed on the columns, the men's shirts neatly folded on the table, and the case filled with winter and summer hats.

Dr. Joyce Shiels was one of the first woman dentists in Minnesota. She practiced in Sandstone from 1915 to 1919. Dr. Shiels charged 25¢ to pull a child's tooth, but she returned the money to any patient who had been good during the procedure. Dr. Shiels frequently visited surrounding towns to provide dental care to patients who could not travel to Sandstone.

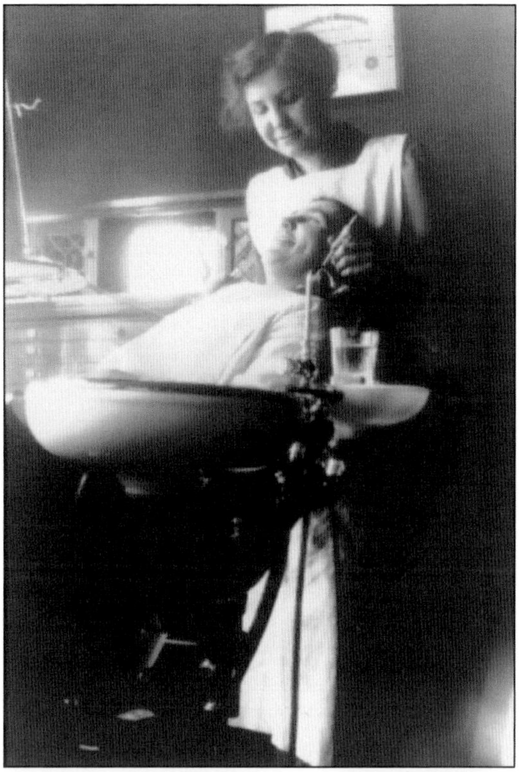

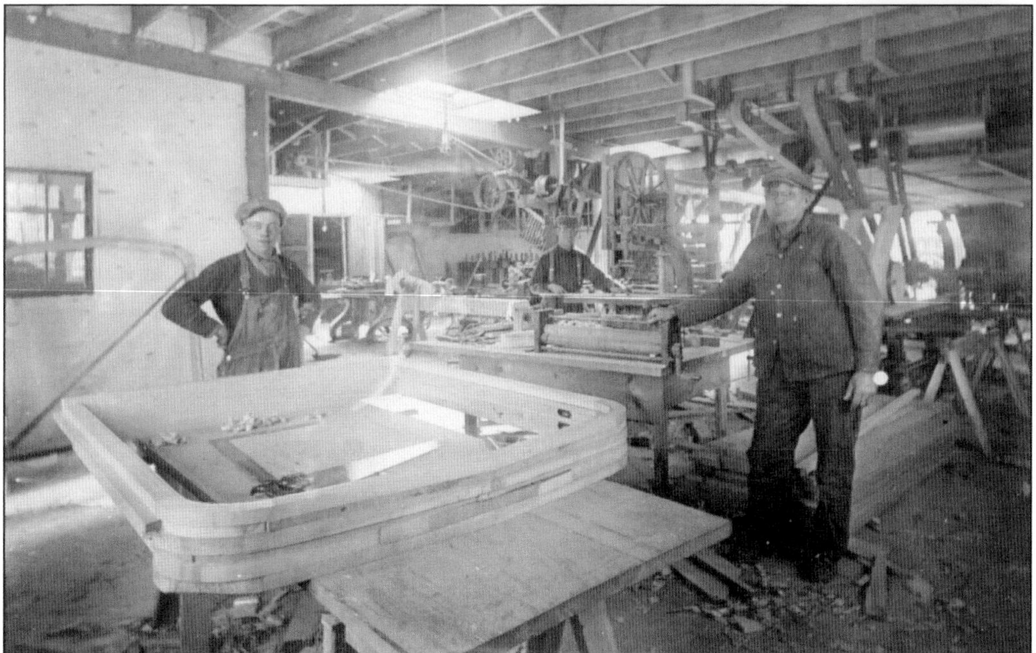

Hanson Sash and Door Factory, on Fourth Street in Sandstone, provided doors and windows for buildings throughout Pine and Carlton Counties. From left to right, Lawrence Dupuis, owner Eric Hanson, and Hans Troolin took at break from their work to pose for this 1920s photograph.

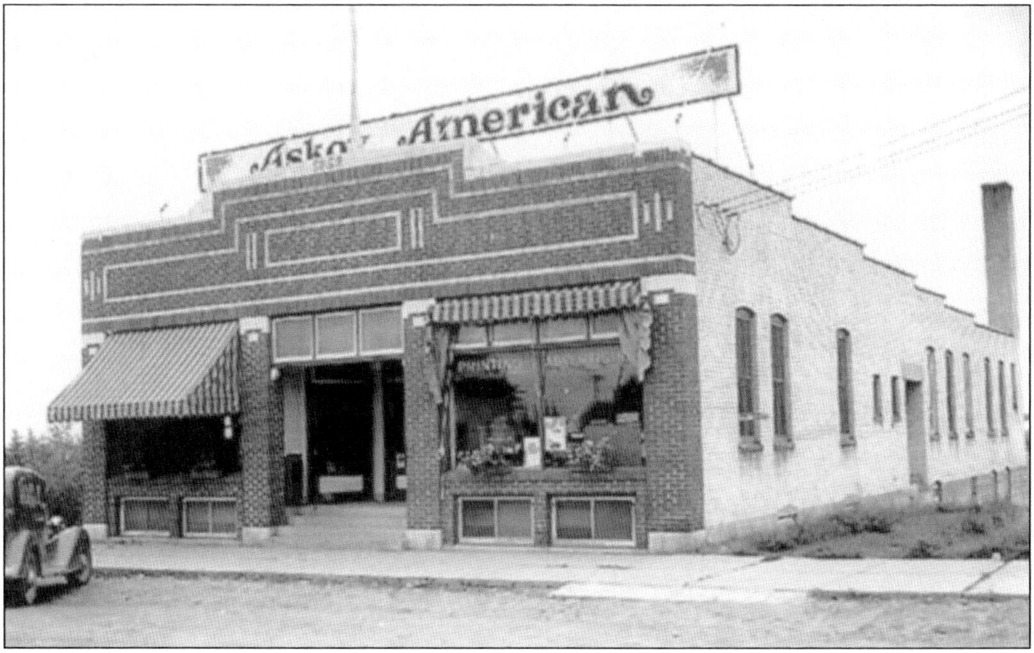

The *Askov American* newspaper was founded in 1914. Like most small town newspapers, it covered local happenings like births, deaths, marriages, organizational meetings, and neighborly visits; provided advertising space to local businesses; and updated readers on state, national, and world news. The paper is still headquartered in the same building on Askov's main street.

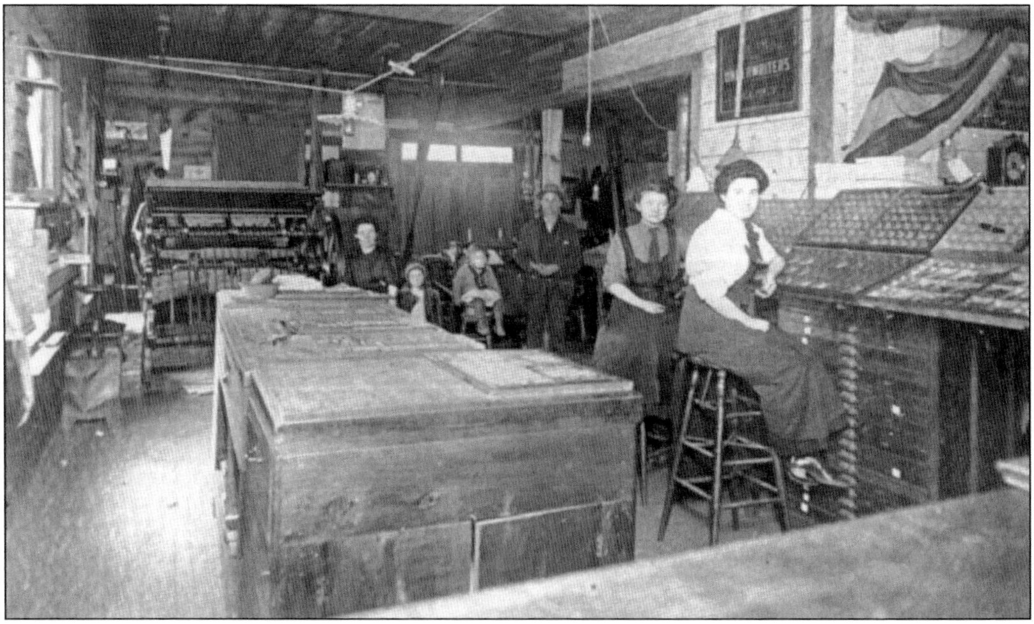

In the *Askov American*'s early days, typesetters, like the ones pictured here, carefully arranged letters and words in special trays to form mirror images of each story. The trays were then inked and run through a press to create copies of the newspaper. It was a time-consuming and somewhat tedious job. Most newspaper offices also offered special order printing of fliers, business cards, posters, and other ephemera.

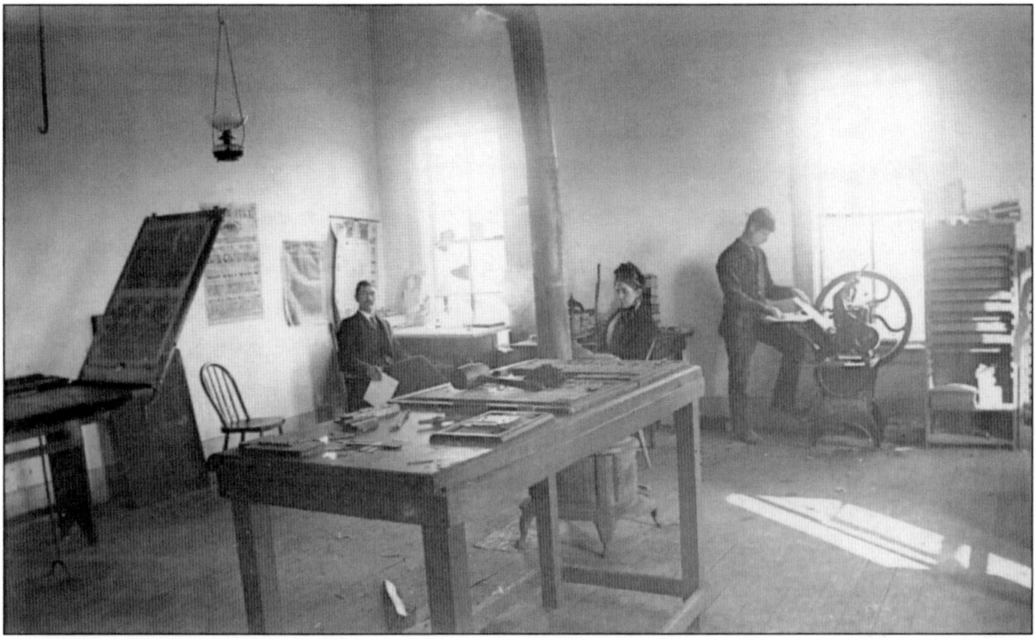

This photograph shows the office of the *Pine County Pioneer* newspaper in Pine City. Notice the unique wheeled handbill press near the window, the typesetting table in the middle of the room, and the paper press on the far left. The office was located in the former county courthouse, which was built in 1872.

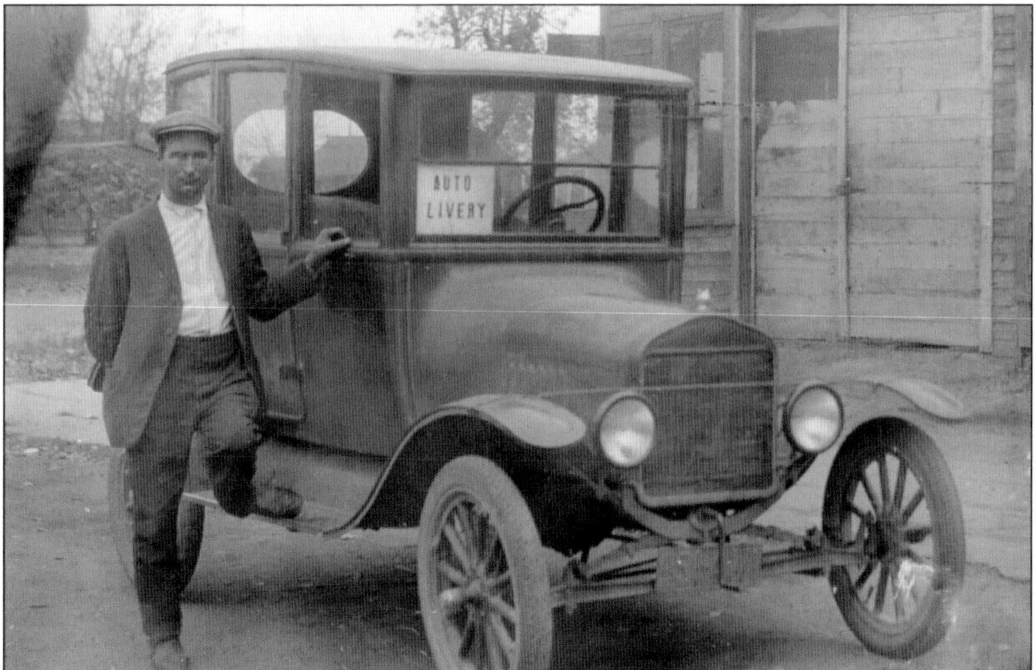

When automobiles made their way to Pine County in the 1900s, the traditional livery stable, which cared for and rented out horses, buggies, and wagons, was gradually replaced by the auto livery, which cared for and rented out the "horseless carriage."

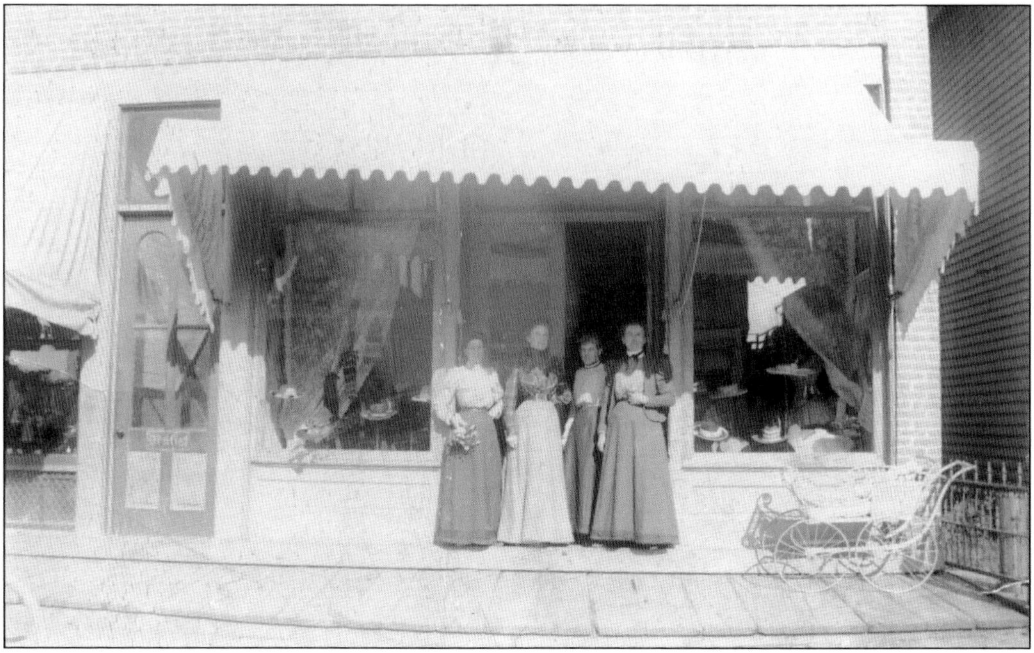

Millinery stores were common in the 1800s and early 1900s. These shops specialized in making and selling women's hats of all colors and styles. This millinery store in Hinckley was owned by Josephine Turgeon (on the left). Rose Turgeon Maloney is second from left.

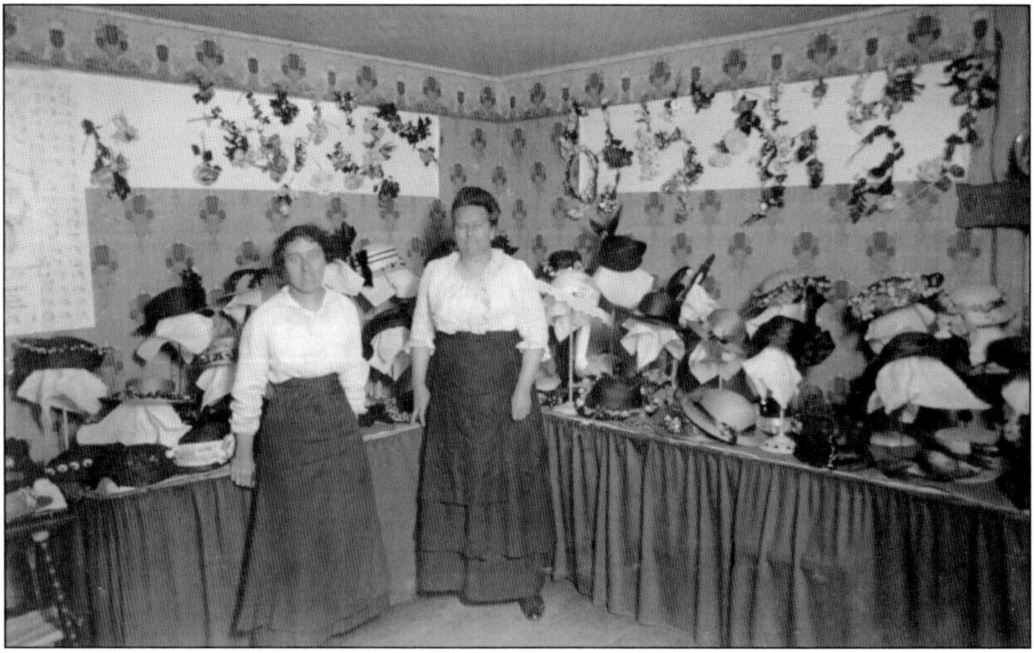

Here is an interior view of one of Hinckley's millinery shops. Ada Conner Healy (left) and Angeline Wallick proudly displayed their goods. Notice the wide variety of hat styles, both formal and casual, and the lively Victorian wallpaper.

Five

EDUCATING THE CHILDREN

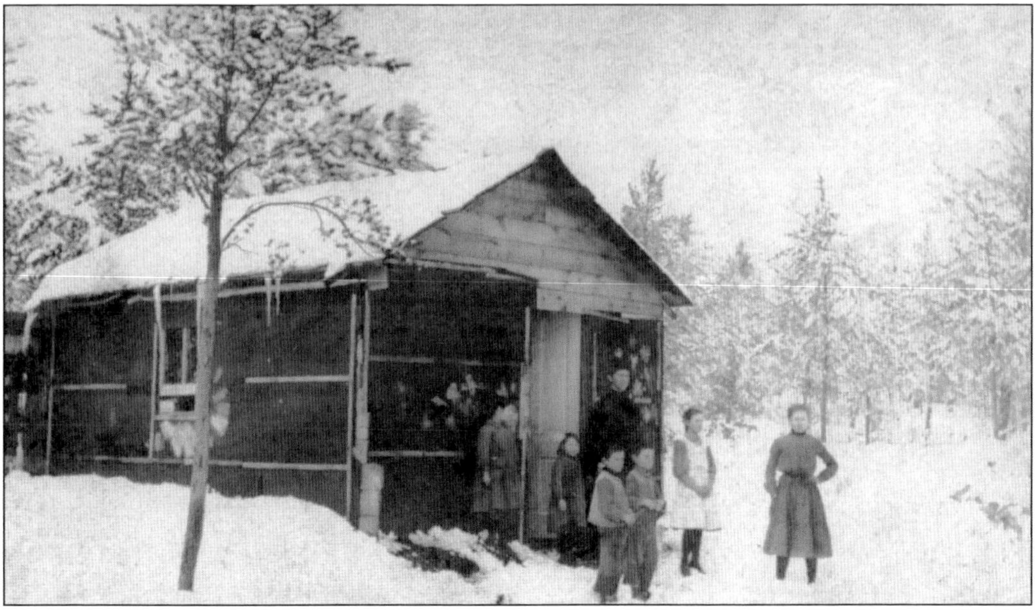

This little schoolhouse near the St. Croix River in eastern Pine County was typical of the area's early schools. Teacher Dora Williams Von Rueden (born 1886) was probably not much older than the five or six students she instructed in "reading, writing, and 'rithmetic." Her school was lined with tar paper to retain as much heat as possible during the winter, but students shivered through their lessons anyway.

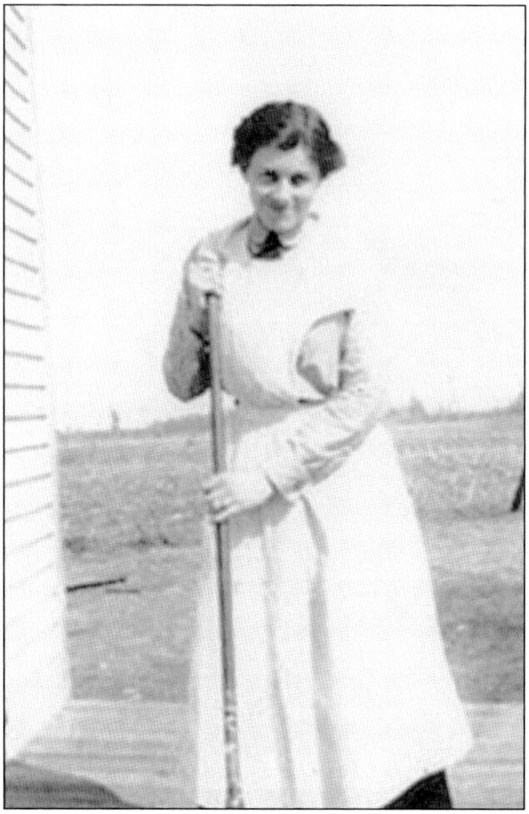

Country schoolteachers, like Ethel Sauer from Meadow Lawn School District No. 73, did far more than conduct classes. Along with giving lessons in everything from reading to personal hygiene, they were responsible for disciplining students, cleaning the school, tending the stove, organizing community events, and maintaining the highest moral standards. Their pay was usually around $40 to $50 per month or less.

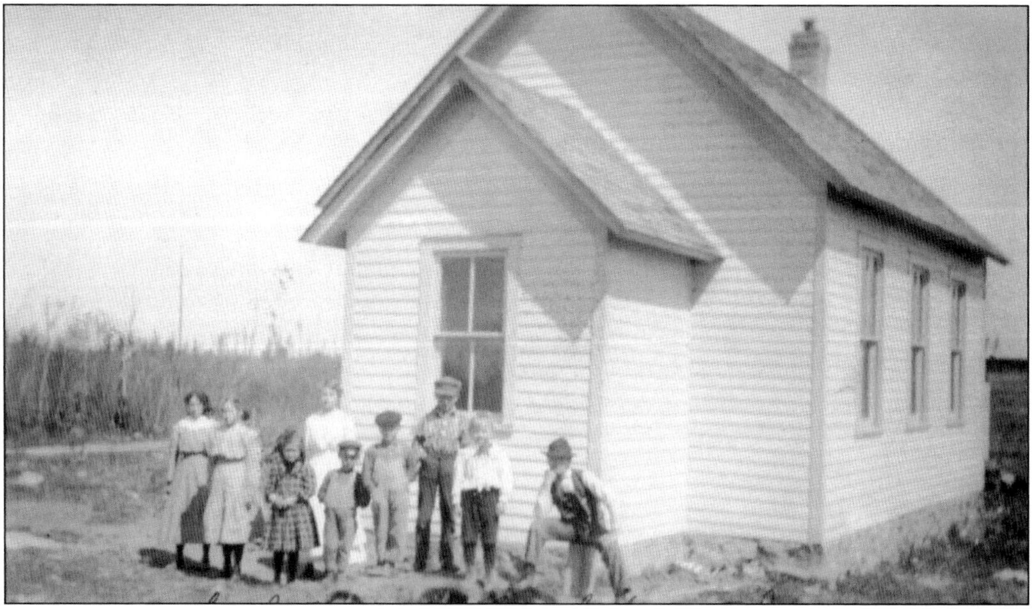

A teacher and her students posed near their rural Sandstone school in 1909. In most country schools, one teacher instructed eight grades, taking time to hear daily recitations and give lessons to each class, even if it consisted of only one or two students. Pupils especially enjoyed recess when they could play games like kittenball, hide-and-seek, fox and geese, or Annie-i-over.

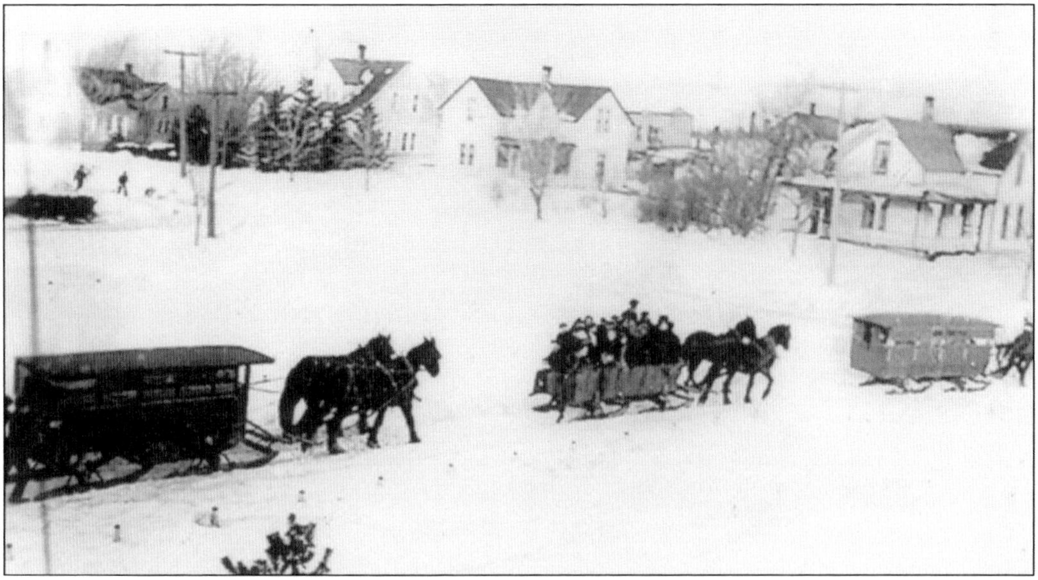

Most rural schoolchildren in Northern Pine County walked to school. A mile or two was considered good exercise rather than hardship, but a few larger school districts operated horse-drawn school busses like these, especially during the coldest winter months. Children still had to bundle up. These busses, which were sometimes merely open sleighs or wagons, lacked heat. Even so, catching a ride to school was better than walking through deep snow.

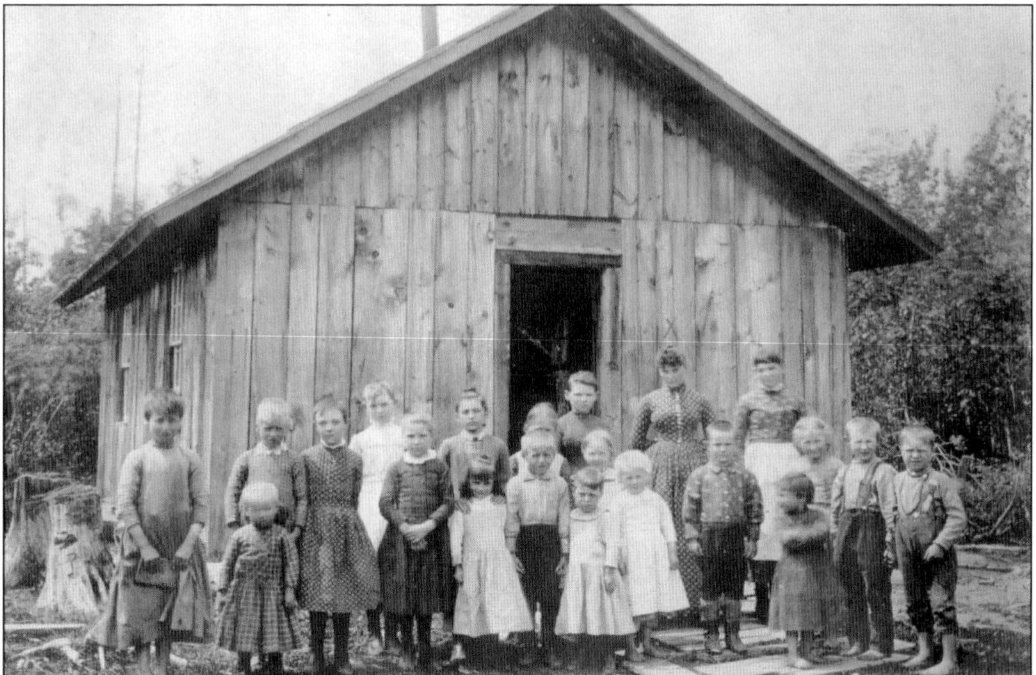

The Mission Creek school was built in 1880 for the children of John B. Martin Lumber Company employees. Mission Creek was a lumber company town, so when the 1894 fire cut short Pine County's logging days, the village was no longer needed, and residents moved on. The little girl on the right with her arms folded is Jamie Johnson, age five.

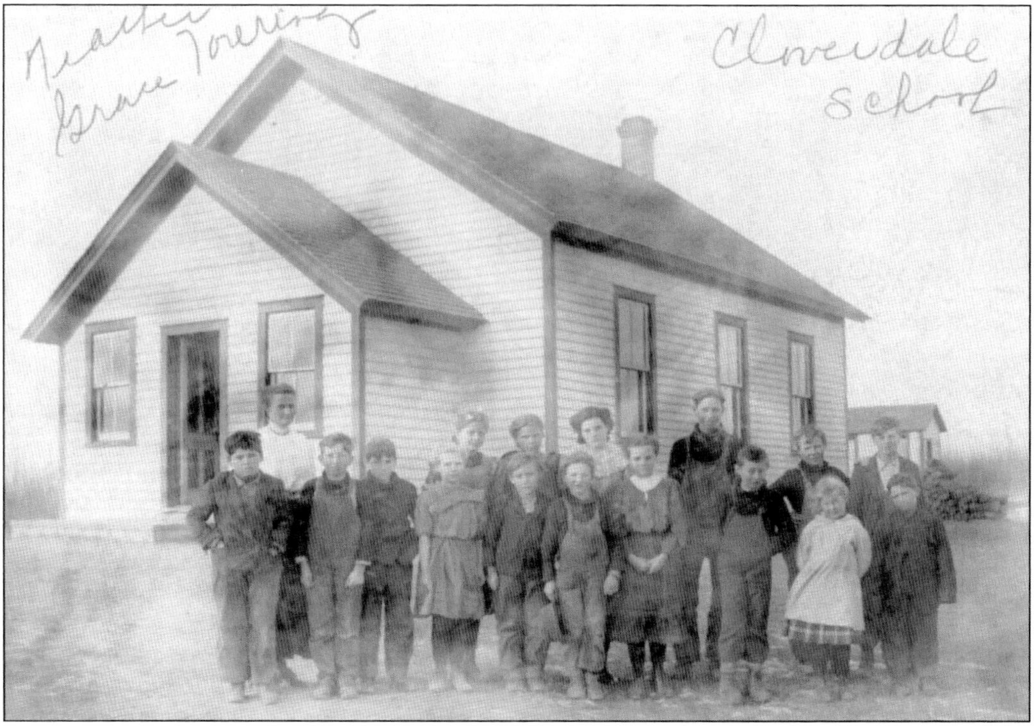

The Cloverdale school, in Arlone Township east of Hinckley, was constructed by Dan McIver in 1913 for $400. Cloverdale was original called Turpville because of the turpentine industry that flourished there in the early 1900s. Teacher Grace Toering posed with her class in this early photograph. The school closed in 1964.

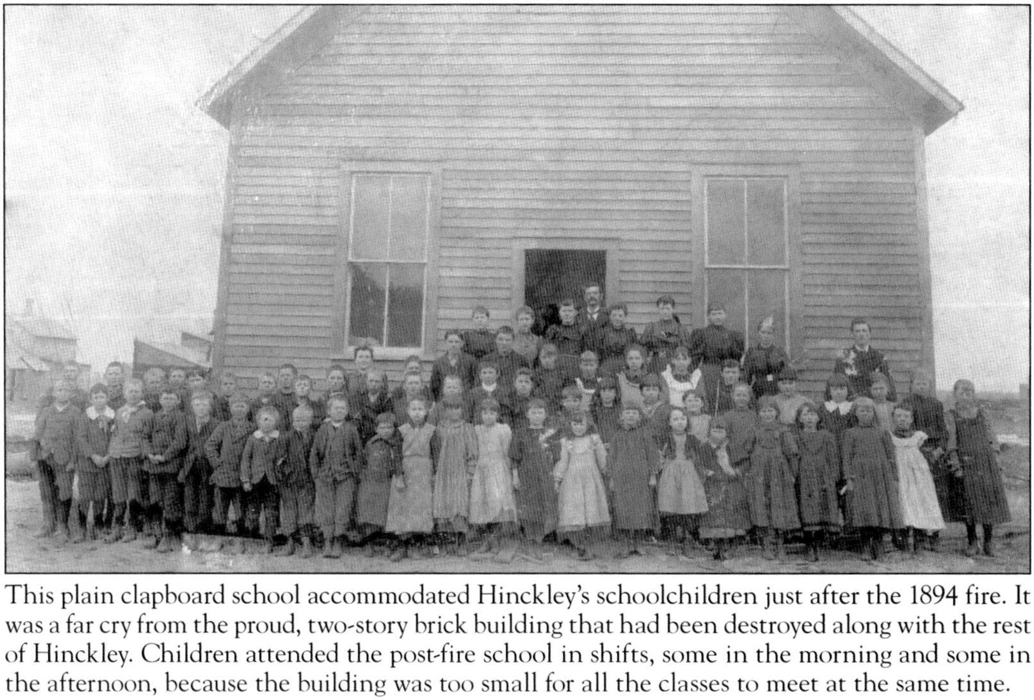

This plain clapboard school accommodated Hinckley's schoolchildren just after the 1894 fire. It was a far cry from the proud, two-story brick building that had been destroyed along with the rest of Hinckley. Children attended the post-fire school in shifts, some in the morning and some in the afternoon, because the building was too small for all the classes to meet at the same time.

The first Hinckley graduating class, Grace Toering, Goldie Hoffman, and Ethel Currie, wore identical dresses and proudly displayed their diplomas when they posed for this 1907 photograph. Very few young people graduated from high school in the early 1900s. Most teenagers married young or went to work on their families' farms and had to be content with an eighth-grade education.

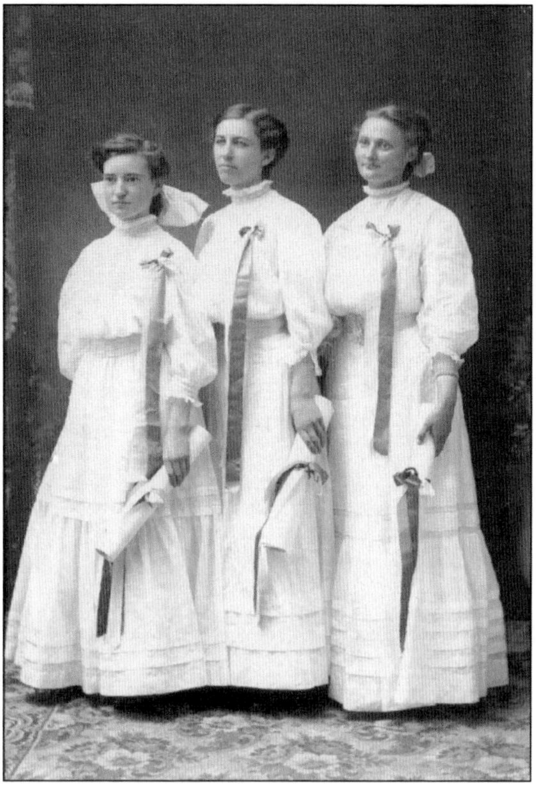

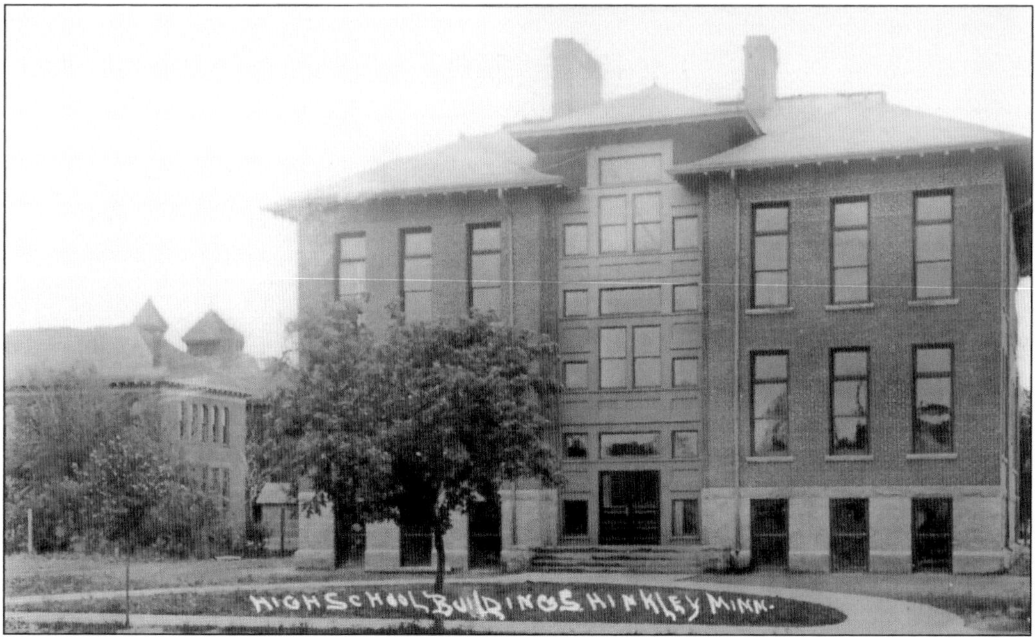

Hinckley's brick high school was completed in 1911. It surpassed earlier schools in size and modern conveniences. Hinckley had come a long way from its first school, which was organized in 1869 in a former dance hall owned by the Brennan Lumber Company. The 1911 building was demolished after a new school was constructed in 1936.

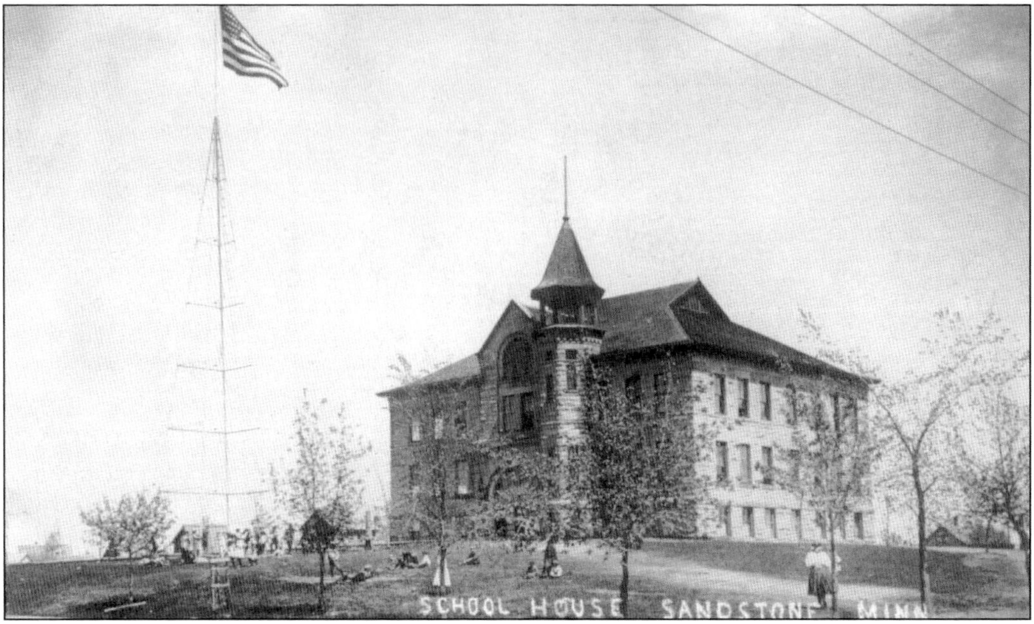

Sandstone's first schoolhouse was actually a warehouse in the quarry. School met for only three days in the fall of 1886 before the teacher died. Schools were built, sold, and rebuilt as the student population grew. Finally, on April 22, 1902, Sandstone dedicated its regal new school building, designed by Minneapolis architect F. B. Kendrick and constructed of local sandstone. The school was destroyed by fire in 1909.

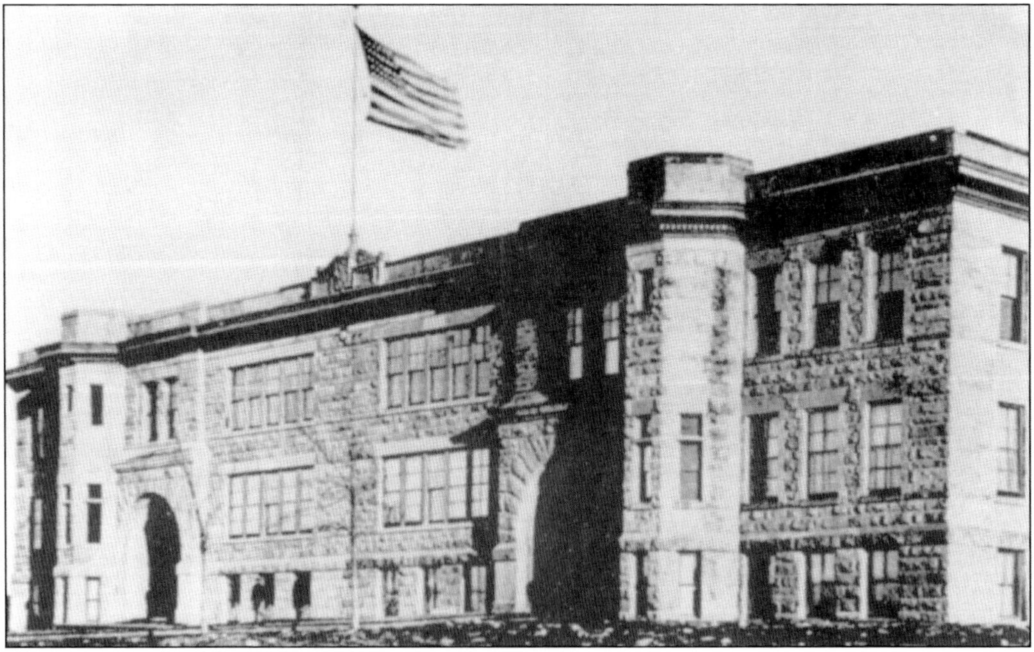

After the Sandstone school burned in 1909, community members purchased $26,000 in bonds to finance a new school, which was completed in the fall of 1910. The school's enrollment that year numbered 400 students, including 50 of high school age. Older students enjoyed forming basketball teams and competing in the new gymnasium.

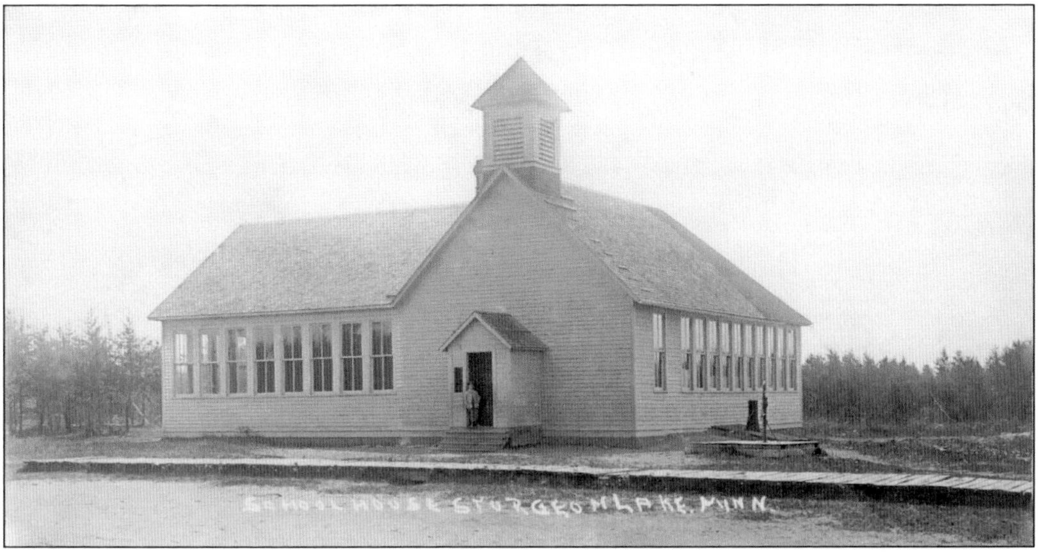

Sturgeon Lake's two-room schoolhouse is pictured here. It replaced its one-room predecessor, which featured a blackboard made from a barn door, in 1900. Somewhat unusually for the era, a married couple, Mr. and Mrs. Wilkens, served as schoolteachers for the upper and lower classes, respectively. A brick school, built as a Works Progress Administration (WPA) project, was completed in 1941.

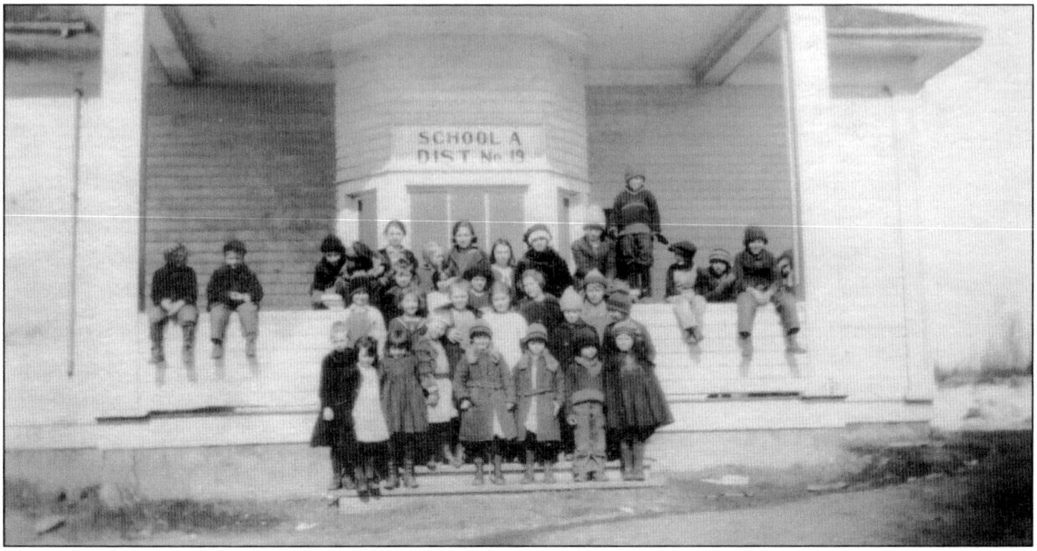

Denham's school district No. 19 was organized in 1889. The first schoolhouse was a log building that was also used by two churches. The structure shown here was constructed in 1903 with a rather unique architectural design. Denham, in the northwest part of the county, was a small town on the Soo Line railroad spur, which transported livestock, cream, wood, farm produce, and dry goods to, from, and through the village.

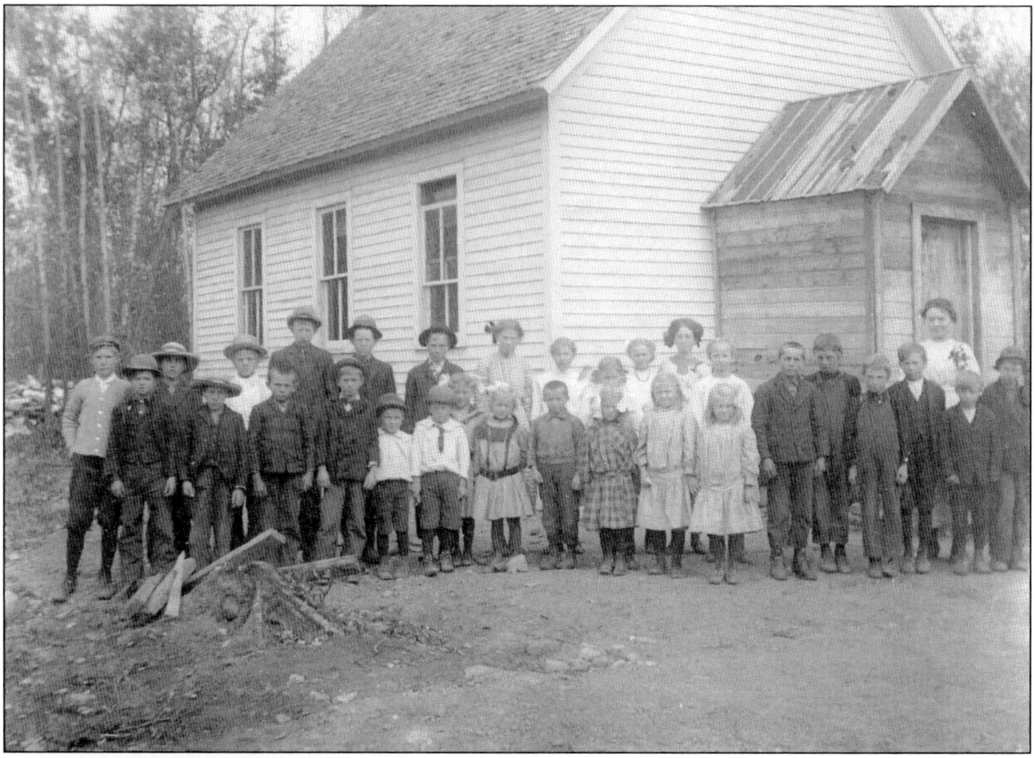

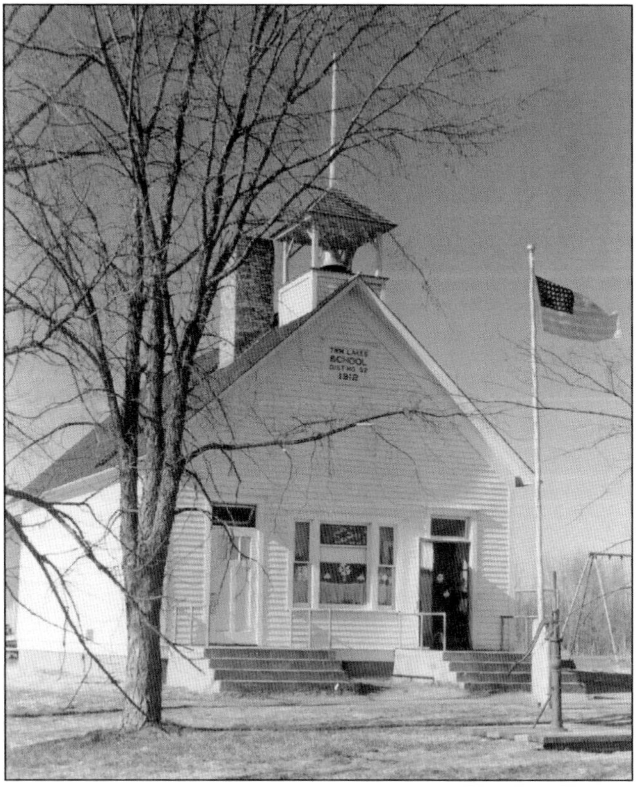

The Sunny Hill School in Birch Creek Township was organized in 1909 and named by Marie Paulson, a student in the district. Kate Barnum, the daughter of a Pine City doctor and an 1894 fire survivor, taught at Sunny Hill. After a few years, the school was moved half a mile to the north to better accommodate settlers' children.

The Twin Lakes or Lake Lena School in Ogema township in far eastern Pine County was established in 1910. Logging company owner David Tozer provided 2 acres for the school, which was built with one door for boys and another for girls. Many Ojibway children from nearby villages attended classes in district No. 92.

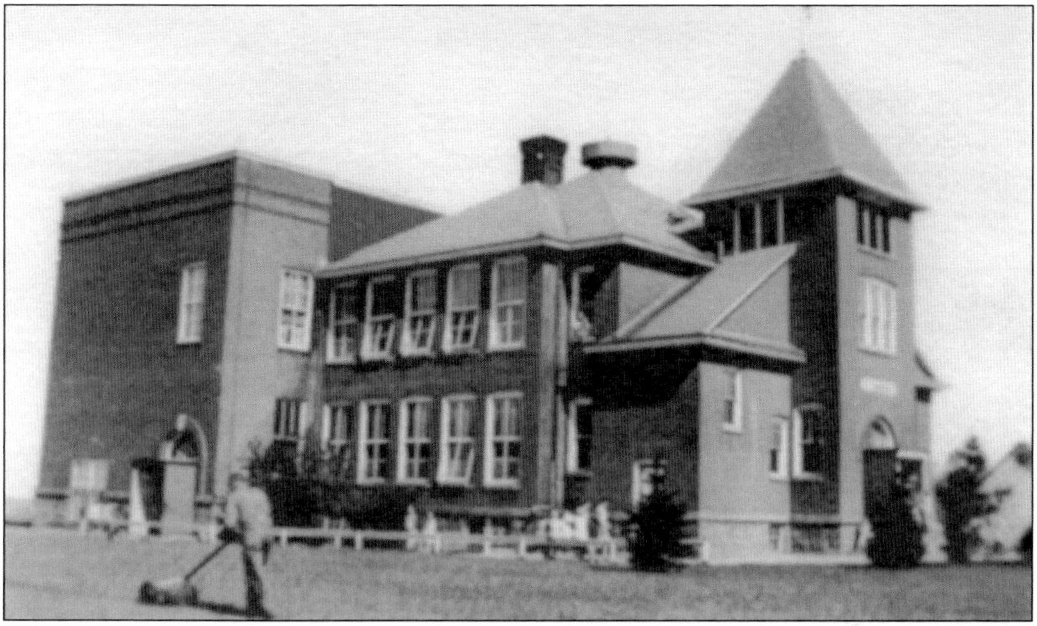

Askov's Hans Christian Andersen School reflects the community's Danish heritage. Built in 1910, this four-room brick schoolhouse was soon too small to accommodate Askov's student population, and another schoolhouse was moved into town to make room for extra classes. All Askov students received lessons in Danish reading, writing, storytelling, and singing as part of their regular curriculum.

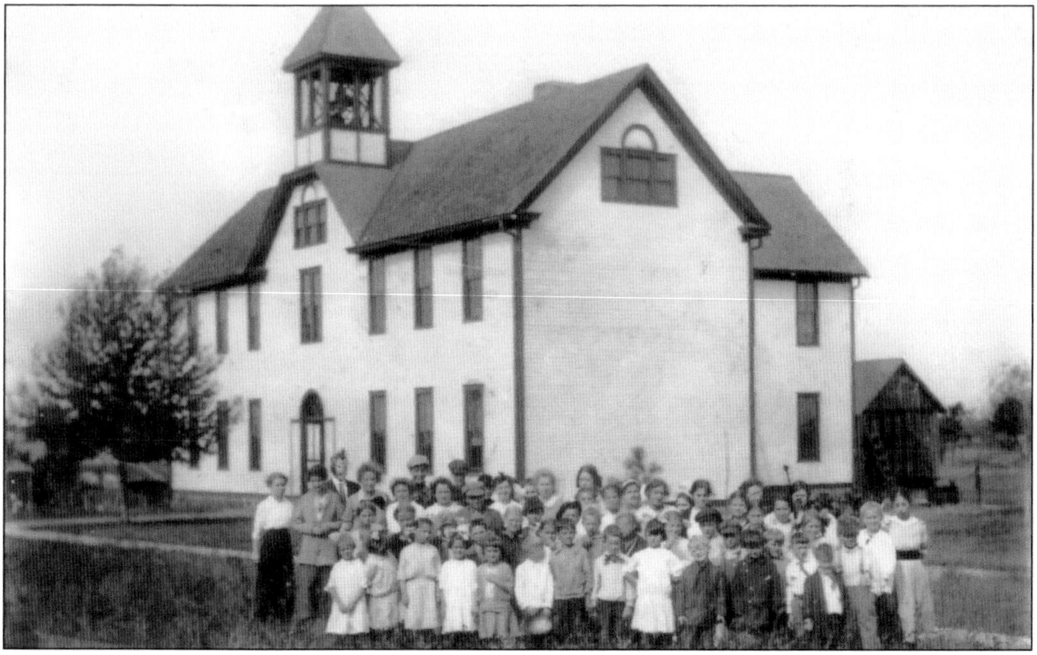

The first Willow River school, organized in 1890, had only one room. A second room was added in 1894 to accommodate the growing school population, but the school burned in 1900. The schoolhouse shown in this 1918 photograph was constructed in 1900 as a one-floor, T-shaped building. A second floor addition was built later.

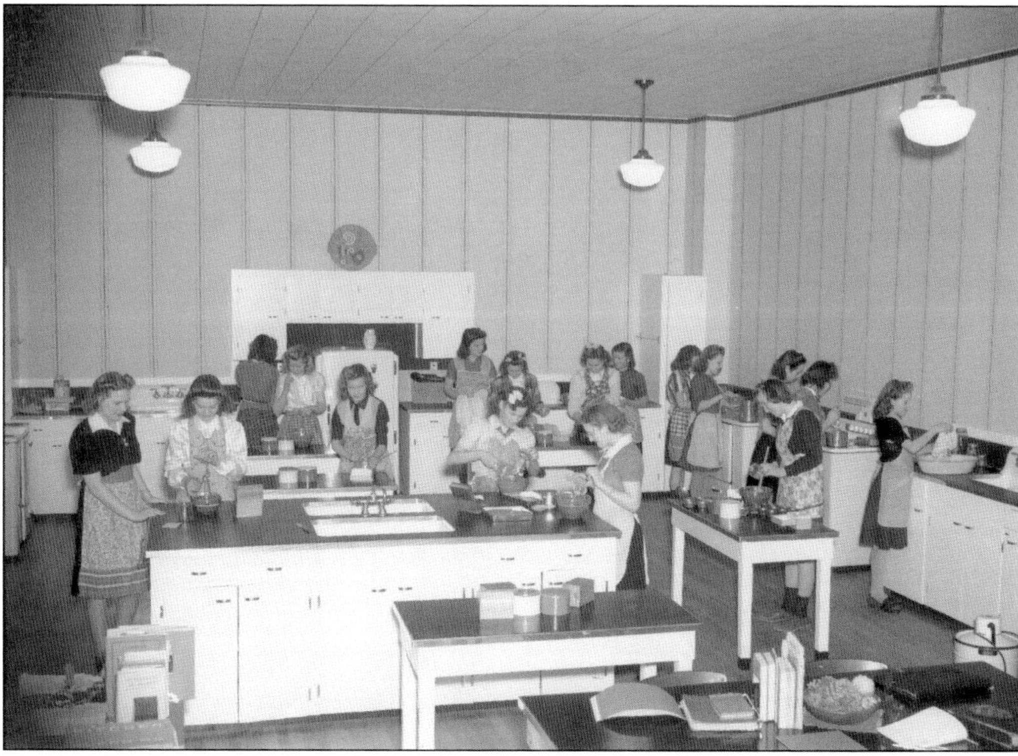

As the Willow River school district continued to expand, the town decided that a new school building was in order. A two-story brick school was completed in 1921. In this 1940 photograph, students participated in a cooking class.

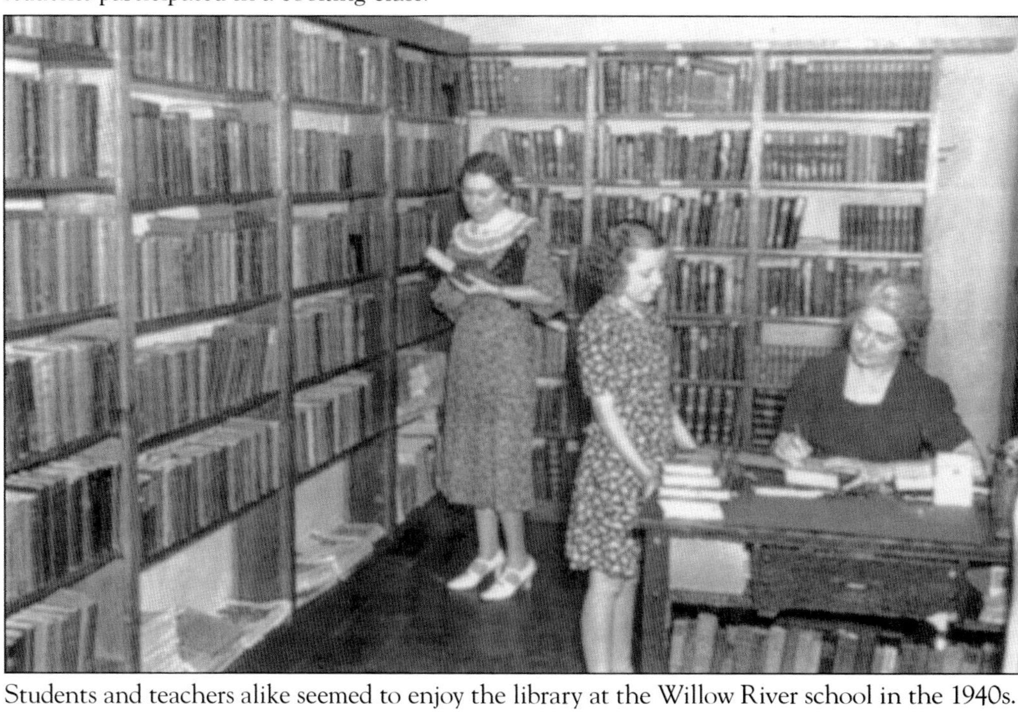

Students and teachers alike seemed to enjoy the library at the Willow River school in the 1940s.

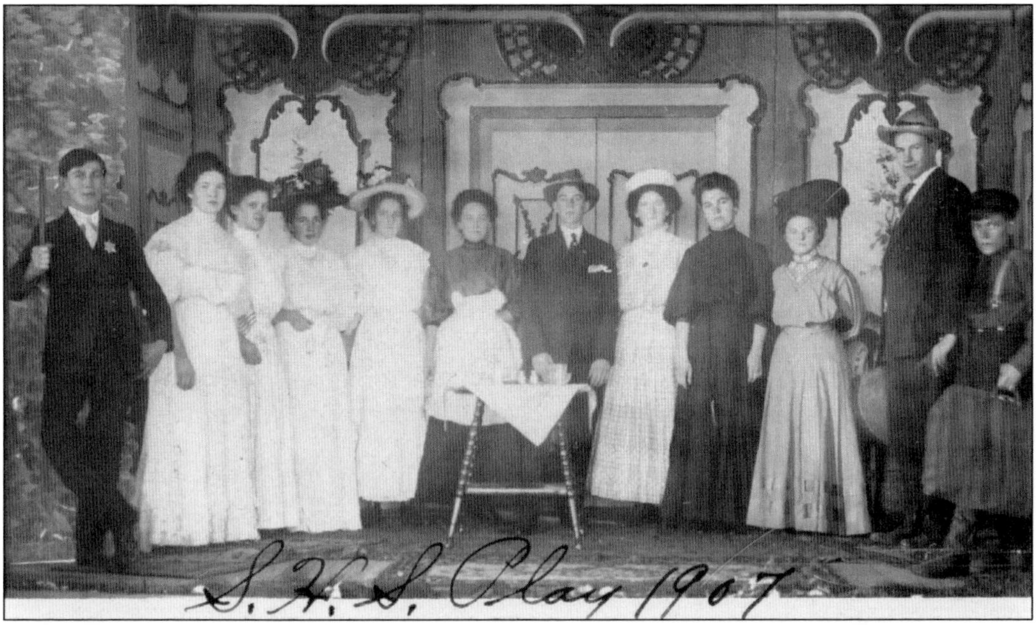

Sandstone students worked hard every year to stage successful class plays, and townspeople came out in droves to watch. The 1907 cast paused for a moment to pose for this photograph.

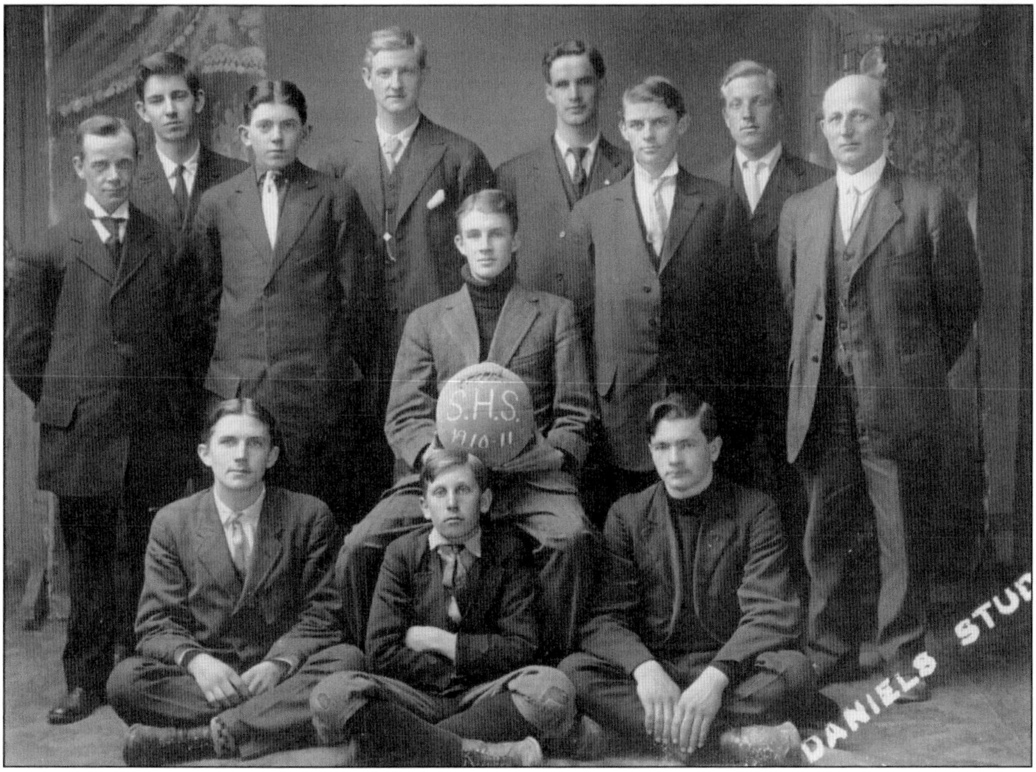

Sandstone was proud of its boys' and girls' basketball teams, both of which were organized during the 1910–1911 school year. The 1910 Sandstone school featured a gymnasium, the first one ever in Sandstone, that was the perfect home for the two teams.

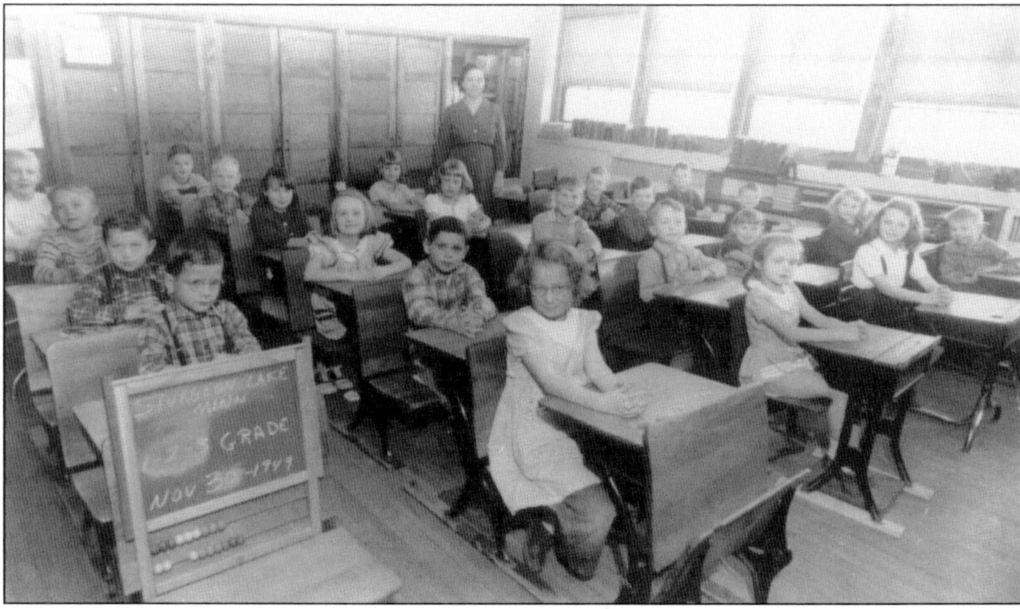

Every year, students in Northern Pine County's schools posed for their class picture. The first, second, and third graders at Sturgeon Lake sat primly at their desks for this 1949 shot.

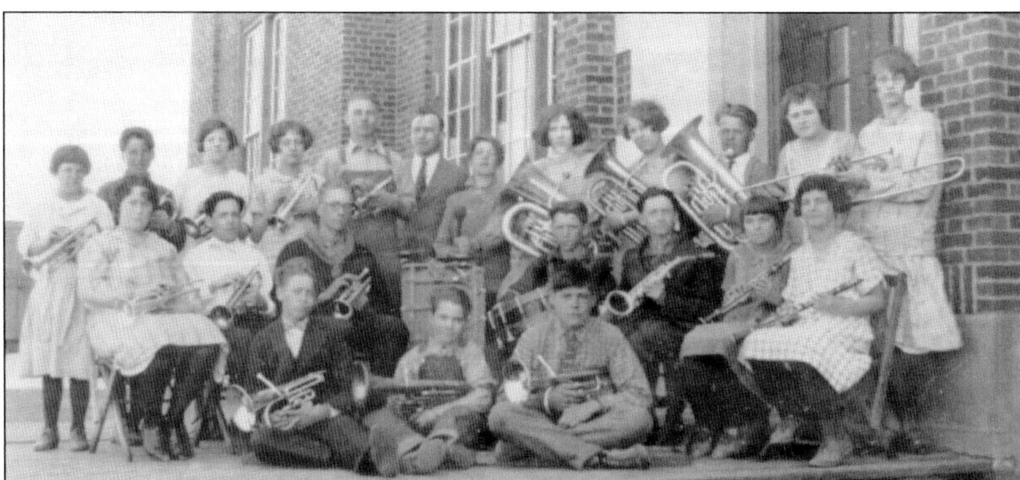

Cloverton school band members showed off their instruments after placing second in a band contest. Cloverton's two-story brick schoolhouse was built in 1920 and served all 12 grades. At its high point in the mid-1920s, it boasted an attendance of 165 students. Cloverton school offered hot lunches, an advanced curriculum that included French, and a sports program featuring track, baseball, basketball, and kittenball.

Six

Keeping the Faith

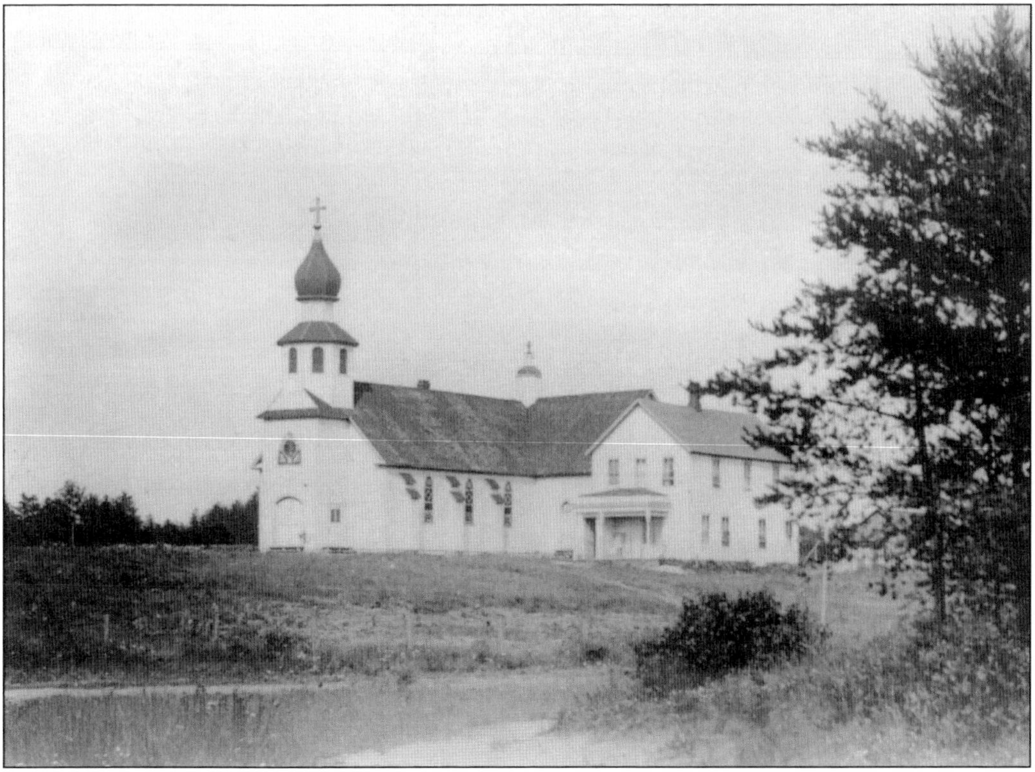

St. Isidore's Catholic Church in Sturgeon Lake was built in 1890 to serve the spiritual needs of the town's Polish and Lithuanian Catholic immigrants. The parish itself was founded in 1887 and held its liturgies in a shoemaker's shop owned by Joseph Gracrek. In 1889, the congregation obtained two parcels of land from the railroad, one for a church and another for a cemetery, for the sum of $1.

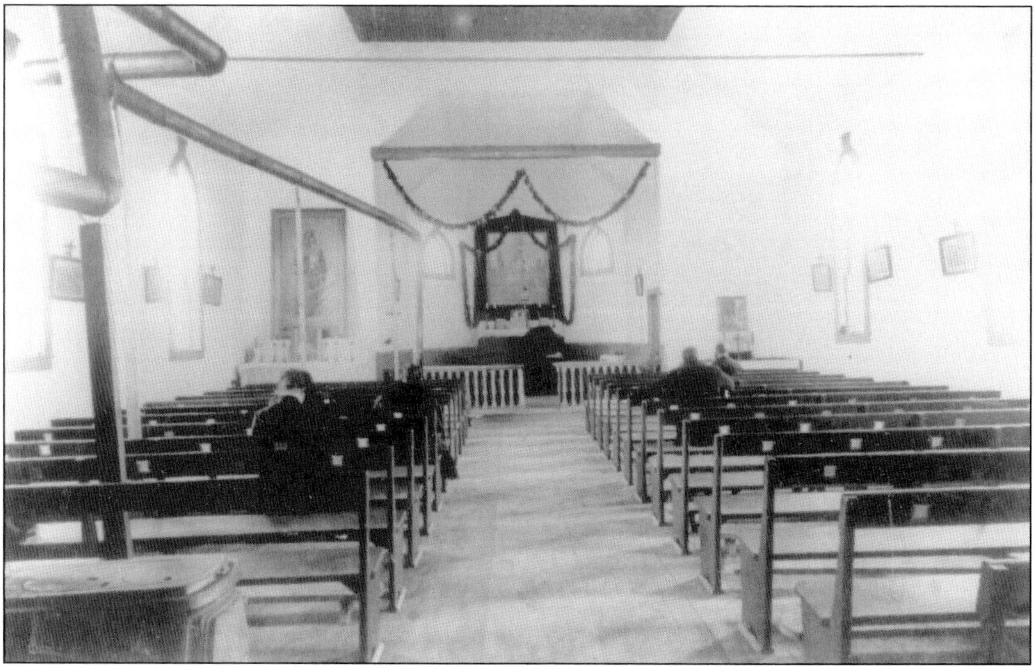

The interior of St. Isidore's was quite simple in the church's earliest days, but it was still well equipped for Catholic worship. Note the altar and Communion rail at the front, the painting of the Virgin Mary above the side altar on the left, the stations of the cross plaques lining the walls on both sides, and the kneelers attached to the back of each pew.

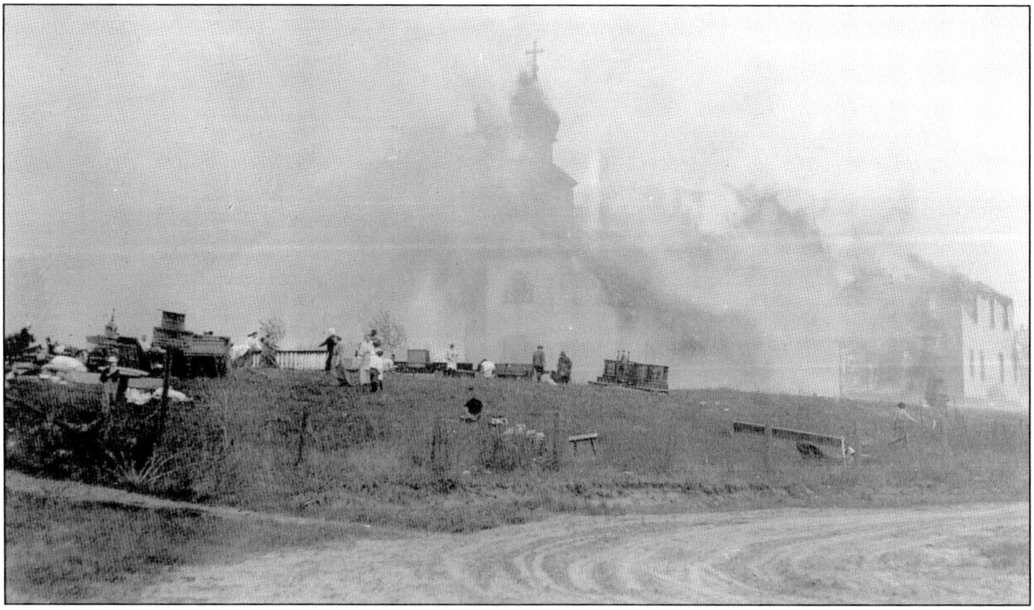

St. Isidore's Church and Rectory burned on May 5, 1915. A grass fire sparked by a passing steam engine spread rapidly to engulf the two buildings. Thanks to quick-thinking parishioners, the altar, pews, statues, furnishings, and vestments were rescued from the burning church. The Sturgeon Lake fire department called in help from other towns to fight the blaze while schoolchildren stood nearby watching.

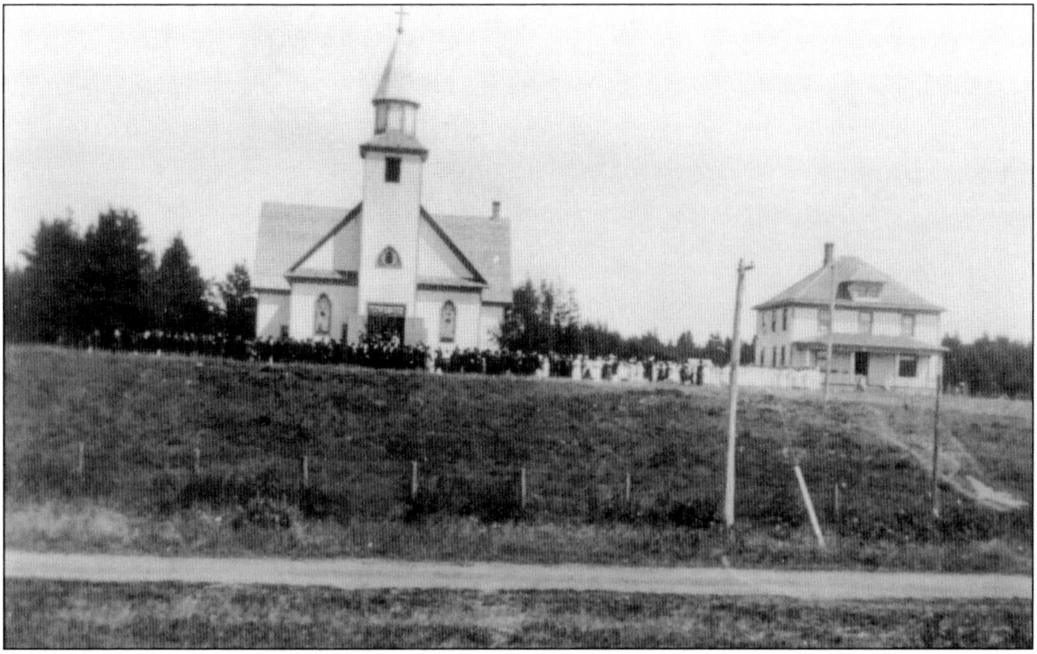

Only 15 days after the fire, a building committee met to plan for a new church and rectory, which were dedicated in September 1916. The church was built by J. J. Pukropp for $2,068.50, and W. Tarnowski constructed the rectory for $1,900. The latter used his own materials for the job, and parishioners agreed to help mix the cement.

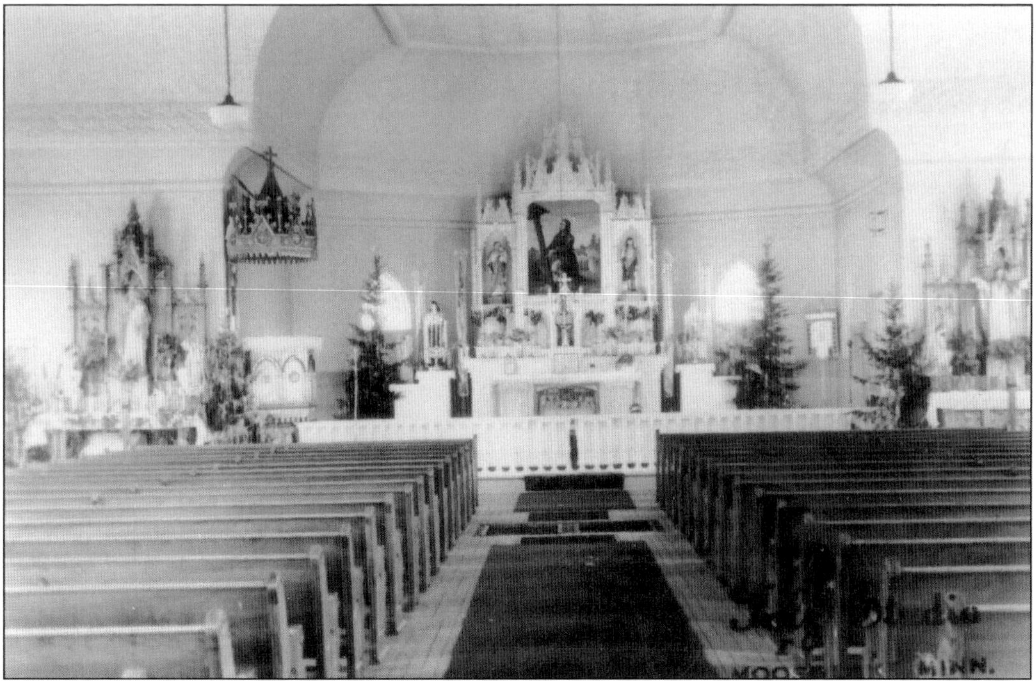

The interior of the new St. Isidore's was more elaborate than that of the old church. In this picture, the church had been decorated for the Christmas season. St. Isidore's is still the spiritual home of Sturgeon Lake's Catholics.

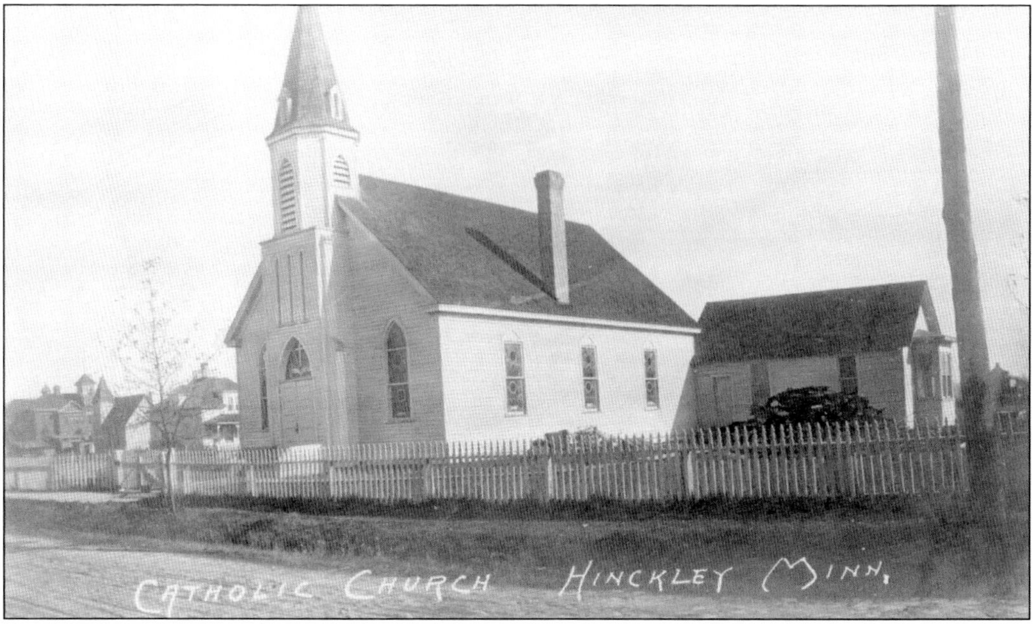

St. Patrick's Catholic Church in Hinckley was organized in 1883. Like the rest of Hinckley, St. Patrick's was destroyed in the 1894 fire. Fr. D. W. Lawler was a member of the volunteer fire department. After attempting to battle the blaze, he ran through town, warning residents to head for the Grindstone River or gravel pit. Father Lawler, unlike many of his parishioners, survived. This picture of St. Patrick's is post-fire.

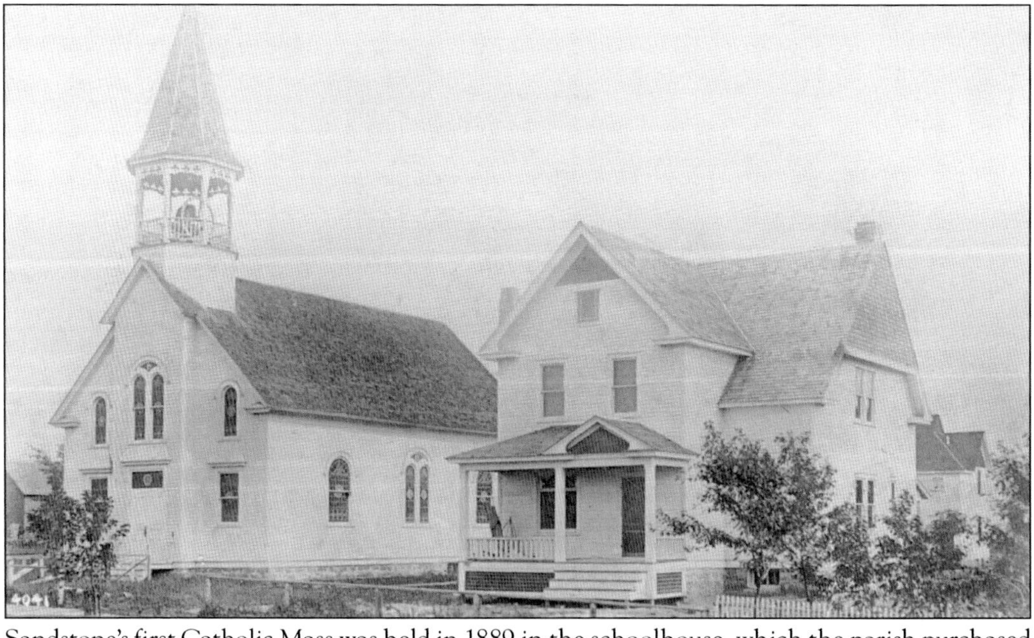

Sandstone's first Catholic Mass was held in 1889 in the schoolhouse, which the parish purchased four years later to serve as its permanent home. After their church burned in the 1894 fire, Catholics met in the nondenominational memorial church for their liturgies until their new church, the one shown here, was finished in 1900. St. Willibrord's Catholic Church served Sandstone's Catholics until 1963 when a new church, St. Luke's, was built.

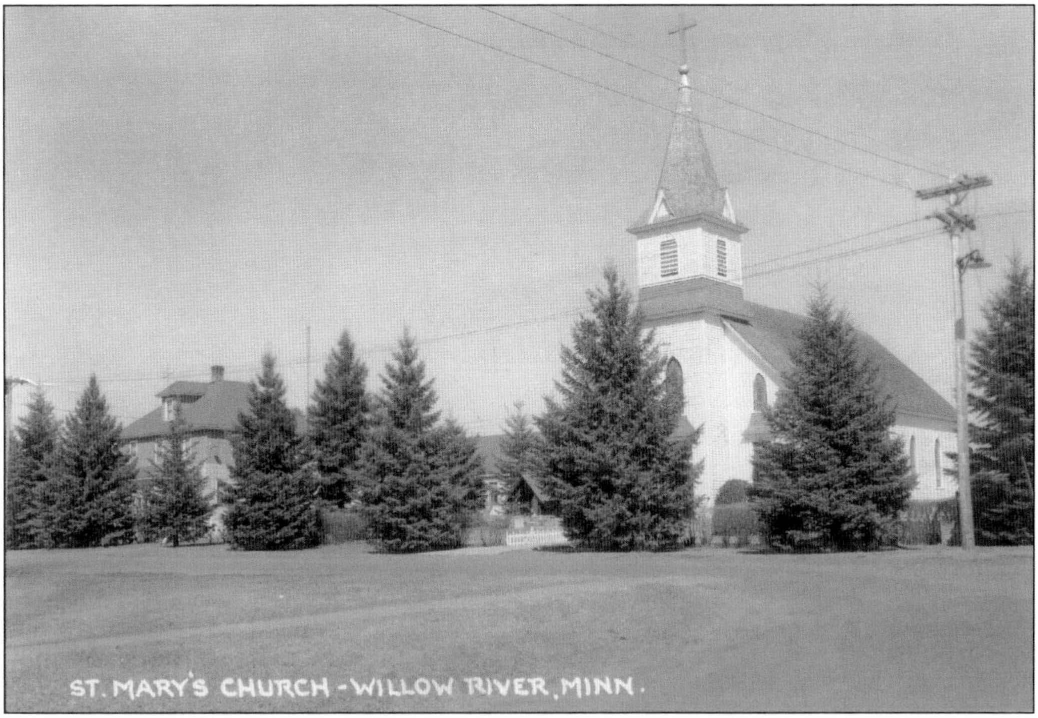

St. Mary's Catholic Church in Willow River was built in 1908. A rectory was added in 1916 to accommodate the first resident priest, Father Meyer.

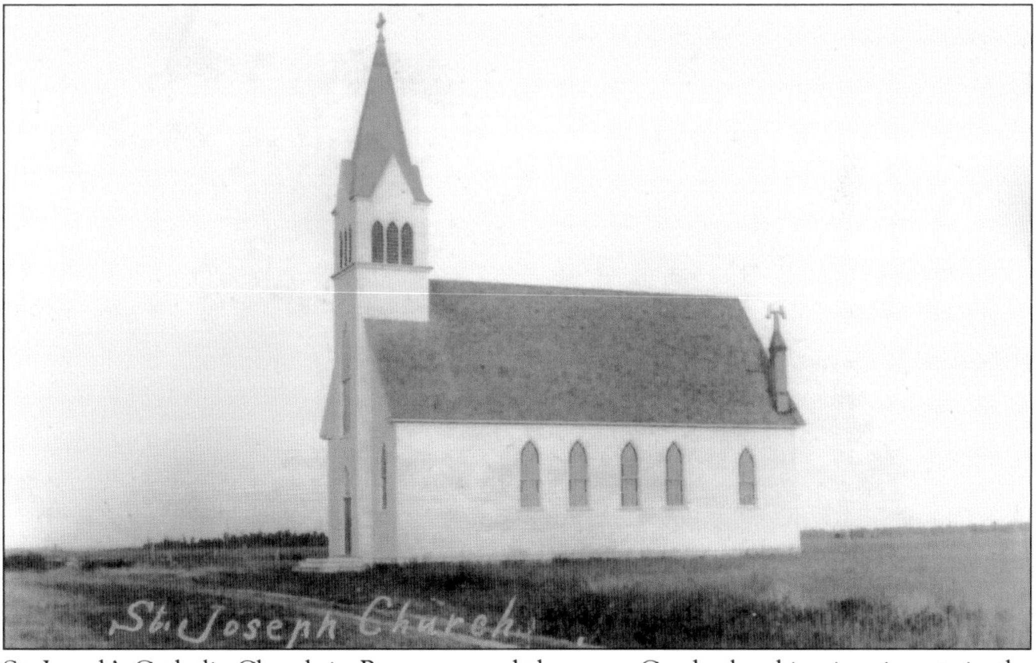

St. Joseph's Catholic Church in Beroun served the many Czechoslovakian immigrants in the area. The first church was an 18-by-30-by-32-foot structure built in 1896. The church pictured here was constructed a few years later and replaced in 1927 by a brick church, which features 12 stained glass windows imported from Austria.

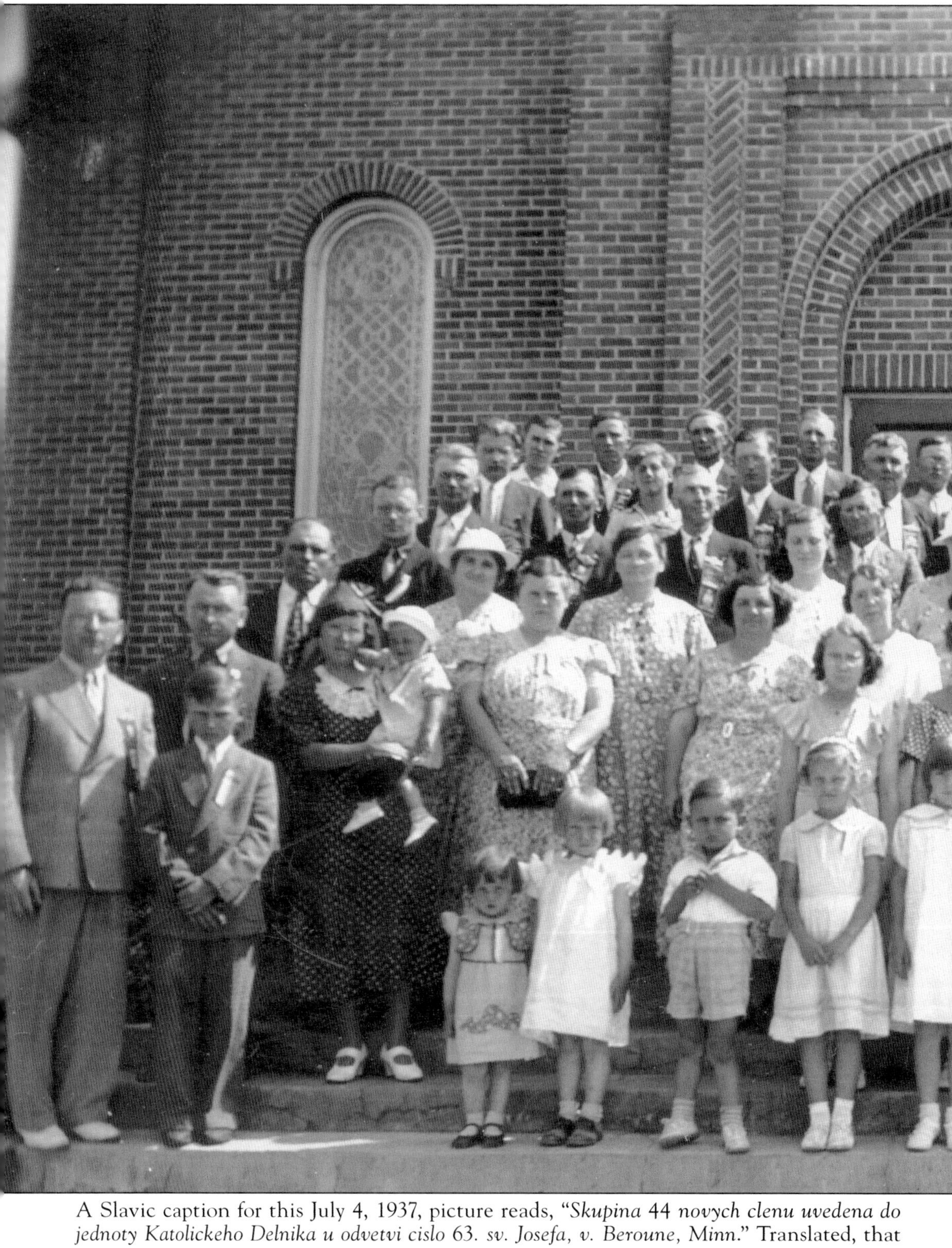

A Slavic caption for this July 4, 1937, picture reads, "*Skupina* 44 *novych clenu uvedena do jednoty Katolickeho Delnika u odvetvi cislo* 63. *sv. Josefa, v. Beroune, Minn.*" Translated, that

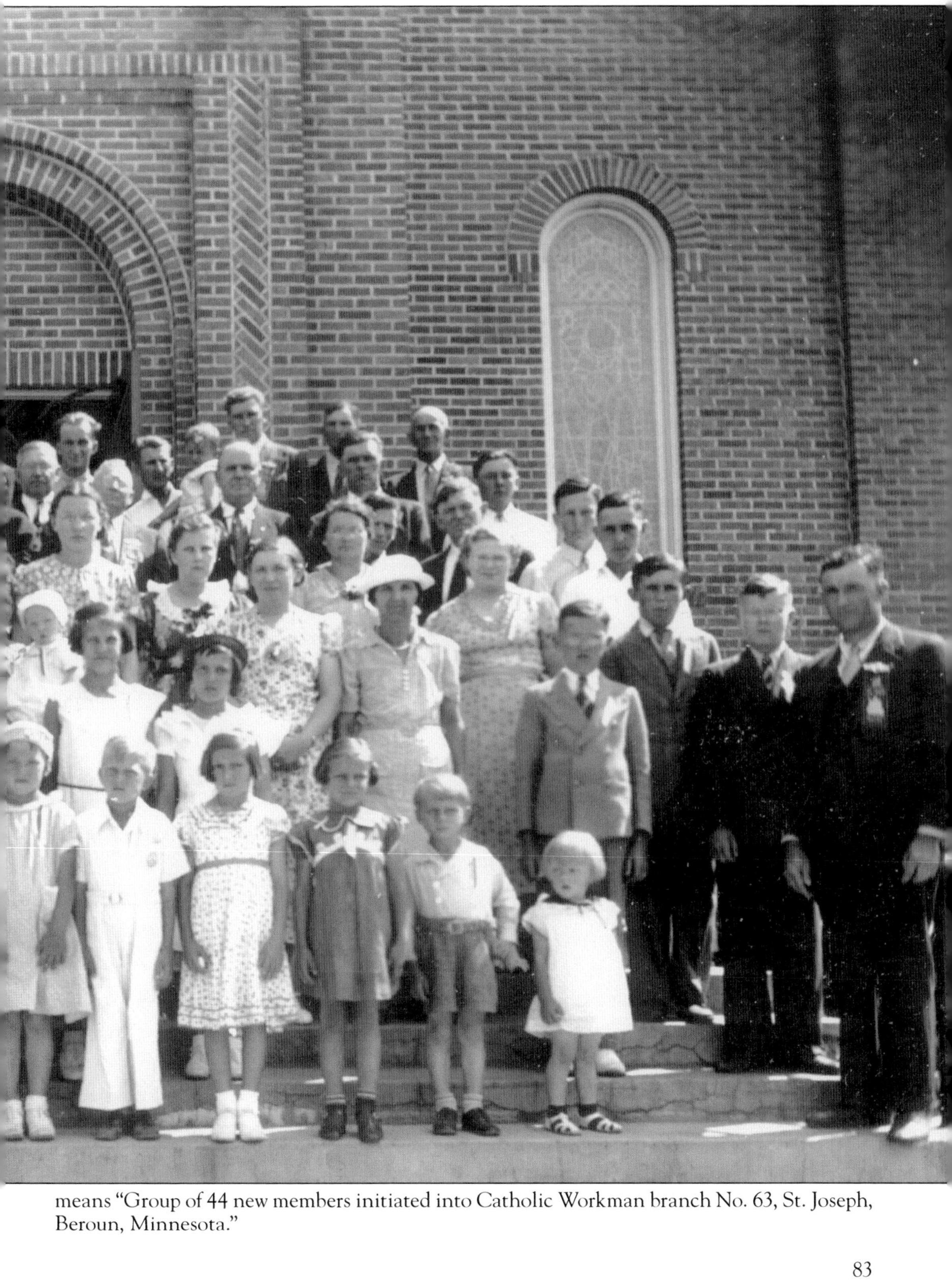

means "Group of 44 new members initiated into Catholic Workman branch No. 63, St. Joseph, Beroun, Minnesota."

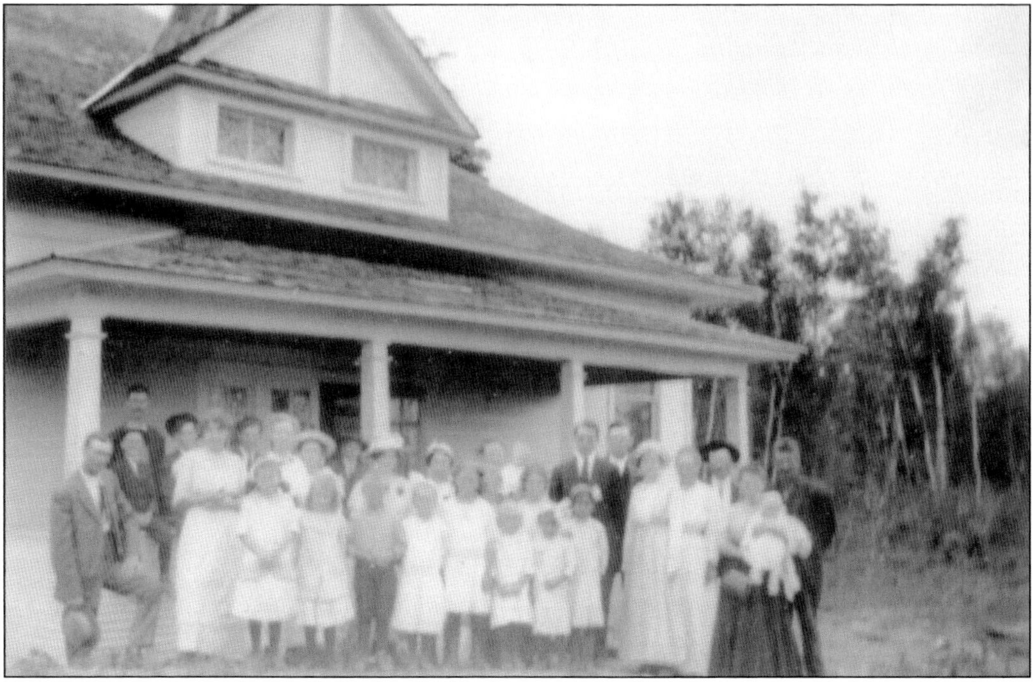

In early days, church services were often held in schools. These Sunday churchgoers gathered in front of the Kingsdale school. Kingsdale was organized in 1912 along the Soo Line Railroad in the easternmost part of Pine County.

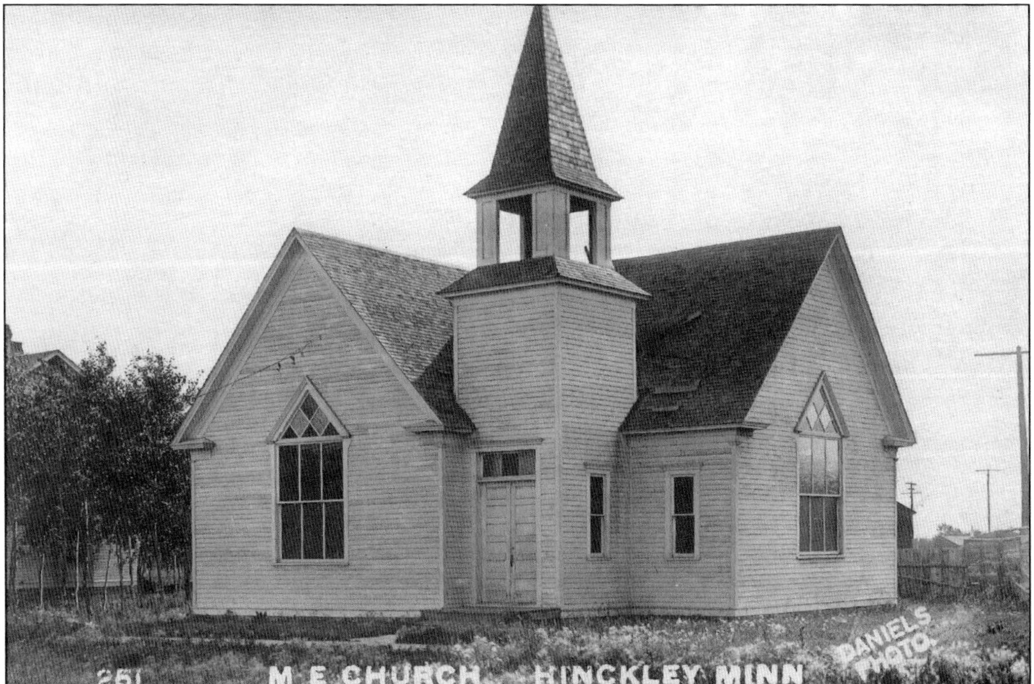

Photographer Ross Daniels snapped this image of the Hinckley Methodist Episcopal Church. The plain clapboard structure was typical of small town churches.

Seven

A Test of Character

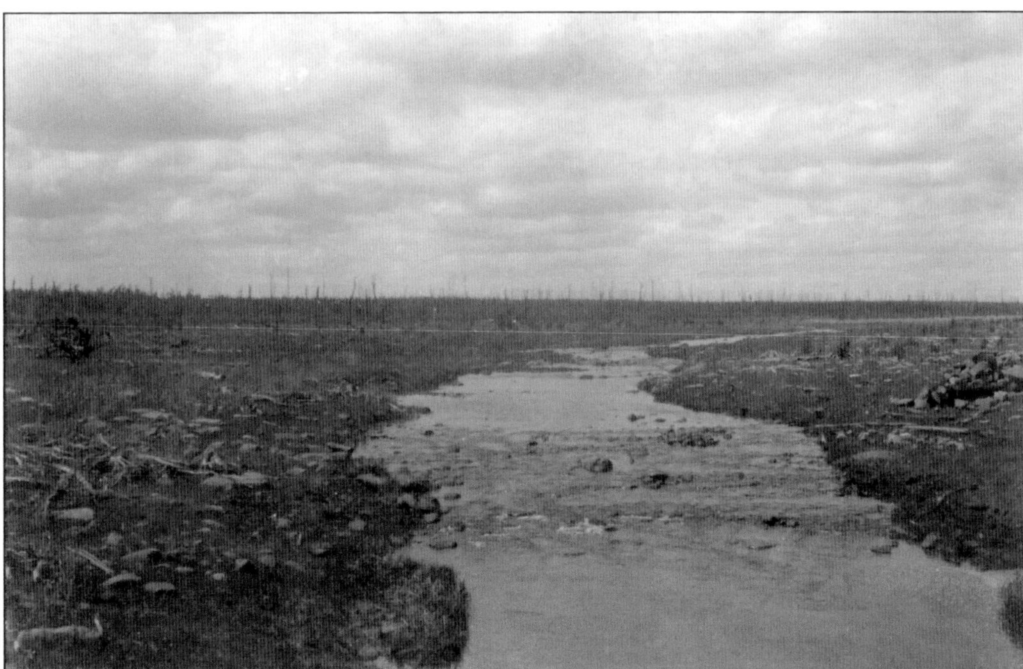

This desolate landscape stood in sharp contrast with the lush pineries of Northern Pine County. Forest fires were often sparked by trains or started by farmers trying to clear the land, but the disaster of 1894 outstripped every other fire in intensity and destruction. There was literally nothing left but a few burned trees and shells of structures.

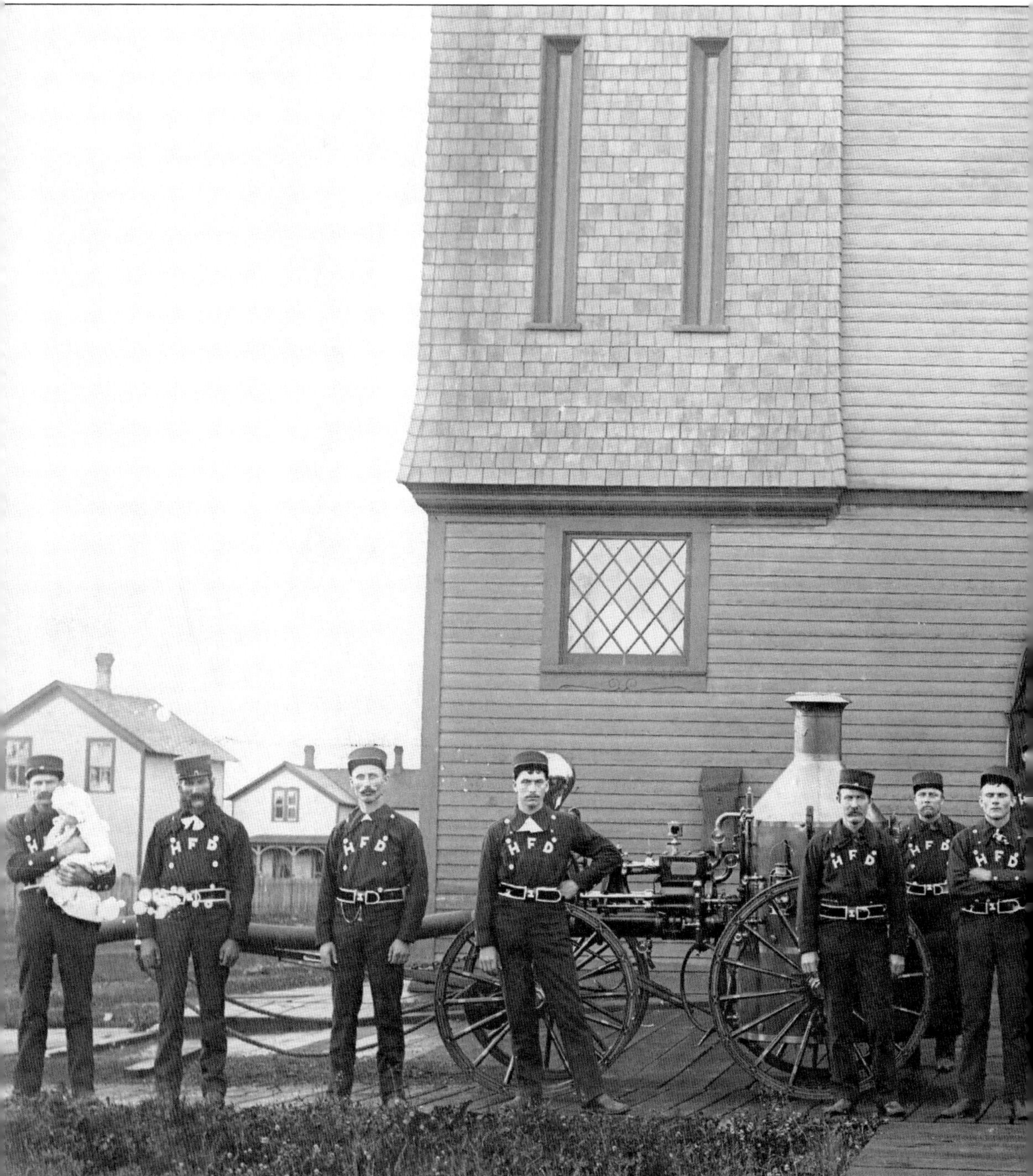

The Hinckley Fire Department is pictured here just before the 1894 fire. The 19 volunteer firemen, led by Chief John T. Craig, were proud of their new fire engine, hose cart, and firehouse. They were positive they could conquer any fire that threatened Hinckley. They were proven wrong on September 1, 1894. By the end of the day, a massive firestorm had burned 300,000 acres, destroyed several towns, killed nearly 500 people, and left thousands homeless. The Hinckley firemen made

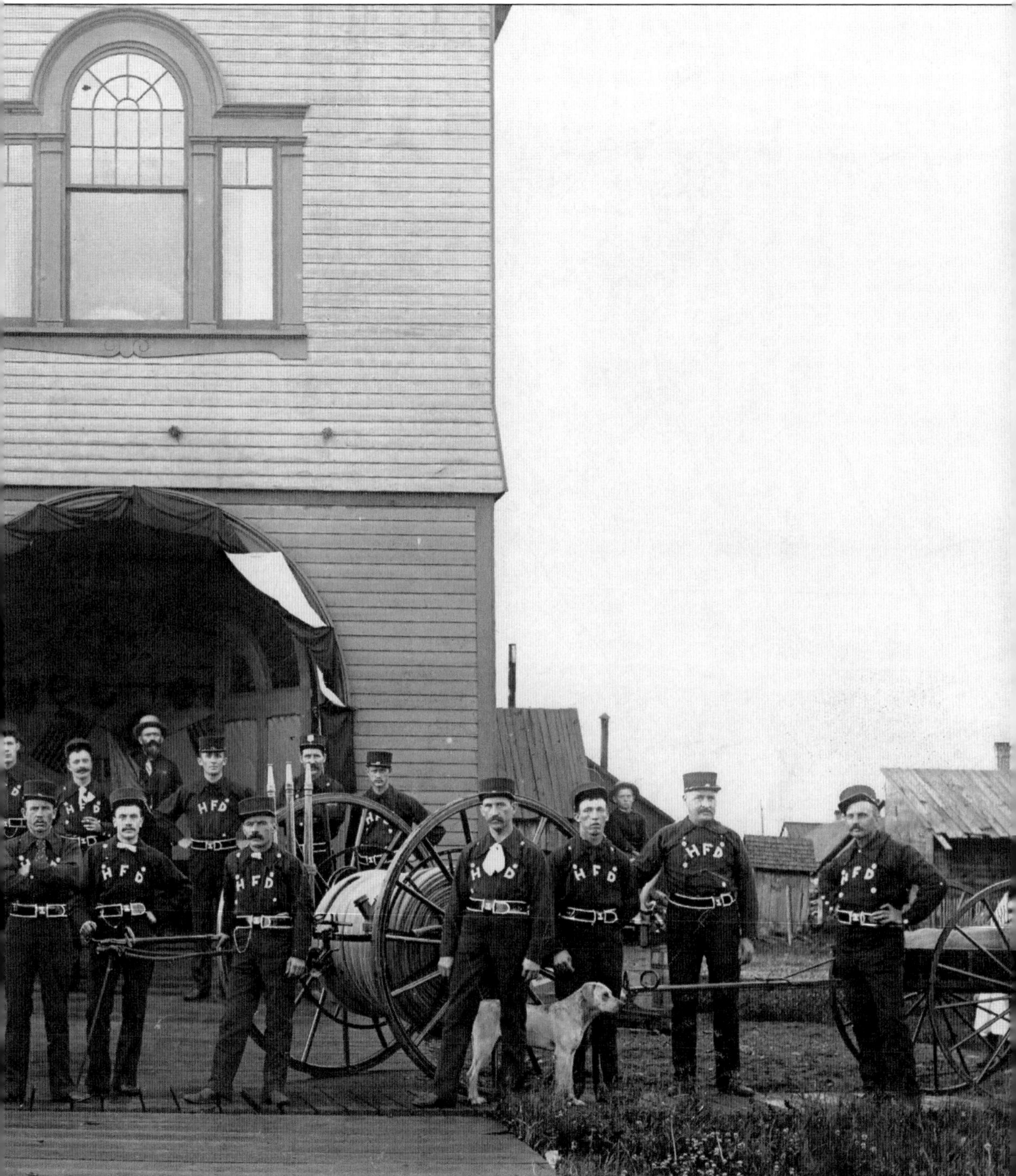

a valiant effort to combat the flames, but they finally had to run for their lives when their hose burned through. Some escaped with their families on the Eastern Minnesota train. Others ran to the Grindstone River or the gravel pit. Still others boarded the St. Paul and Duluth train, which burned at Skunk Lake 7 miles to the north.

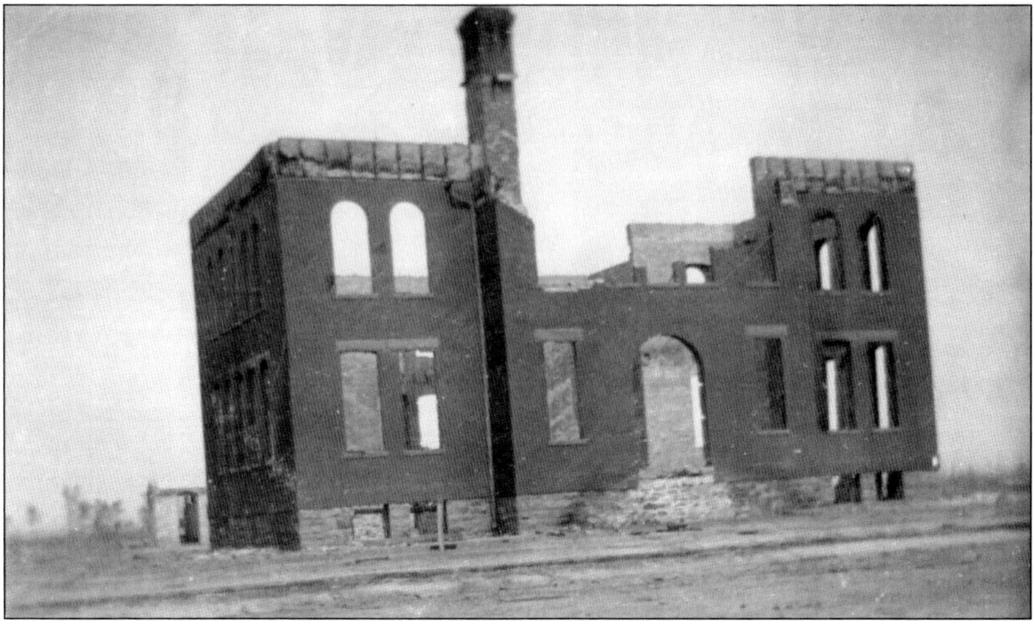

A blackened shell of Hinckley's new schoolhouse stood amidst the ruins of the town after the fire passed through. Schoolchildren had been looking forward to returning to class on September 3. Instead, fire victims, men, women, and children, huddled together in shelters in Pine City, Duluth, or the Twin Cities, mourning lost relatives and friends and wondering if life would ever be the same.

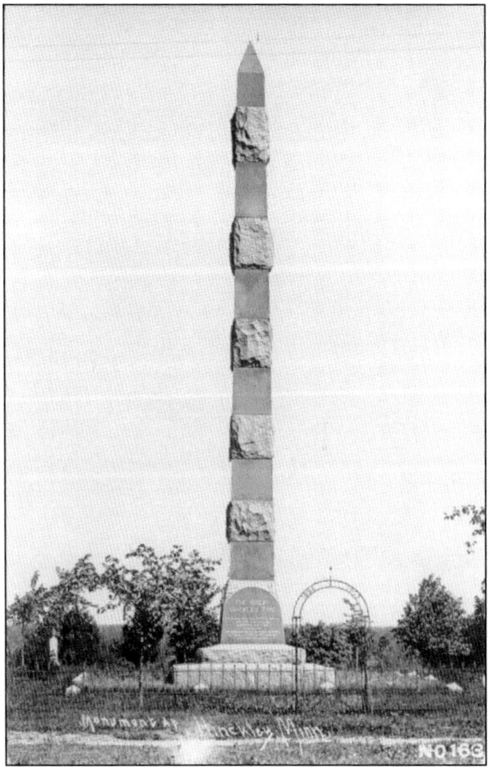

On September 1, 1900, exactly six years after the great fire, Northern Pine County citizens dedicated this moment. It marks four trenches in the Memorial Cemetery where 248 unidentified fire victims lie buried. Their families and fellow residents wanted to make sure their lost loved ones were never forgotten.

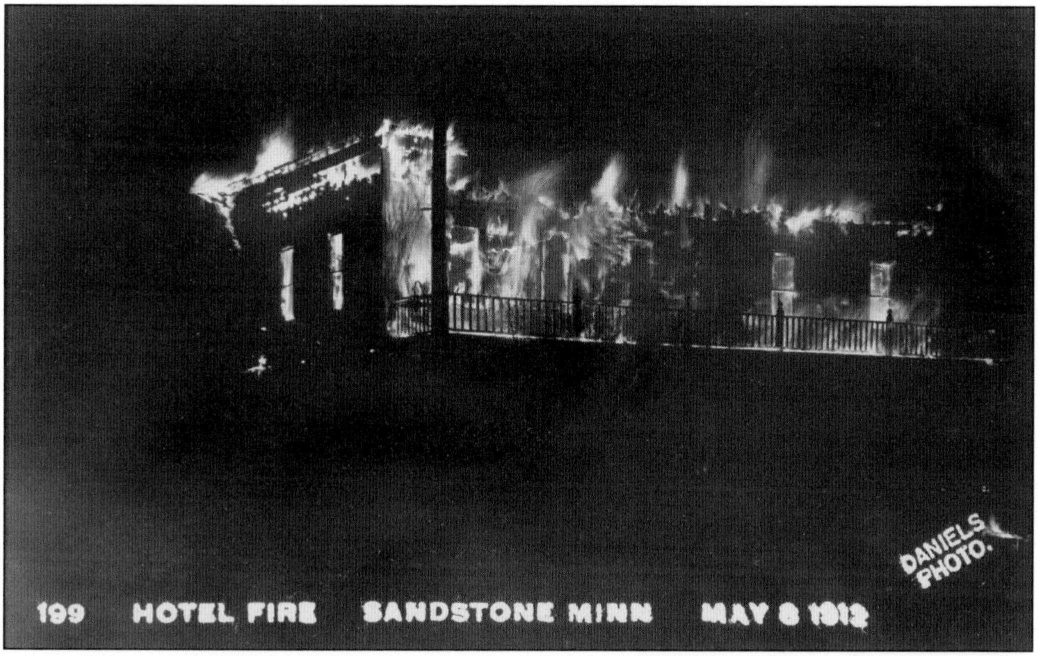

The family-owned Welsh Hotel was located at the corner of Fifth Street and Commercial Avenue in Sandstone. Around 2:00 in the morning on May 8, 1912, Mrs. Welsh woke to the smell of smoke. She managed to awaken the rest of her family, and everyone in the hotel escaped unharmed.

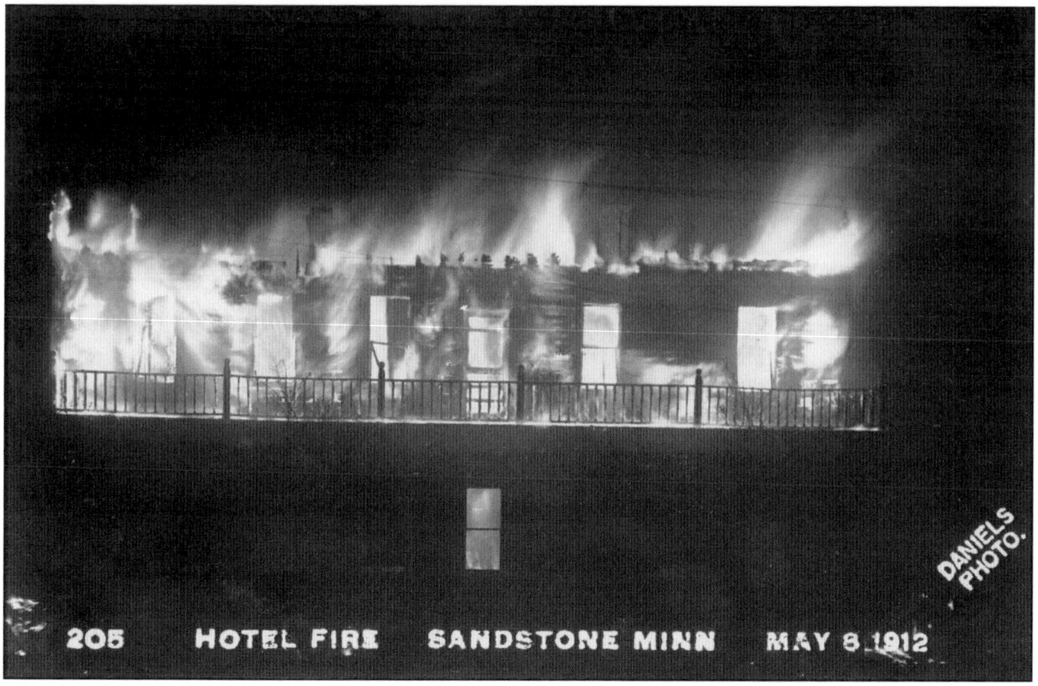

The fire department arrived on the scene and rescued some of the hotel's furnishings. They were unable to make much headway against the fire, however, for the town's water pressure was almost nonexistent. The building was entirely destroyed with an estimated loss of $5,500. The owners carried only $3,500 in insurance.

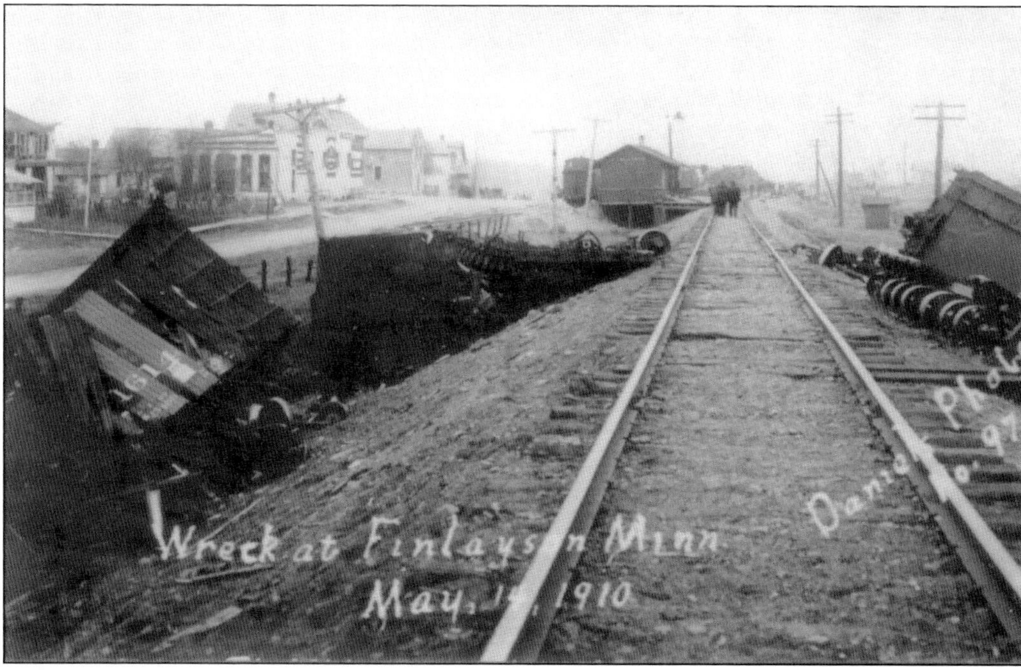

Finlayson residents were awakened by a tremendous crash early Sunday morning, May 14, 1910. Thirteen freight cars from the northbound train had jumped the track. Their cargo, mostly grain and merchandise, was scattered, and several cars were on fire. Two men, fireman Frank St. John and head brakeman William Young, were killed in the wreck, which was caused by an unknown person turning the rail switch.

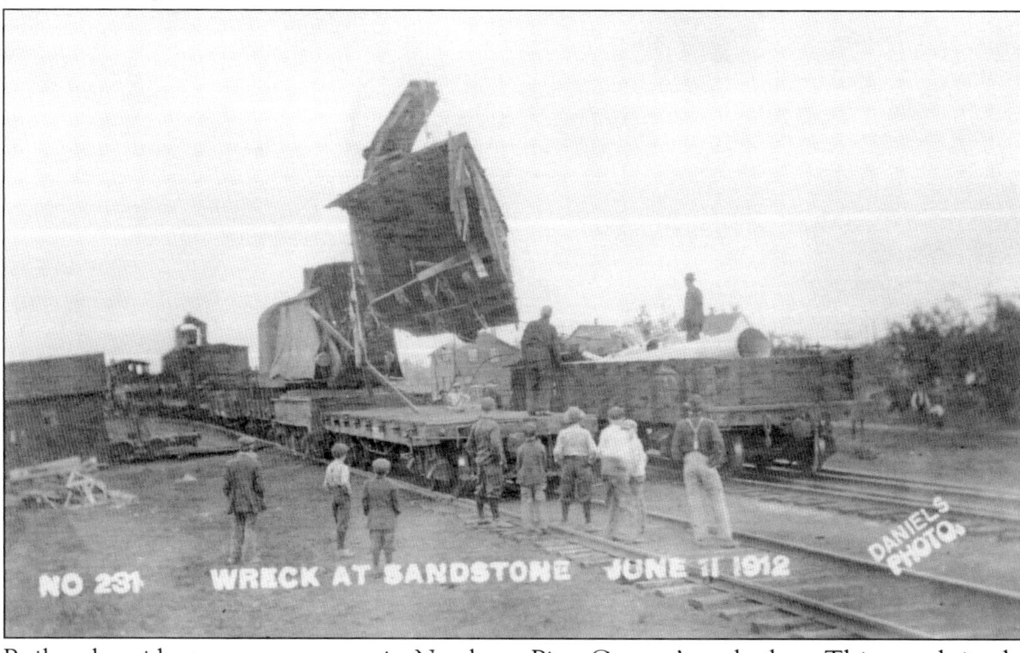

Railroad accidents were common in Northern Pine County's early days. This wreck in the Sandstone rail yards occurred on June 11, 1912. Although no one was hurt, the clean-up process still required much time and effort.

Sandstone children enjoyed climbing on the wreckage from the 1912 accident.

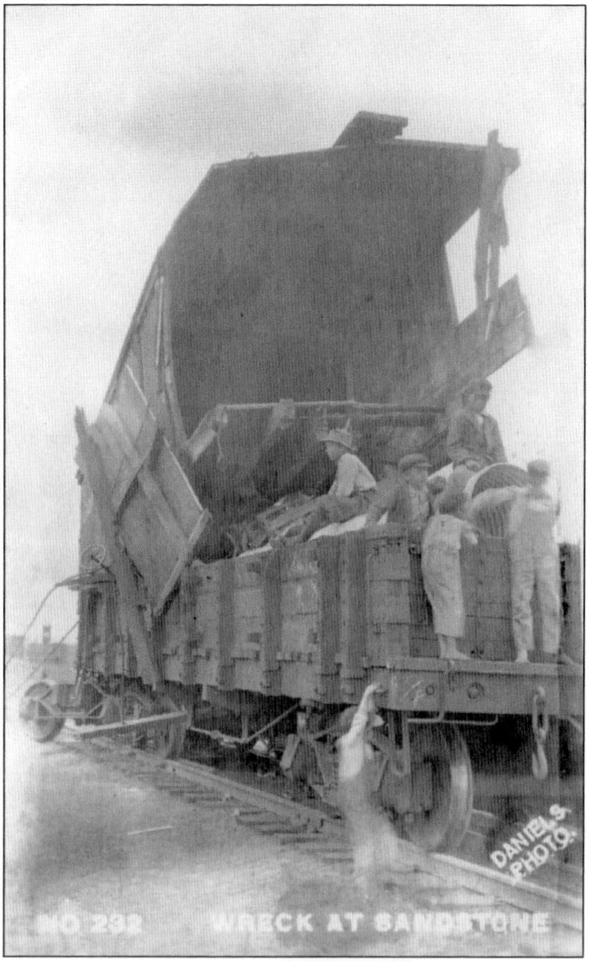

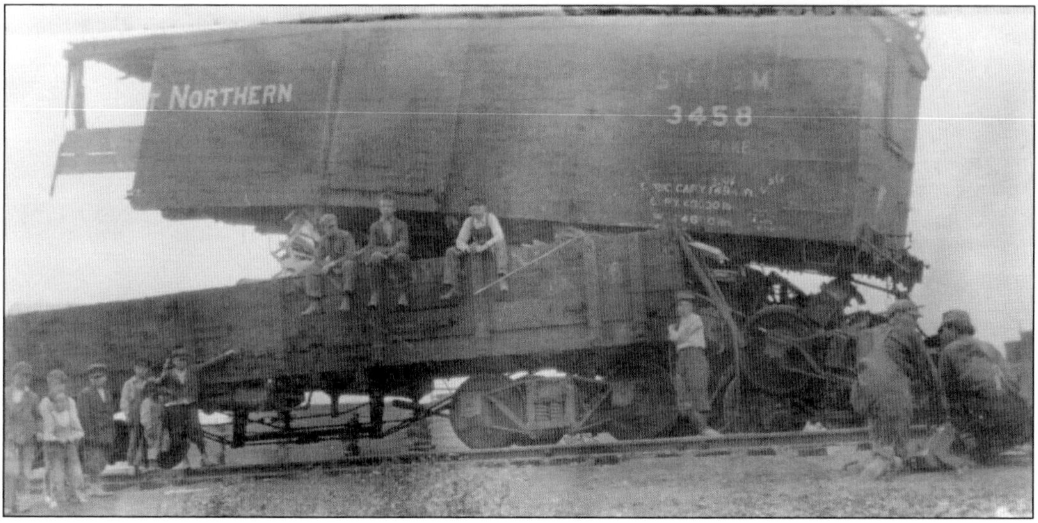

A Great Northern boxcar was poised precariously atop another railroad car as the clean up of the 1912 wreck continued.

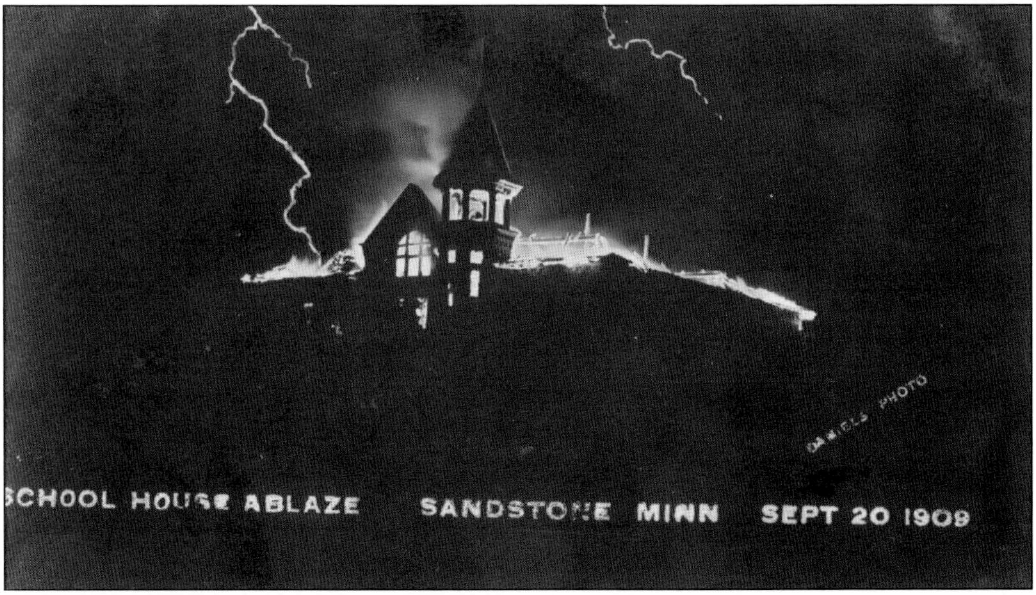

Sandstone's 1901 school building was the pride of the community. It was constructed of locally quarried sandstone for approximately $23,000. On Monday, September 20, 1909, the unthinkable happened. A bolt of lightning from a severe electrical storm made direct contact with the school, and flames erupted from the roof. Photographer Ross Daniels captured the lightning strike and resulting fire.

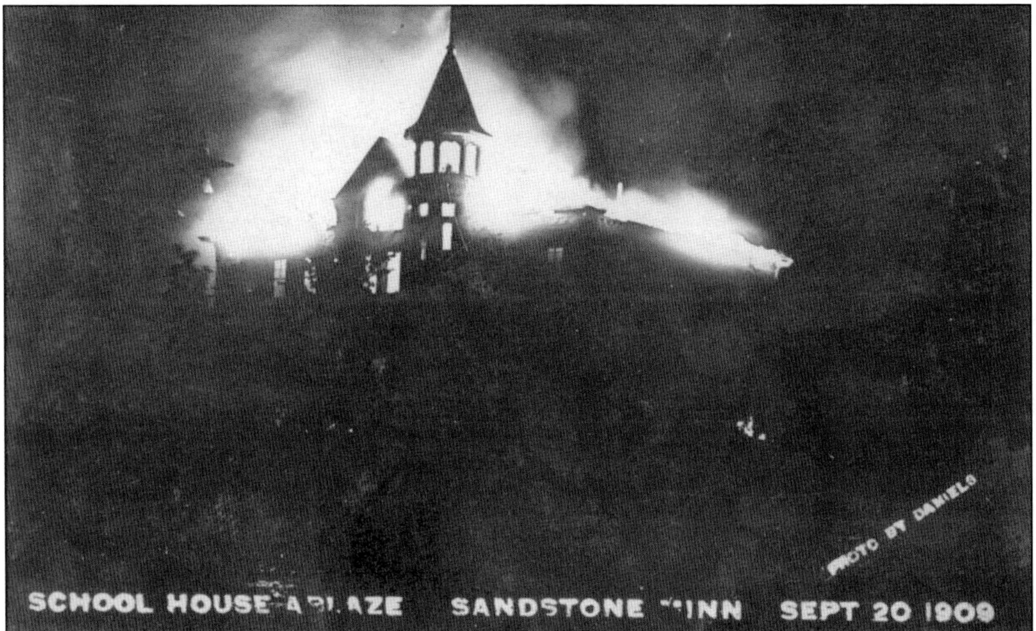

Sandstone's fire department responded quickly to the alarm, but since lightning had struck the town's electric water pump, firemen had to cope with low water pressure. The village telephone system had been knocked out by the storm, making it impossible to call for help. While firemen worked to contain the blaze, debris shot high into the air and landed several blocks away. Heavy rain prevented other buildings from catching fire.

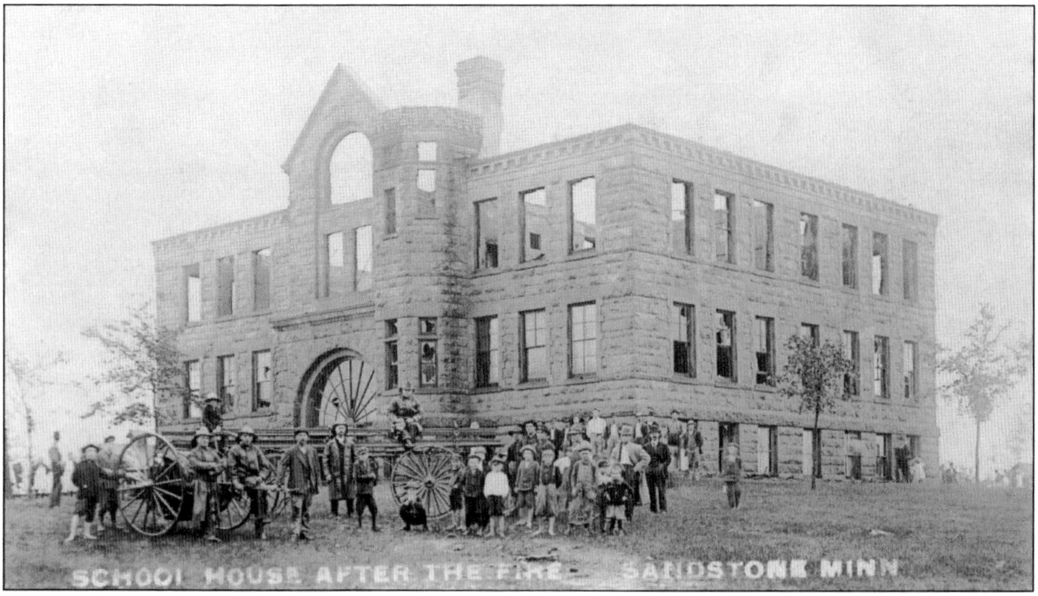

Citizens came out the next day to survey the damage, although many of them had braved the downpours overnight to witness the blaze in person. Firemen posed with a group of sad schoolchildren in front of the ruins. The school's top floors were completely destroyed, the first floor badly damaged, and the basement soaked. The building was valued at $35,000, but insurance adjustors allowed only $14,497.62 to cover the loss.

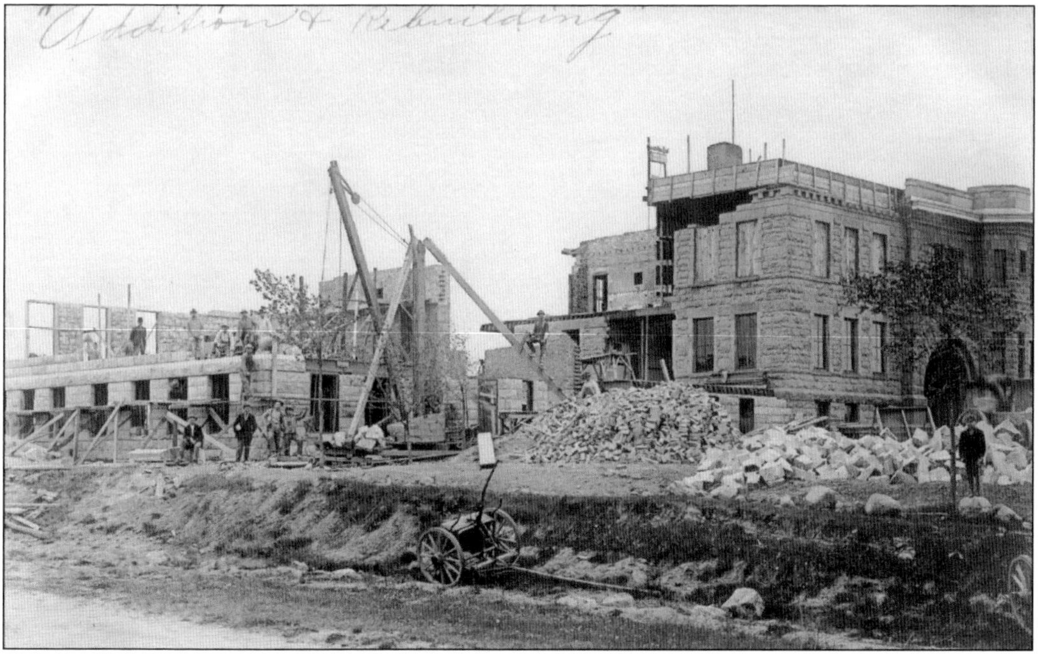

While children attended classes in rented spaces, the school board began plans to rebuild. Townspeople provided funds through bond sales, local builder E. O. Hanson won the contract, and the new, larger school soon rose from the shell of its predecessor. Students were thrilled to learn that their new school would feature a gymnasium and drinking fountains. The rebuilt Sandstone school was completed in the fall of 1910 for $30,390.

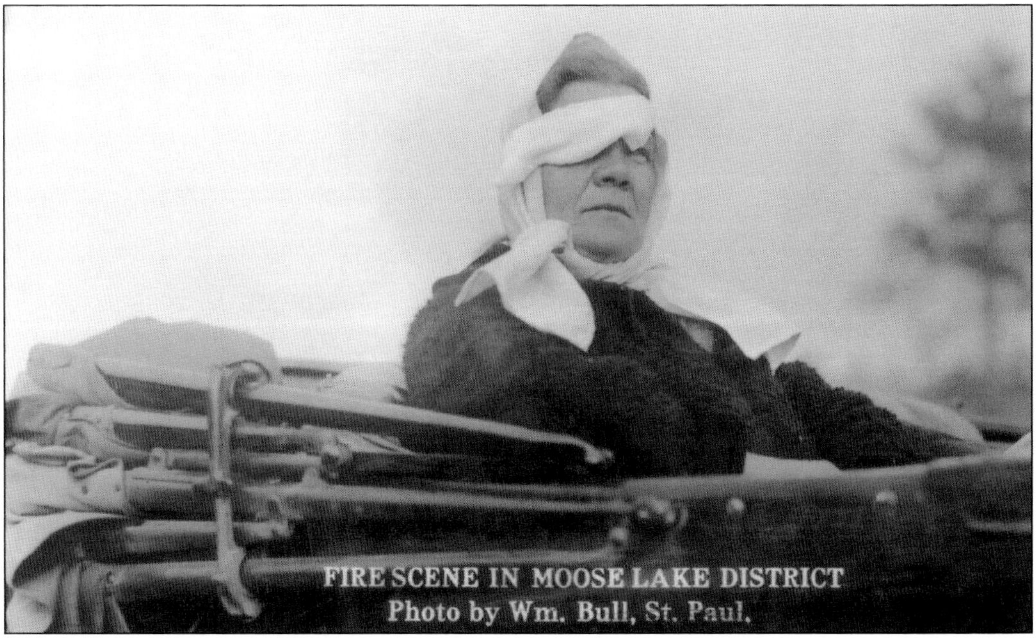

On October 12, 1918, Northern Pine County was once again tried by fire. Sparks from a passing train caught in the dry timber left behind by loggers, and a massive forest fire spread out of control through parts of Pine, Carlton, and St. Louis Counties. In Pine County, Bruno, Willow River, Surgeon Lake, and their surrounding areas were affected. The woman pictured here was a injured survivor.

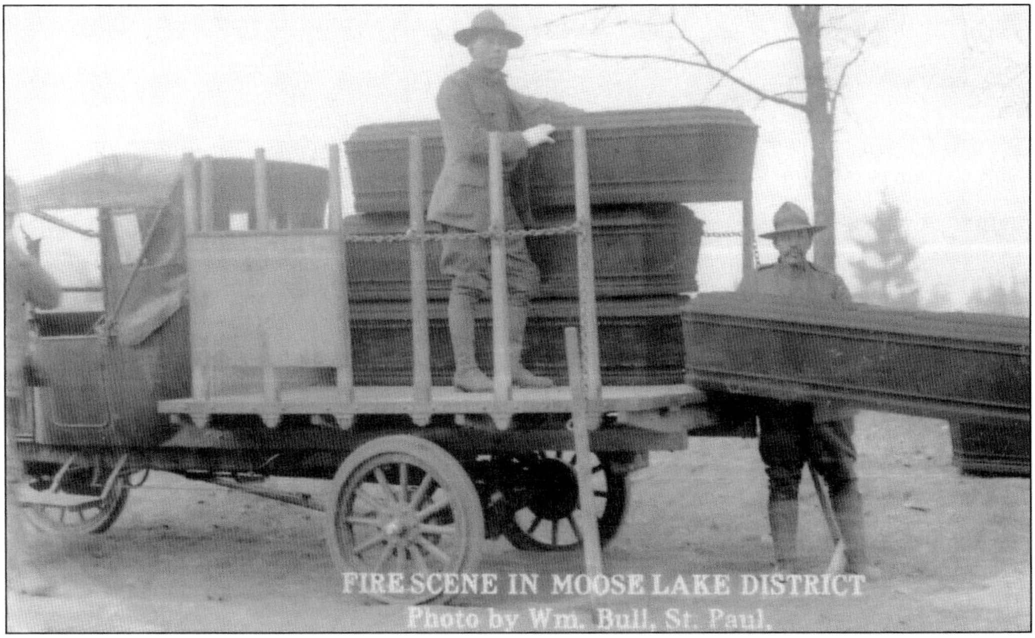

When the fire finally burned itself out late in the evening of October 12, there were 453 people dead, 85 seriously burned, and over 2,000 more injured. The fire had burned 1,500 square miles, destroyed 4,089 houses, 6,366 barns, and 41 schools, and left thousands of people homeless. The Home Guard and Red Cross arrived on October 13 to aid fire victims.

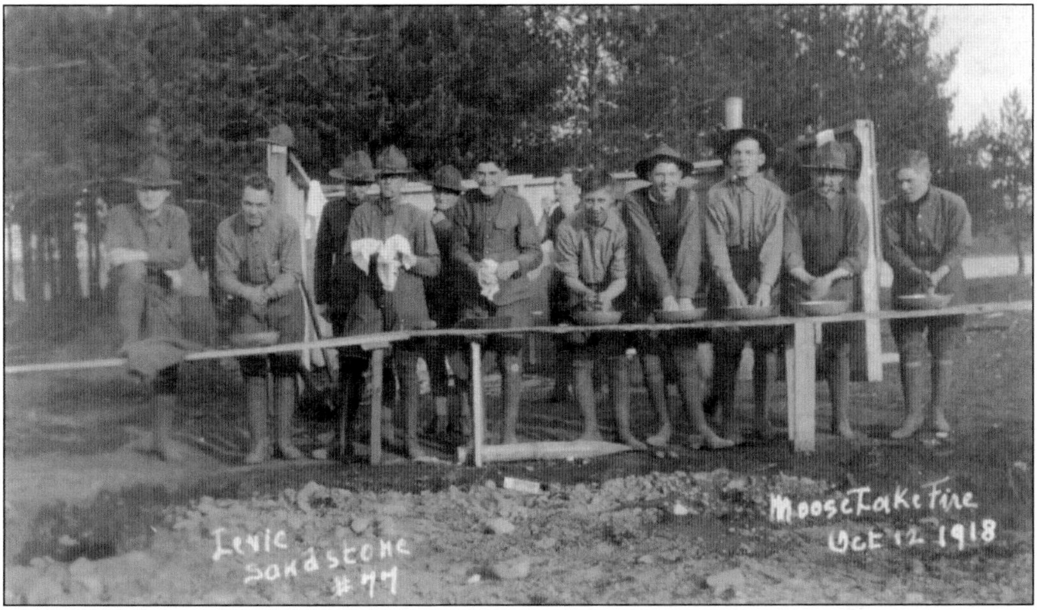

Home Guard members gathered and buried the dead while Red Cross workers provided shelter, food, medical care, and transportation to fire victims. The Red Cross also donated building materials so families could construct small homes before winter. By November, several hundred of these shelters dotted the countryside.

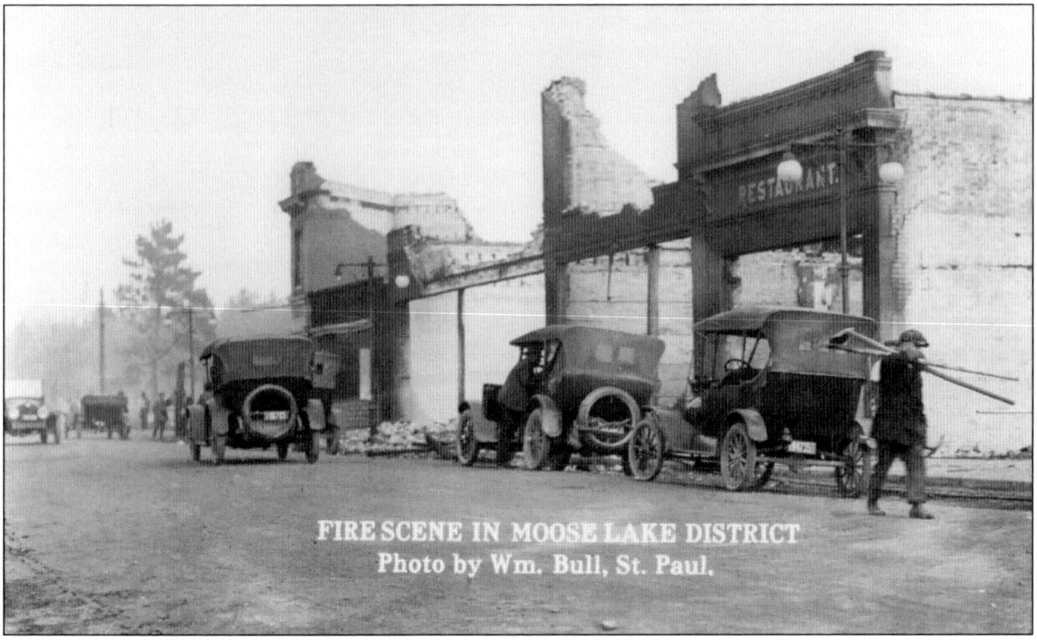

Over 52,000 people were affected by the 1918 fire, and property damage soared to nearly $100,000. A hundred more lives were claimed by an outbreak of the Spanish flu that followed closely after the fire and preyed on weakened fire victims. In the end, the people of Northern Pine County recovered and resumed their daily lives, both saddened and strengthened by the trial they had survived.

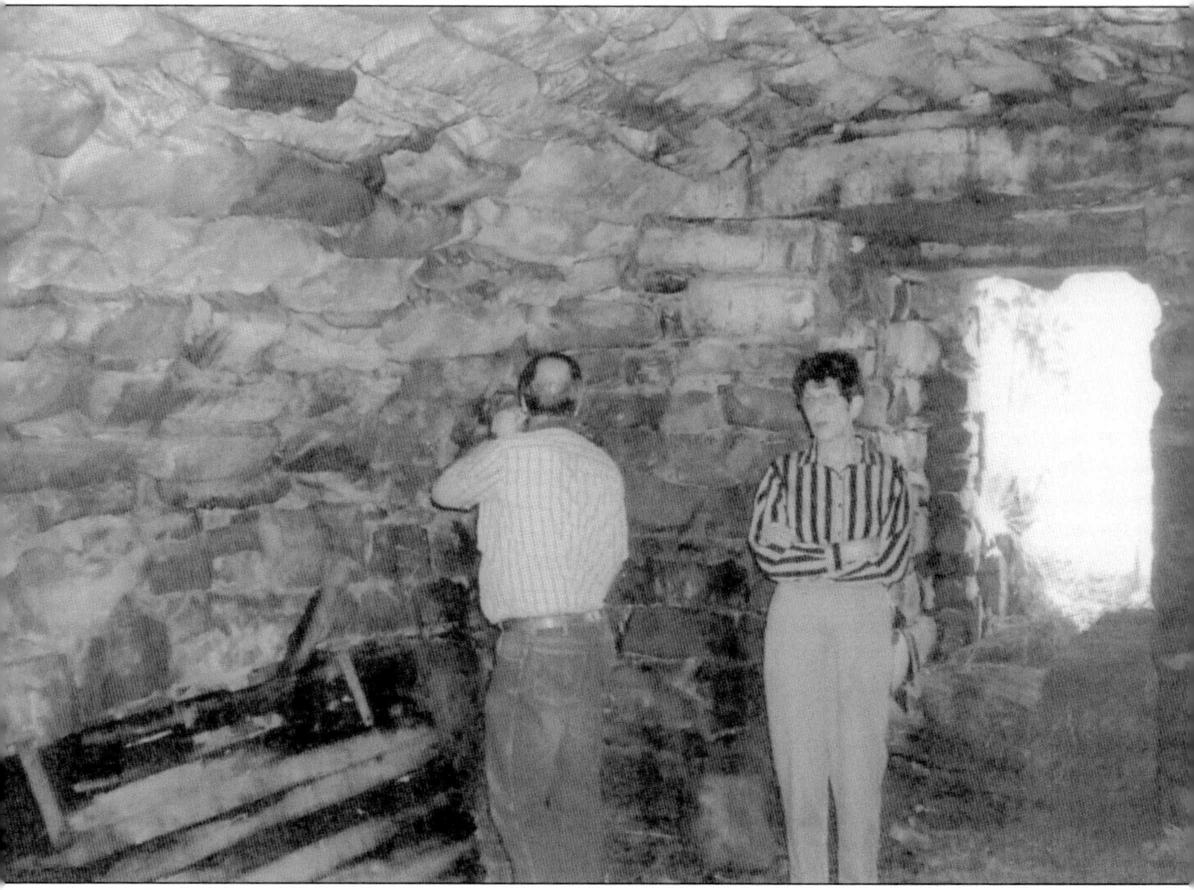

Northern Pine County's people have always been strong in character, especially when they were tested. The Samuelson family was no exception. John and Hattie Samuelson's daughter Minnie was to be married to John DeRosier on September 1, 1894. Amidst the wedding festivities, the family and their guests did not notice the firestorm bearing down upon them until it was almost too late. Chaos ensued as people pushed and shoved, trying to escape the Samuelsons' burning house. They dashed toward the root cellar, piled in, and huddled together, terrified and praying as the door began to burn. Fortunately, someone bumped into a container of milk, and everyone began dousing themselves and the burning door. They all survived, and Minnie and John were married a few days later in Duluth. The root cellar still exists along Highway 61 between Hinckley and Sandstone.

Eight

Life in Northern Pine County

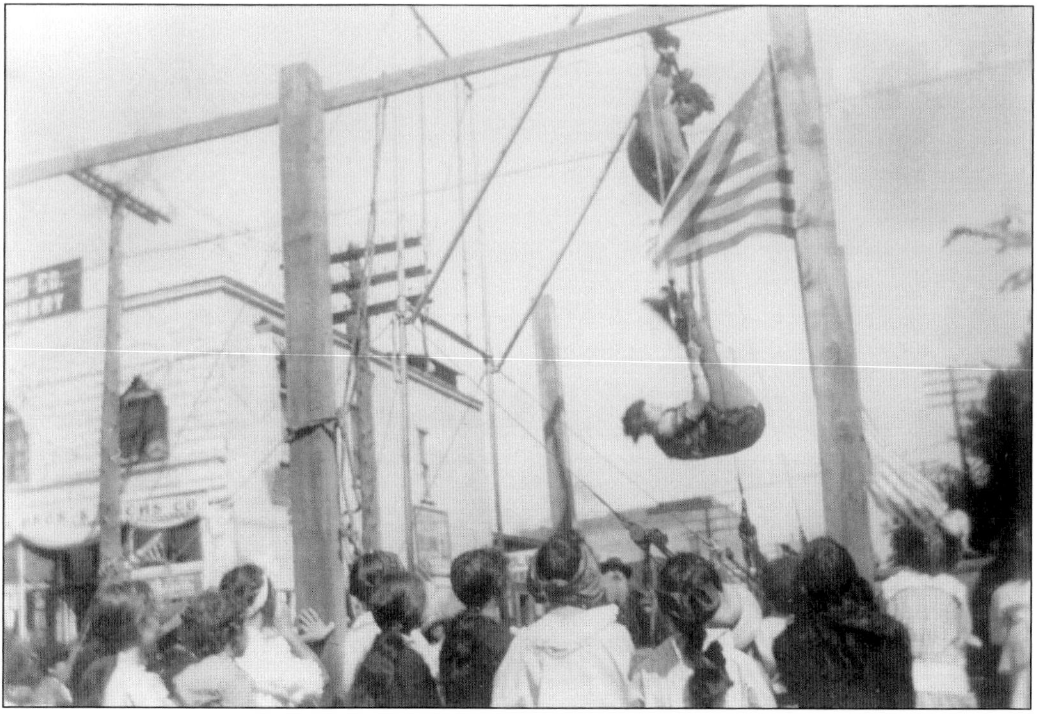

Hinckley residents turned out in droves to see the circus that arrived in town in 1918. In the days before radio and television brought entertainment straight into people's homes, spectacles like circuses were marvelous and exciting novelties that offered a reprieve, however brief, from daily chores.

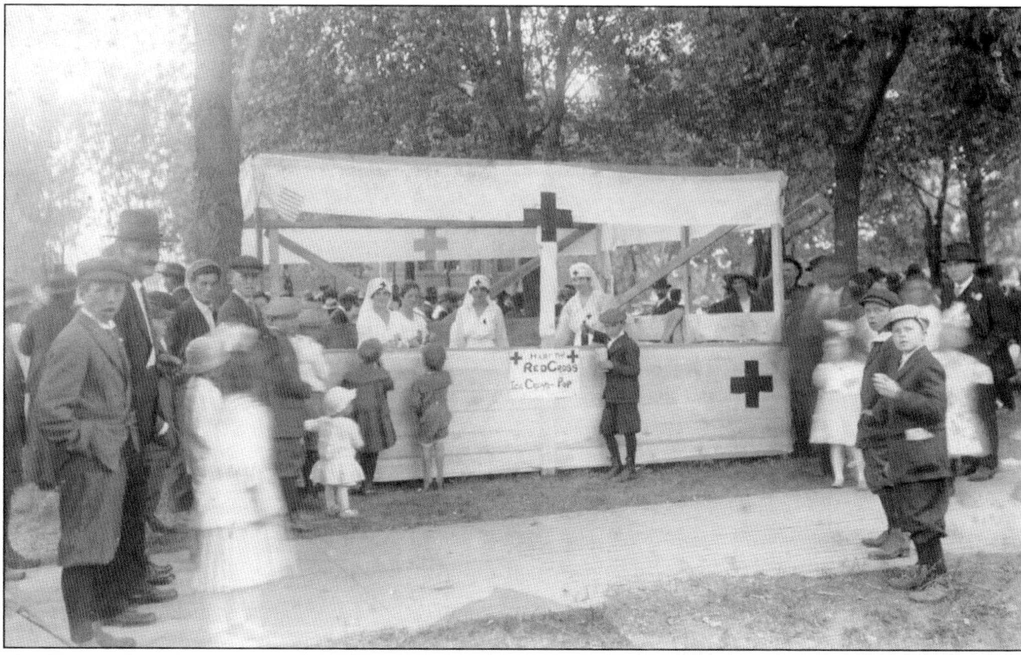

On September 1, 1917, nearly 4,000 Pine County residents gathered in Hinckley to honor the county's newest World War I soldiers. The day was a festive one with music, a picnic, a parade, patriotic speeches, a drill exhibition, and a dance. The Red Cross sold ice cream and soda pop to raise money for its activities.

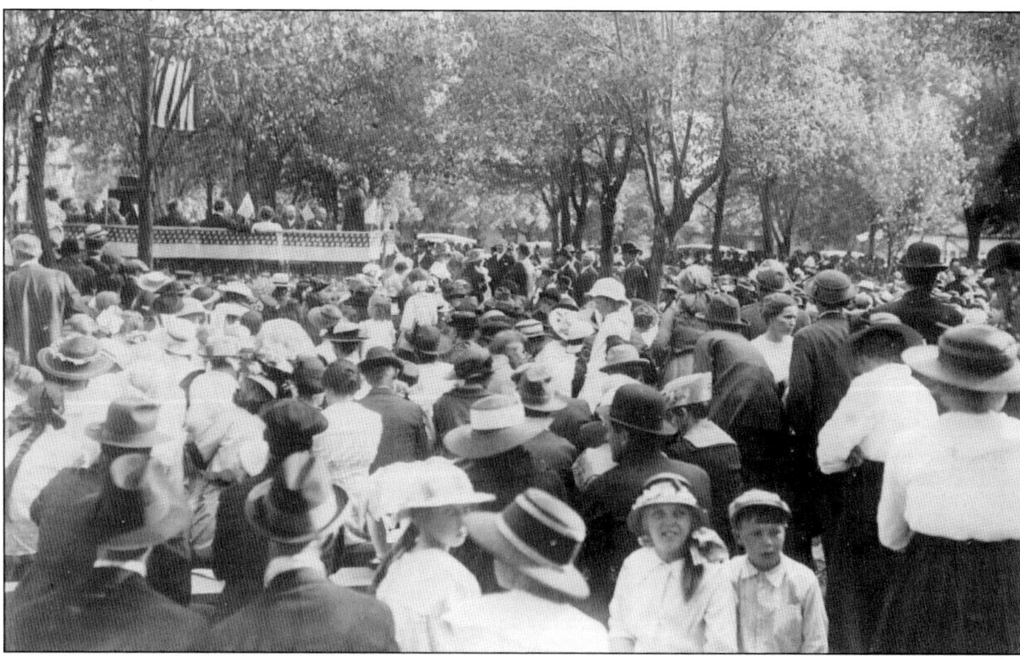

Electric lights were strung along Hinckley's street to give the town a citified appearance. The main stage was decorated in red, white, and blue, and crowds flocked around it to listen to speakers like Civil War veteran Judge Long and George W. Empey, who challenged, "Wake up, Pine County!"

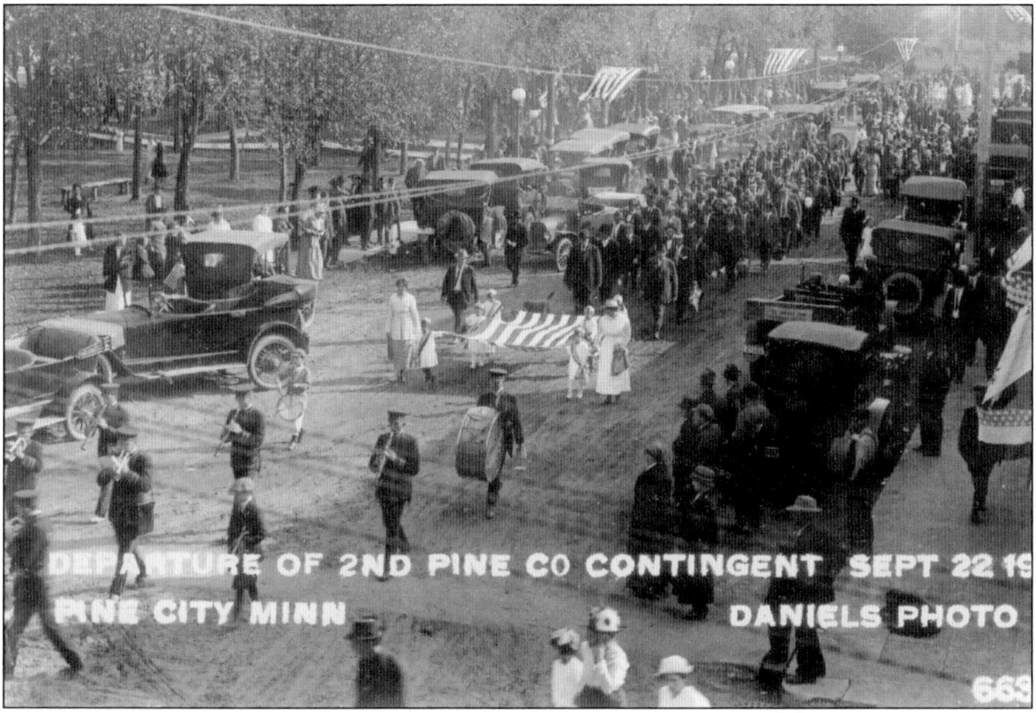

Pine County's citizens gathered again on September 22, 1917, this time in Pine City, to see their boys in uniform off to war. Musical programs, a parade, and speakers were the order of the day, and a huge crowd thronged in the street to cheer and wave as the soldiers marched by. Some members of the crowd waved a banner that proclaimed "Berlin or Bust!"

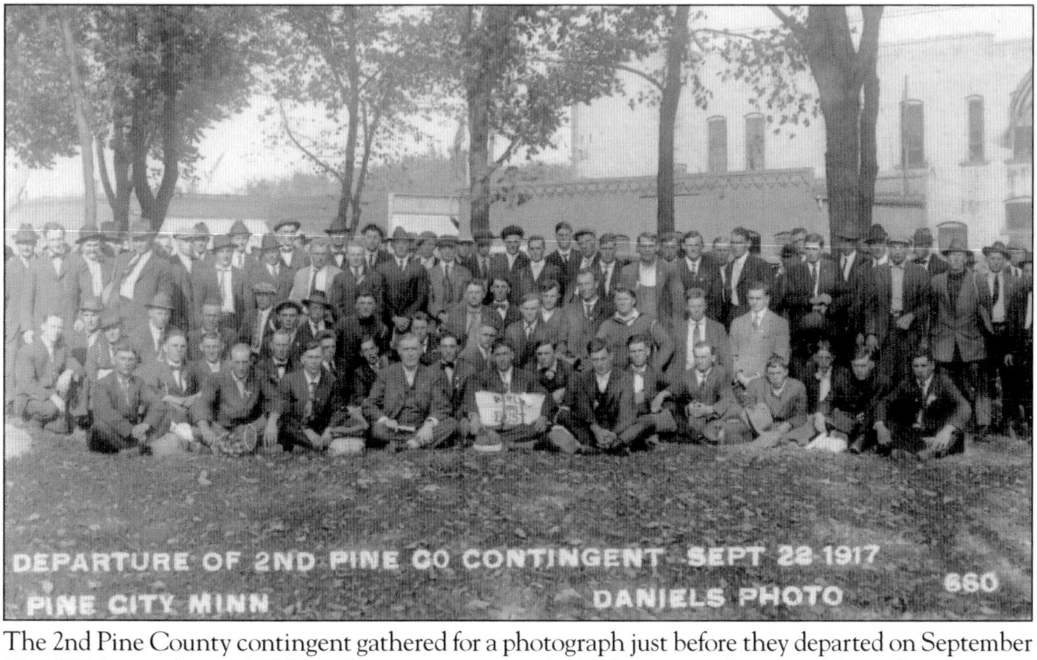

The 2nd Pine County contingent gathered for a photograph just before they departed on September 22, 1917. In total, over 350 Pine County men were drafted into or volunteered for military service during World War I. Some of them never came home.

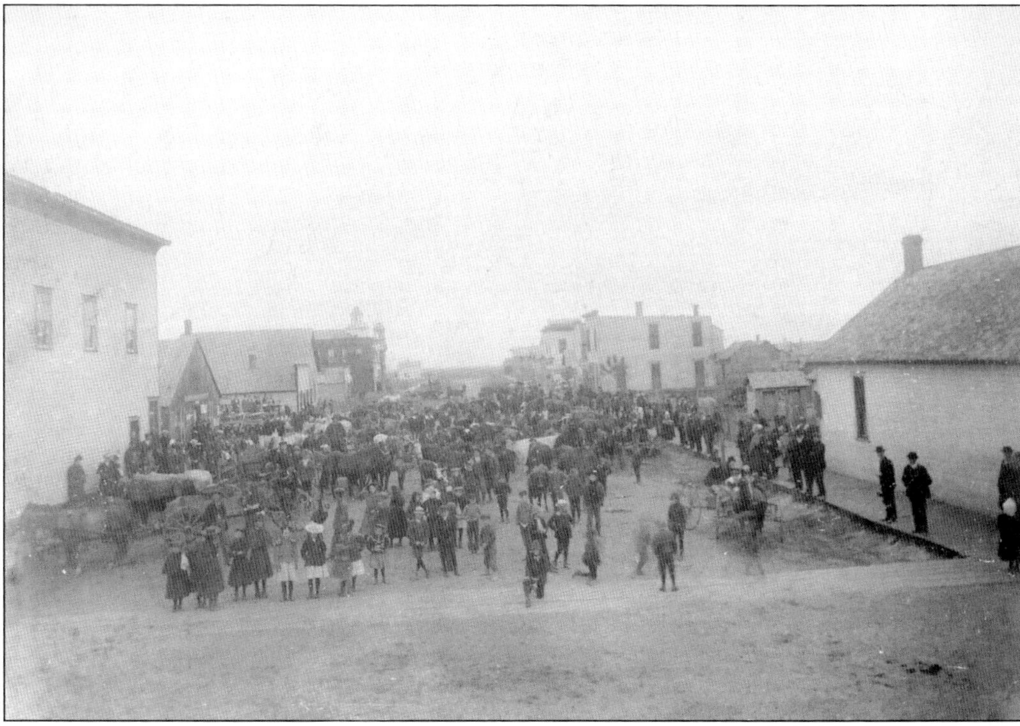

Cattle and horses filled Hinckley's streets during this early Market Day. Young and old alike flocked to town to see the sights, buy or sell, and chat with friends and neighbors.

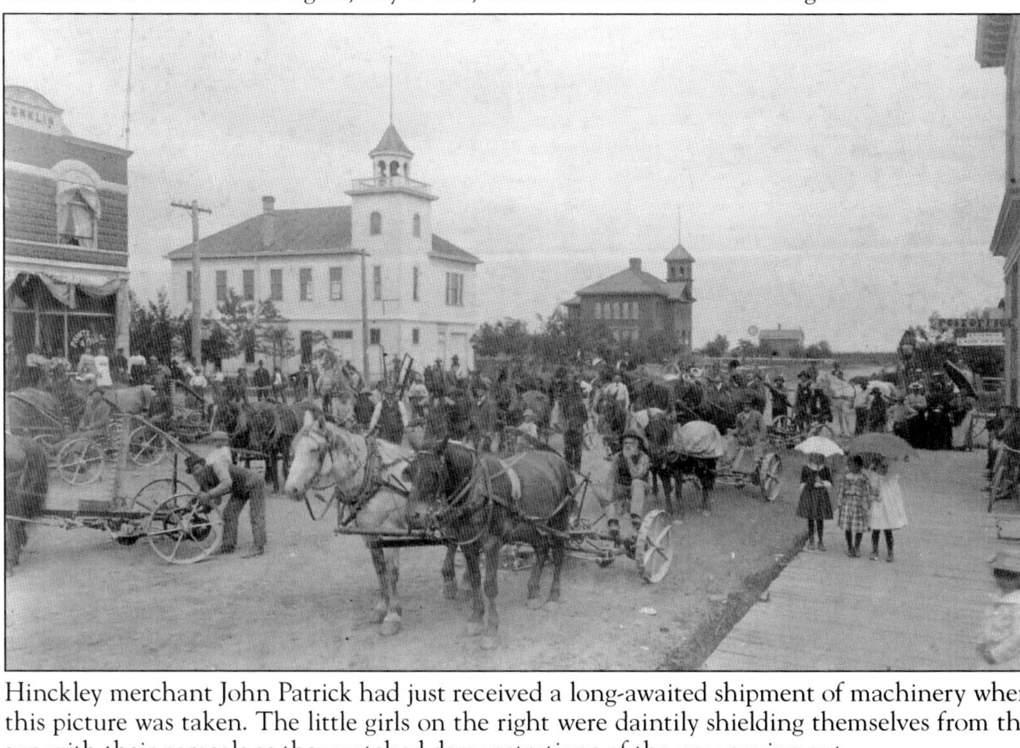

Hinckley merchant John Patrick had just received a long-awaited shipment of machinery when this picture was taken. The little girls on the right were daintily shielding themselves from the sun with their parasols as they watched demonstrations of the new equipment.

Hinckley residents gather along their business district sidewalks to watch the Hinckley fire department in action in 1915. Hopefully, the department was merely providing a demonstration for the annual Corn and Clover Carnival.

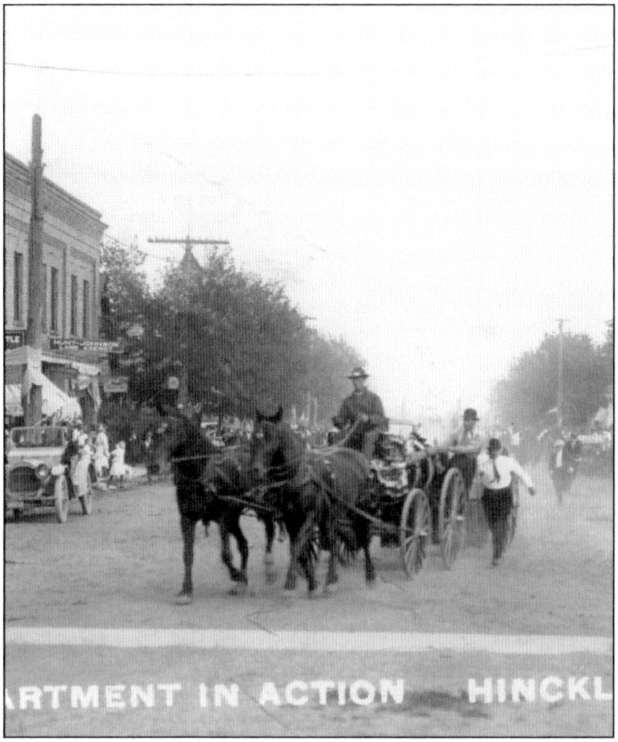

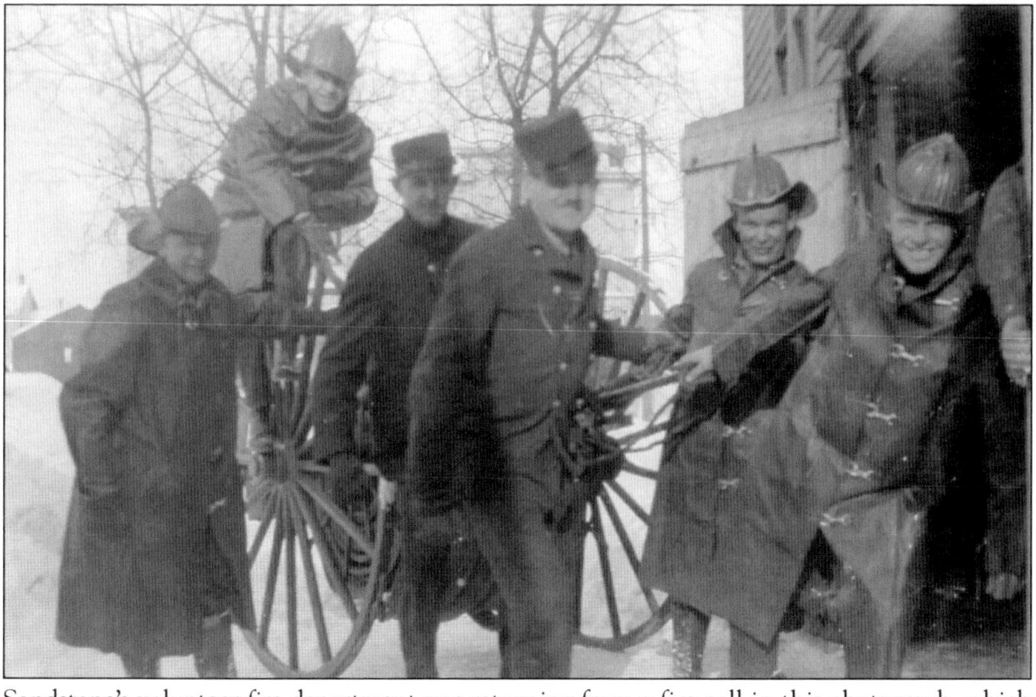

Sandstone's volunteer fire department was returning from a fire call in this photograph, which was taken about 1900. Judging by their smiles, the fire must have been safely extinguished. Since its organization in 1891, Sandstone's fire department has taken great pride in its equipment and its members' skills.

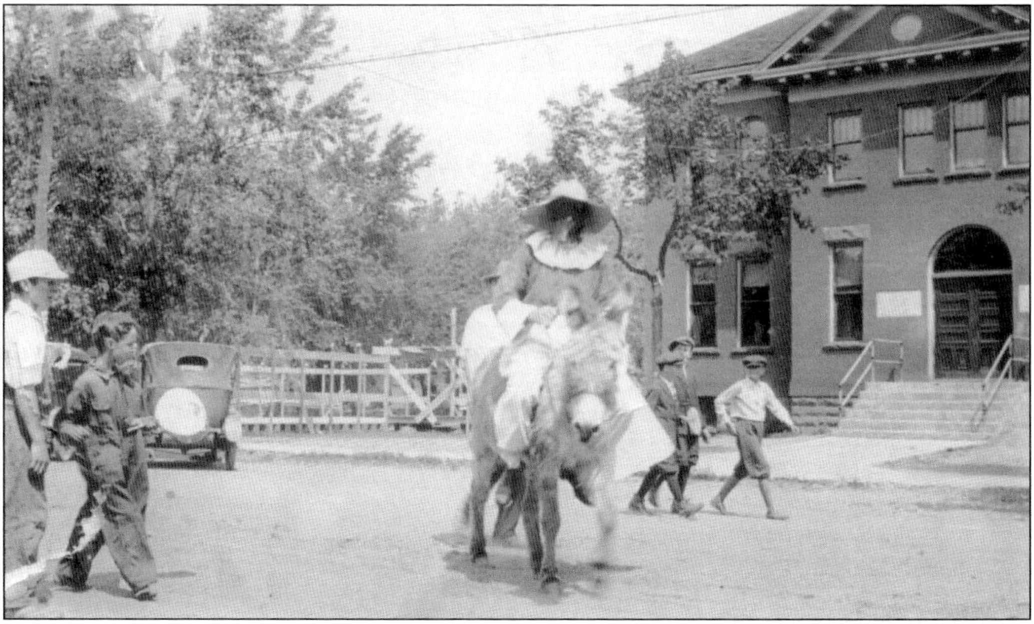

The Corn and Clover Carnival was, and still is, Hinckley's annual celebration. This man won $10 for the best costume in the festival's parade.

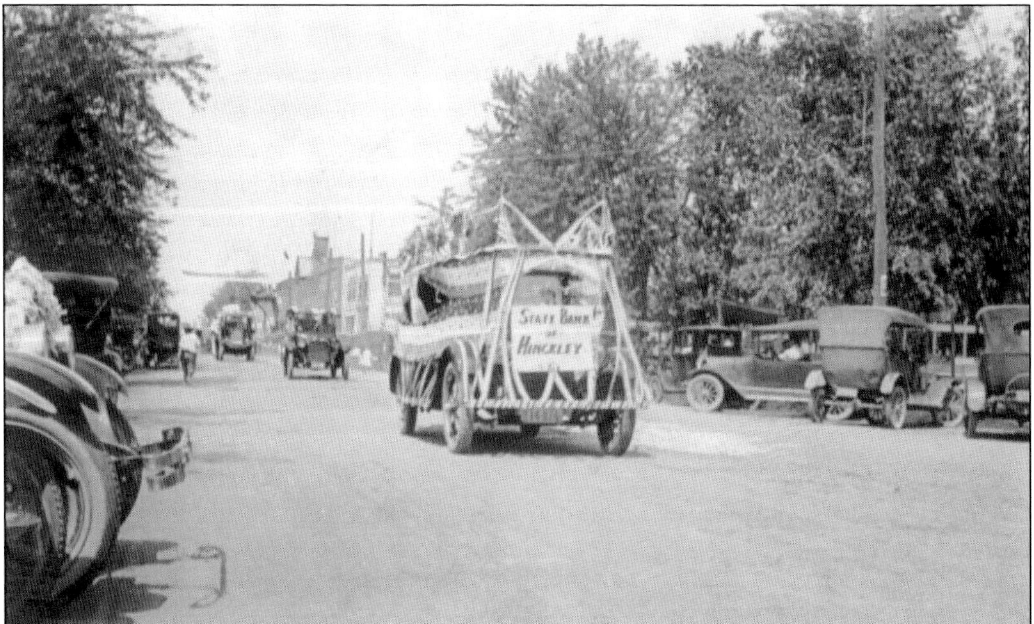

The State Bank of Hinckley decorated a car in a patriotic theme for the annual Corn and Clover Carnival parade.

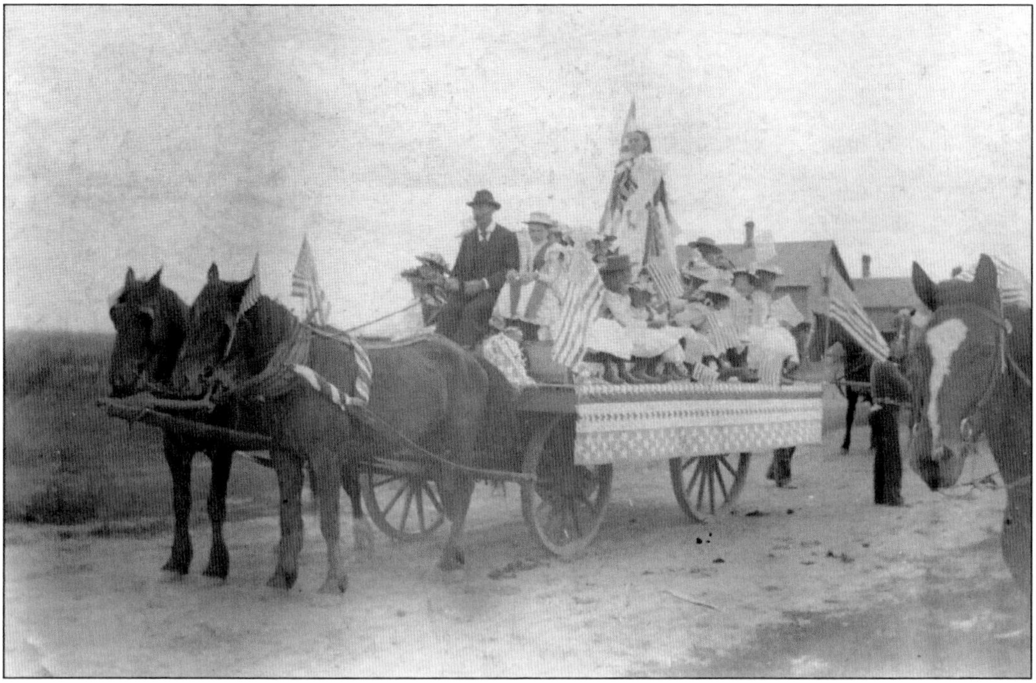

Patriotism again dominated the decorations on this horse-drawn float. The float's little occupants were looking especially festive in their white dresses and Sunday best hats.

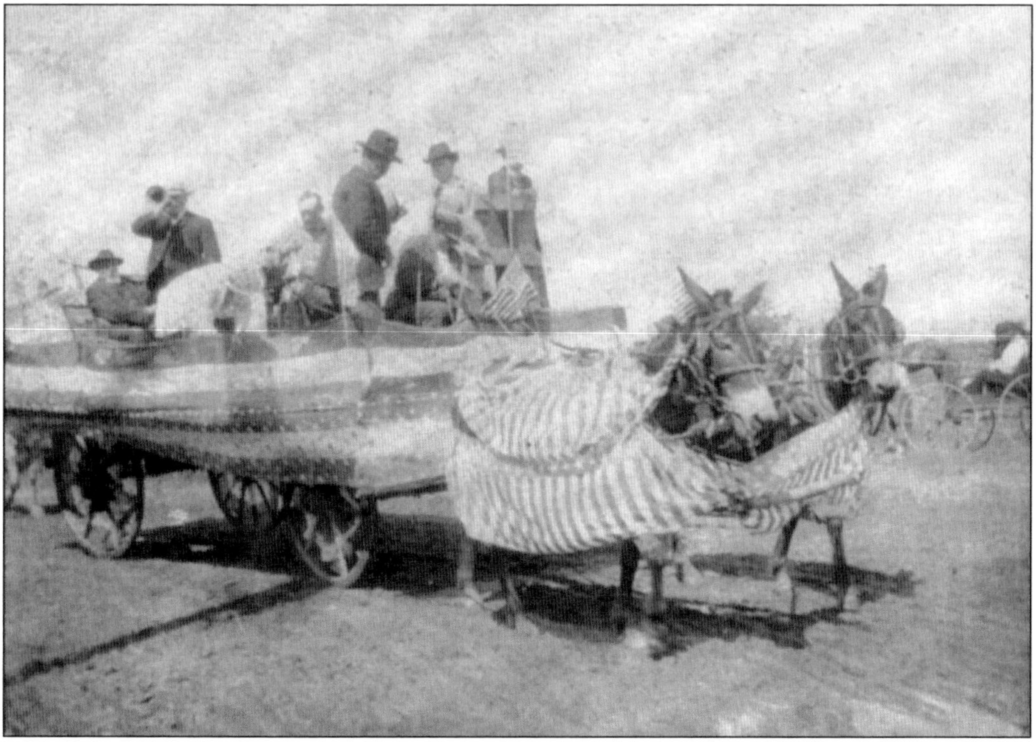

These donkeys and the wagon they were pulling were all decked out for a Fourth of July parade. Ed Linehan was seated on the left.

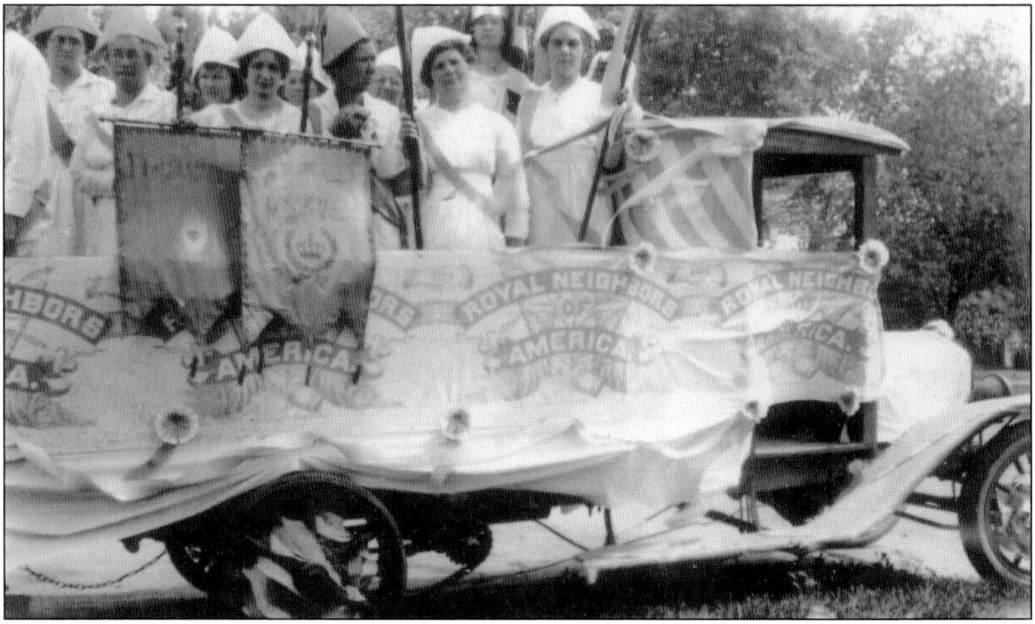

The Royal Neighbors of America was founded in 1888 as a social organization for the wives of Modern Woodmen of America members. In 1895, the society began offering life insurance. According to the organization's charter, its goal was to bring "joy and comfort into many homes that might otherwise today be dark and cheerless . . . by affording the mother an opportunity to provide protection upon her life."

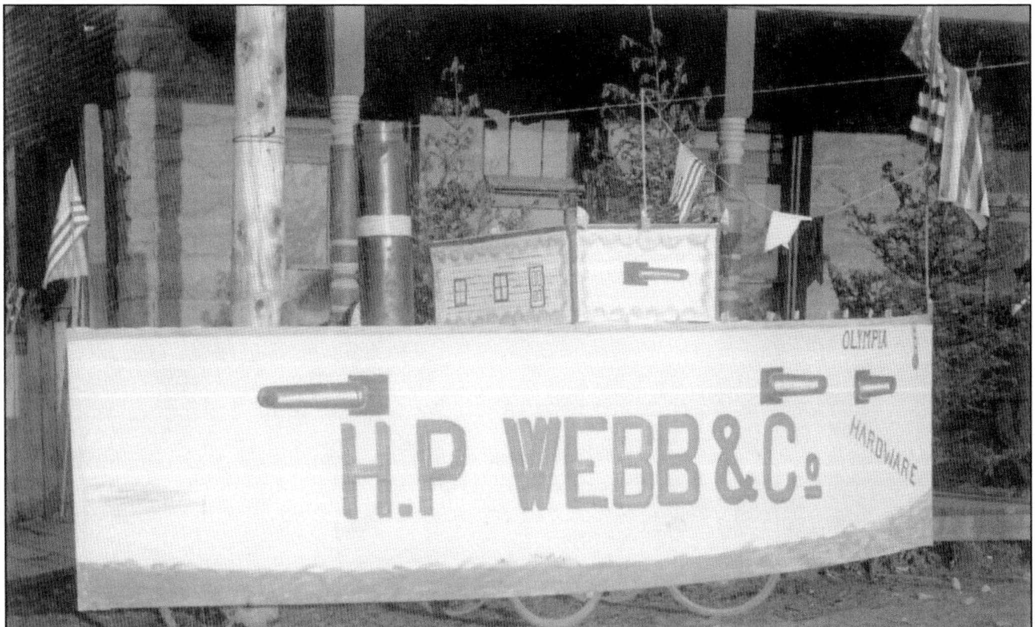

H. P. Webb and Company Hardware built this float for Sandstone's 1904 July 4th parade. The float recreated the famous ship *Olympia*, which was launched in 1892, served as a U.S. flagship during the Spanish-American War in 1898, and led the way in conquering the Spanish fleet at Manila Bay in the Philippines on May 1, 1898.

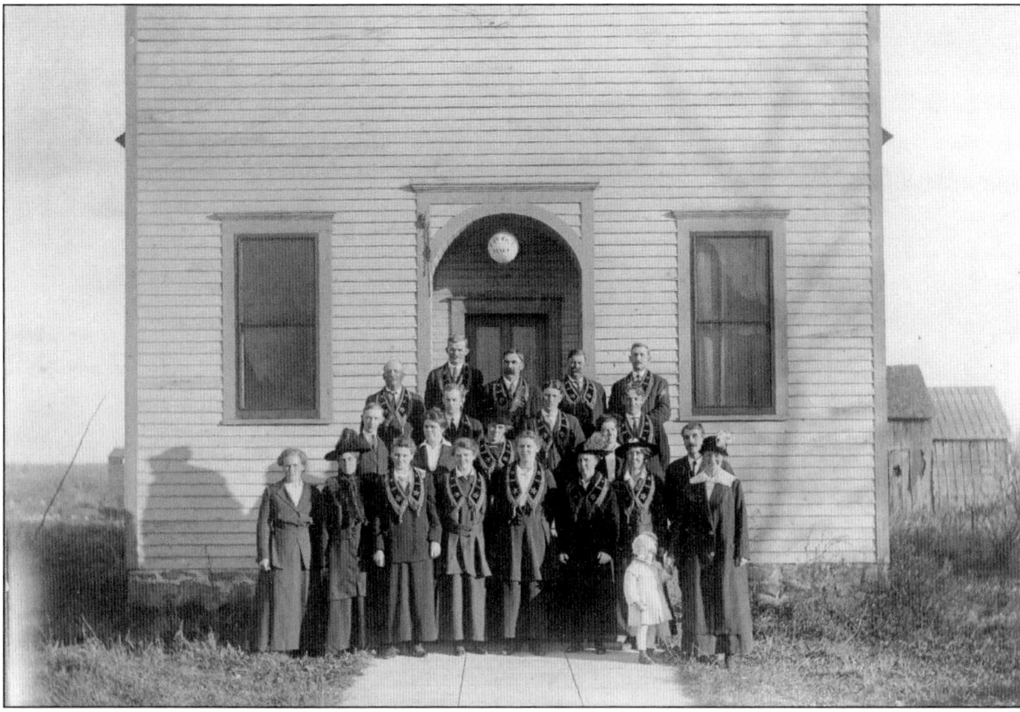

The International Order of Good Templars (IOGT) was a temperance group active throughout the country in the early years of the 20th century. Sandstone's IOGT gathered for their picture in 1908. Their efforts to outlaw alcoholic beverages were successful. Sandstone residents voted to make their town dry in 1909 and between 1914 and 1935. Saloon owners, however, were not happy to find themselves out of business.

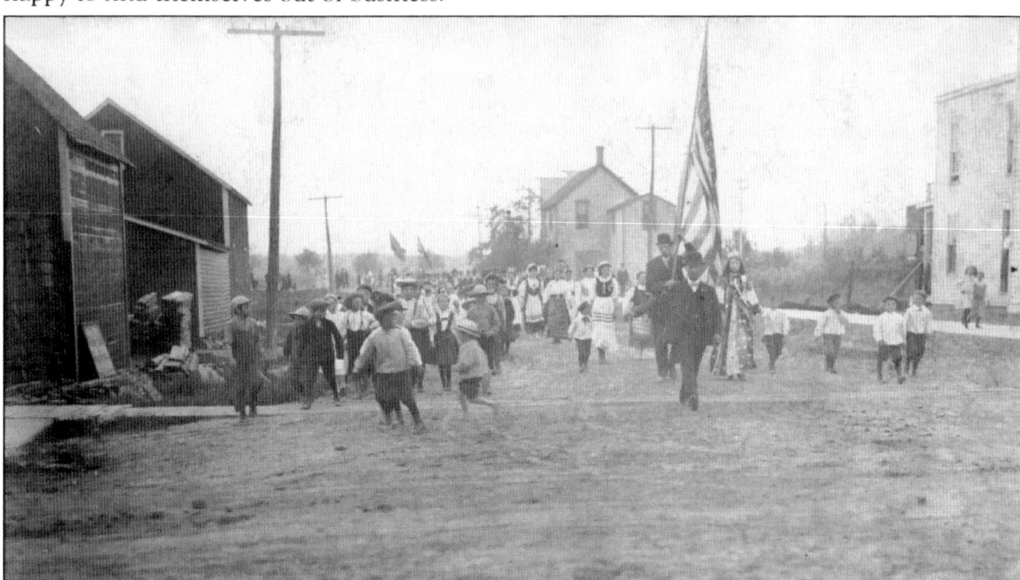

Sandstone's IOGT sponsored a 1909 parade to promote their cause of temperance. Participants combined American patriotic symbols with costumes from their native countries as they marched through the village streets.

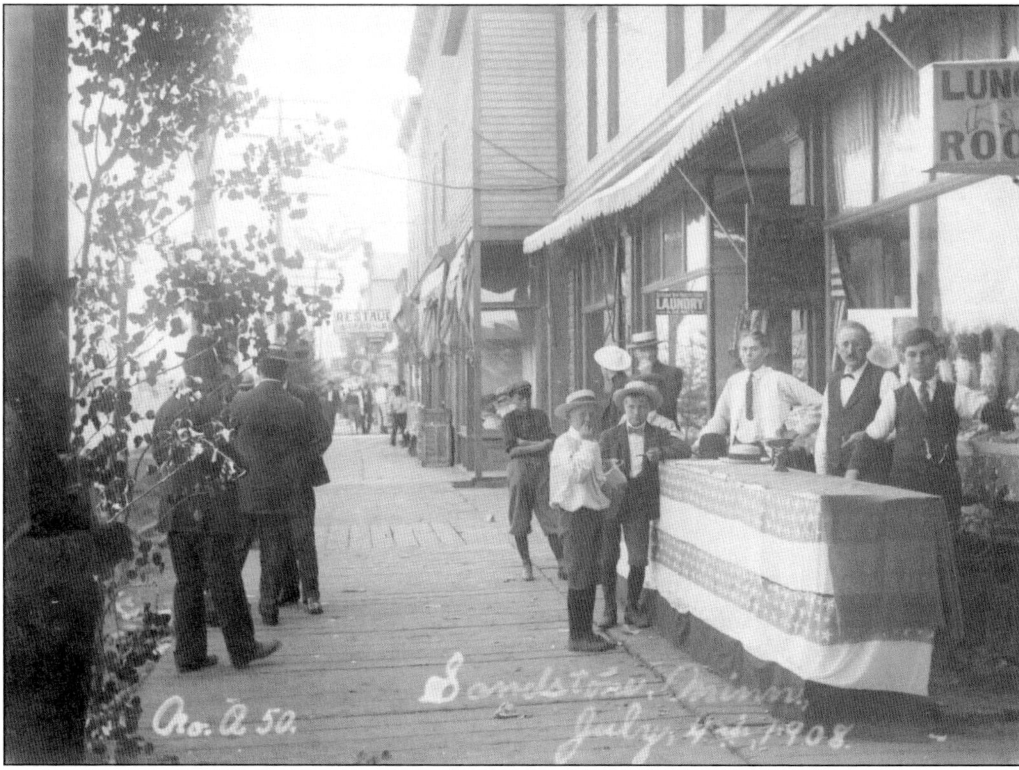

July 4th celebrations drew communities together for patriotic speeches, music, entertainment, sporting events, fireworks, and, of course, plenty of special foods like ice cream and lemonade. These Sandstone residents were enjoying their July 4th in 1908.

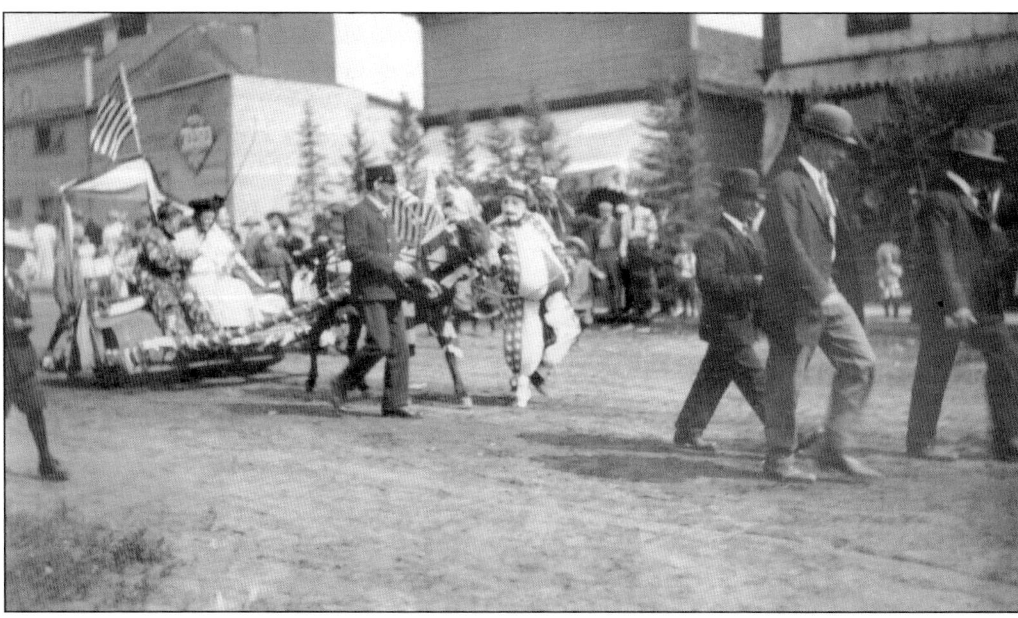

The 1909 July 4th parade in Sandstone was a typical small town spectacle with clowns, floats, and even a dressed up donkey.

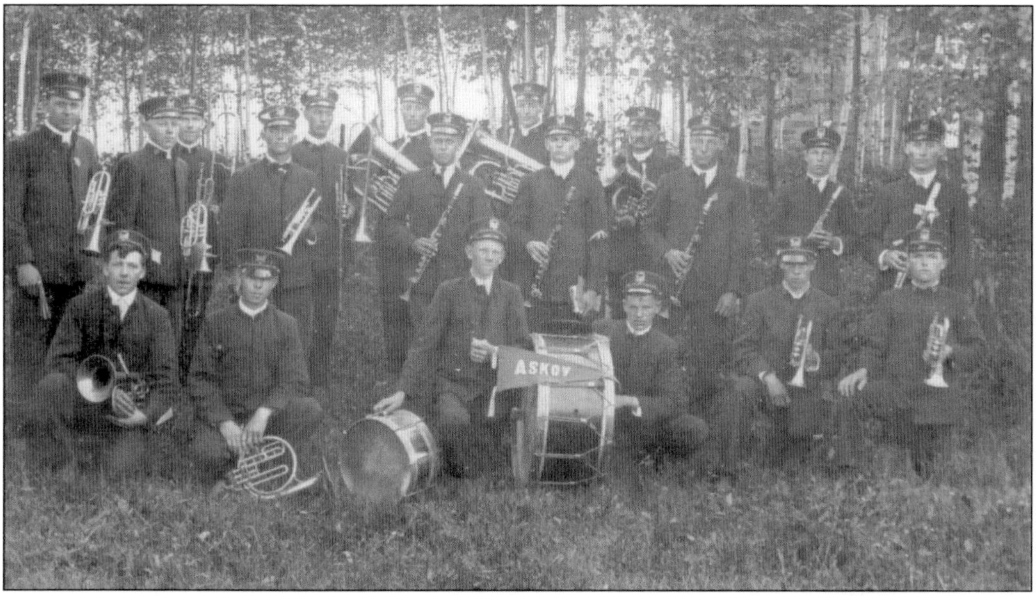

Northern Pine County communities were proud of their city bands. The Askov band, led by director Hjalmar Petersen (standing, far left), posed with their instruments for this 1910s photograph. Band members were Hefluf Rasmussen, Valdermar Hojberg, Henry Andersen, Charles Krantz, Einar Dixen, Arnold Sorensen, Jorgen Petersen, Albert Johnson, Martin Sorensen, Carl E. Sorensen, Folmer Sorensen, Albert Sorensen, John Sorensen, Thorkild Ravnholdt, William Jensen, Hans Masbaek, Alfred Jacobsen, and Thorvald Jensen.

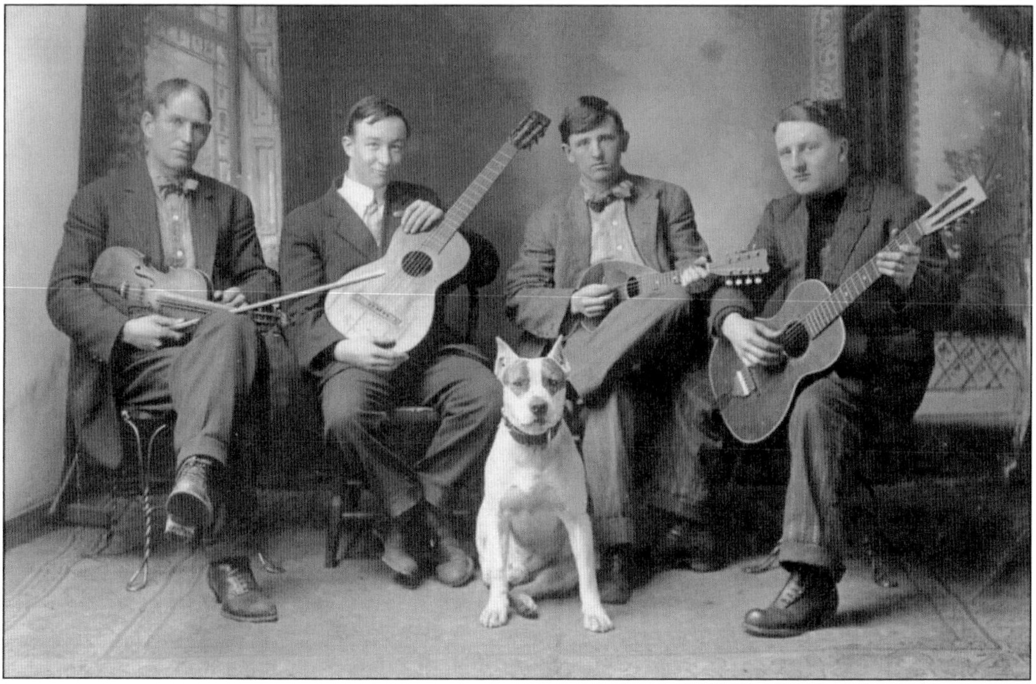

Local musicians often formed small groups to entertain their friends and neighbors at community events like dances, parties, and programs. This string quartet from Hinckley was comprised of, from left to right, Joe McKay, Happy O'Malley, Jess Ingram, and Spud Ingram.

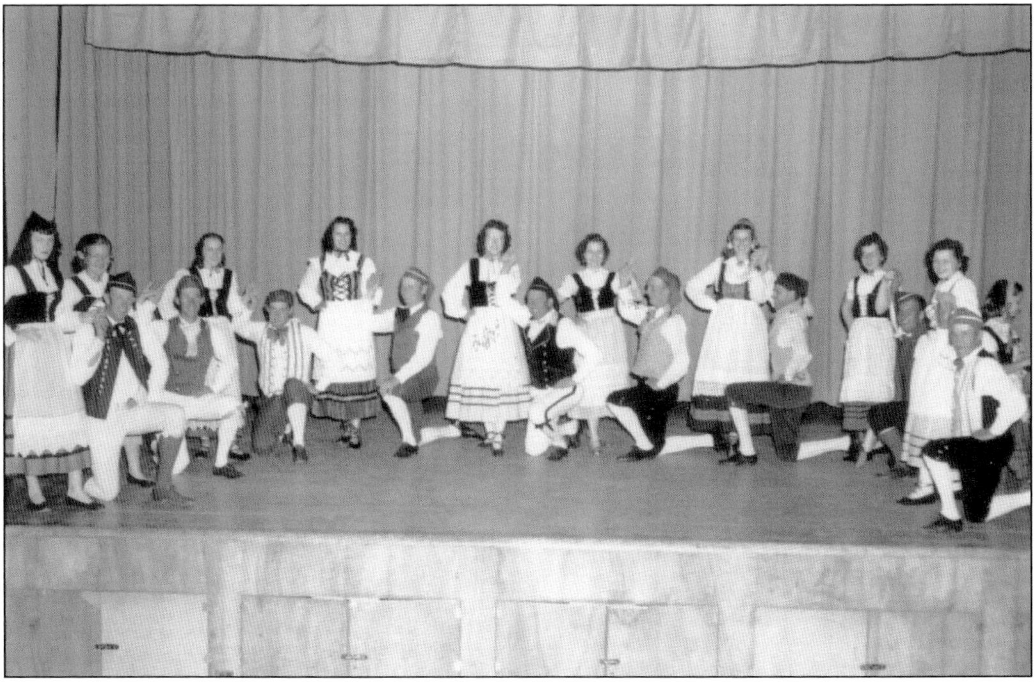

Danish folk dancing was popular in Askov for many years, especially during the 1950s when this group of local dancers performed in Duluth and the Twin Cities.

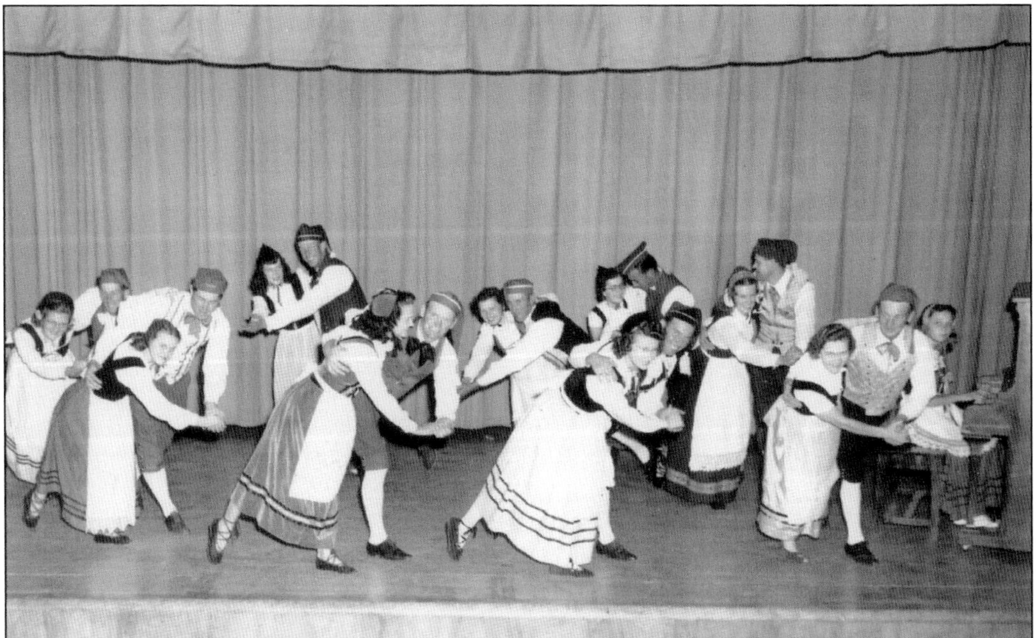

Dancers helped the Askov community celebrate annual Danish festivals including Fastelavn (Shrove Monday), St. Hans, Mid-Somernat, Host Fest, and Mortengaas.

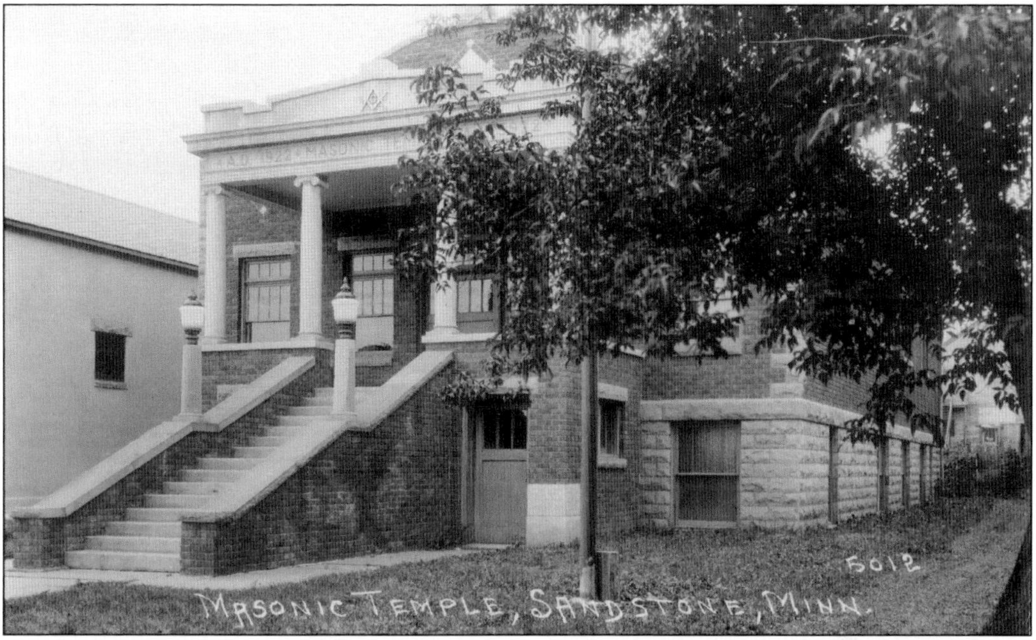

Sandstone's Masonic Temple was built by local contractor Gust Gjertson in 1922 for $16,000. The village's Masonic Lodge received its dispensation to function on April 20, 1900. Founding members included Dr. Duke Cowan, William Aiken, Sherman Brownlee, August Parish, Henry Webb, Louis Edstrom, Gust Westberg, Albert Webb, and Mark Robey. The Masons met at Dr. Cowan's office and then above the Sandstone State Bank until their permanent building was constructed.

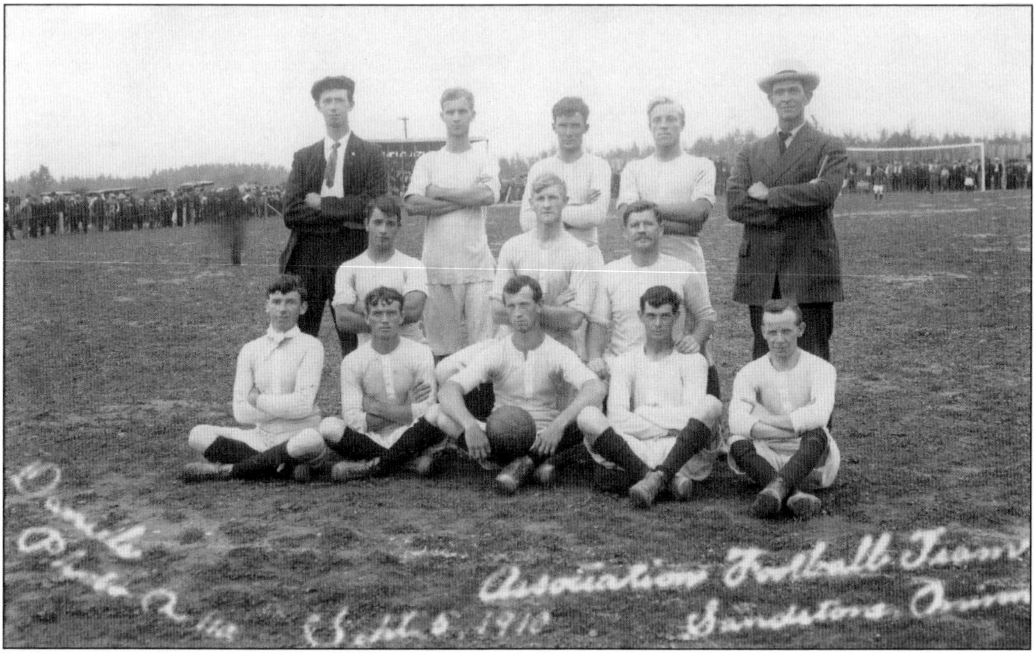

Sandstone's English stonecutters brought their love for soccer with them when they came to America to work in the quarry. The Sandstone soccer team is pictured here in 1910. Other Pine County towns formed teams to offer the Sandstone players some competition.

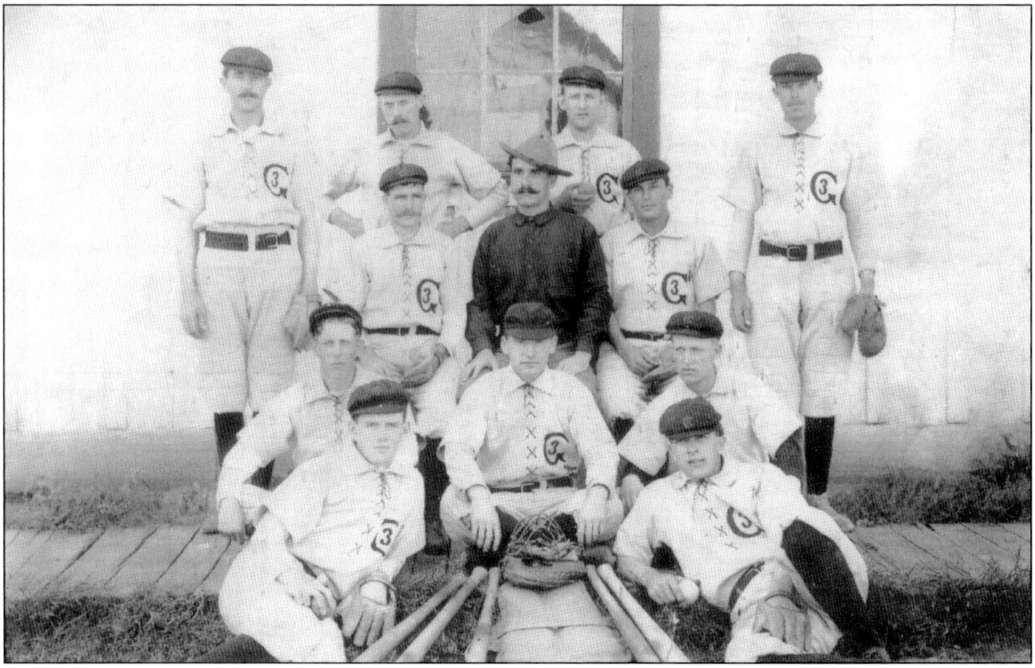

From the earliest days, baseball was a primary sport in Northern Pine County. Town teams played each other throughout the spring and summer. Sometimes two teams formed in the same town for a special entertainment. Just after the 1894 fire, for instance, Hinckley's Fats played Hinckley's Thins to raise money for fire relief. Hinckley's first post-fire town team is pictured here.

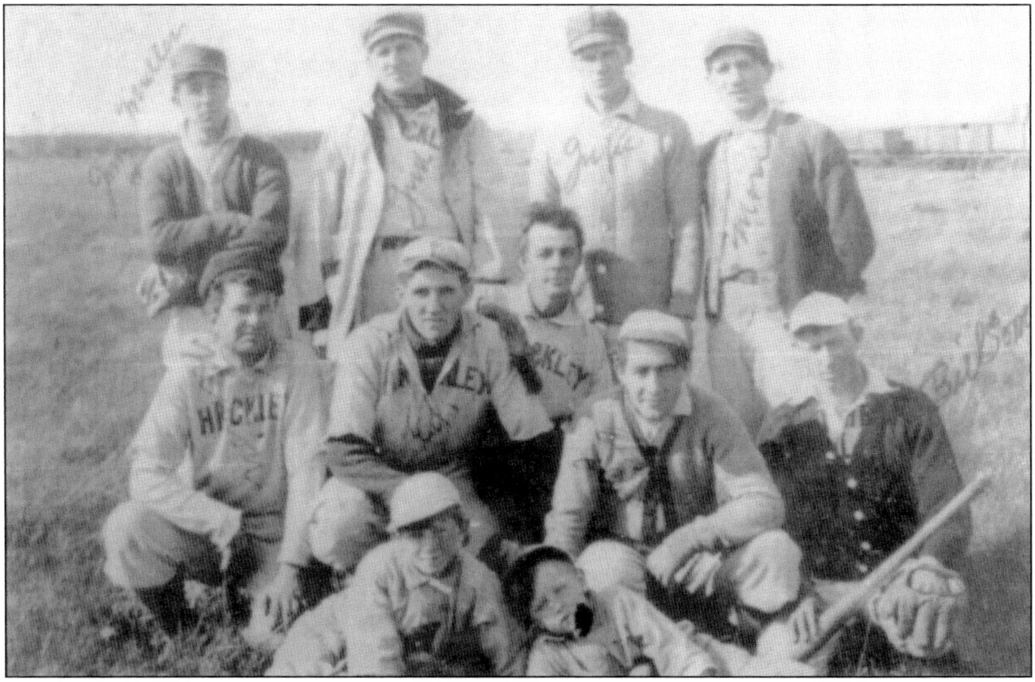

Hinckley's baseball team was organized before the 1894 fire and still plays today as the Hinckley Knights.

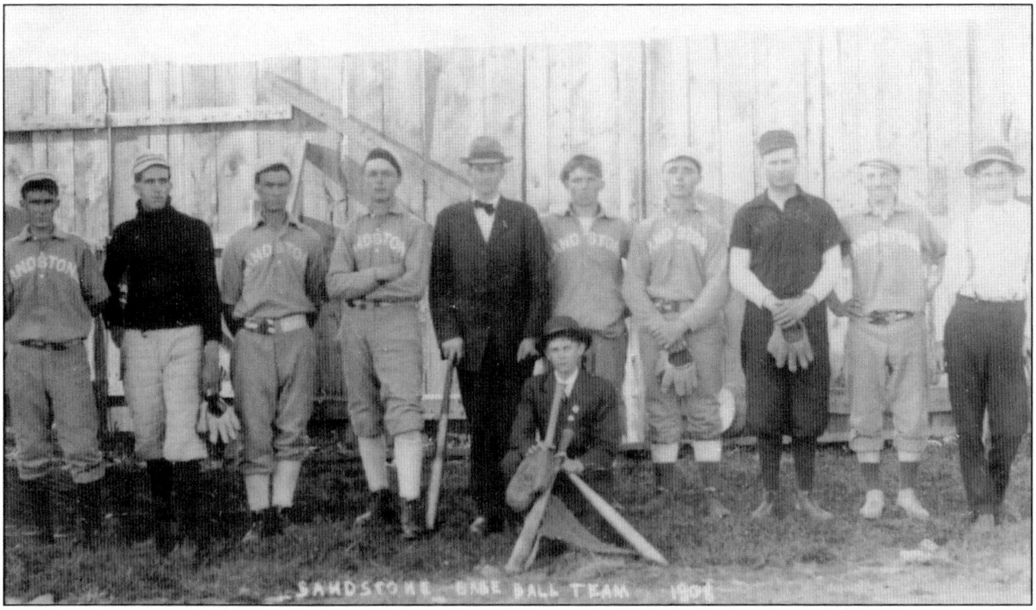

Except for the two fellows on the right, Sandstone's 1908 baseball team looks a little gloomy. Perhaps they were having a difficult season.

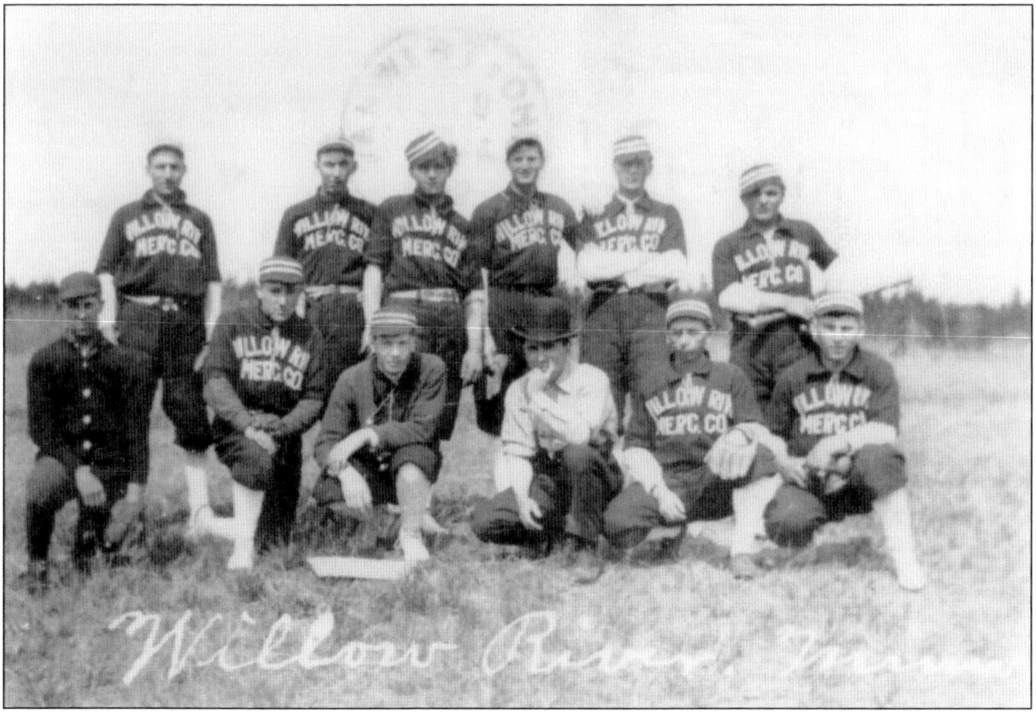

This team was sponsored by the Willow River Mercantile Company. Willow River is proud of its sporting heritage. The town was the home of Pro Football Hall of Fame member Ernie Nevers, who also played three seasons of professional baseball with the St. Louis Browns.

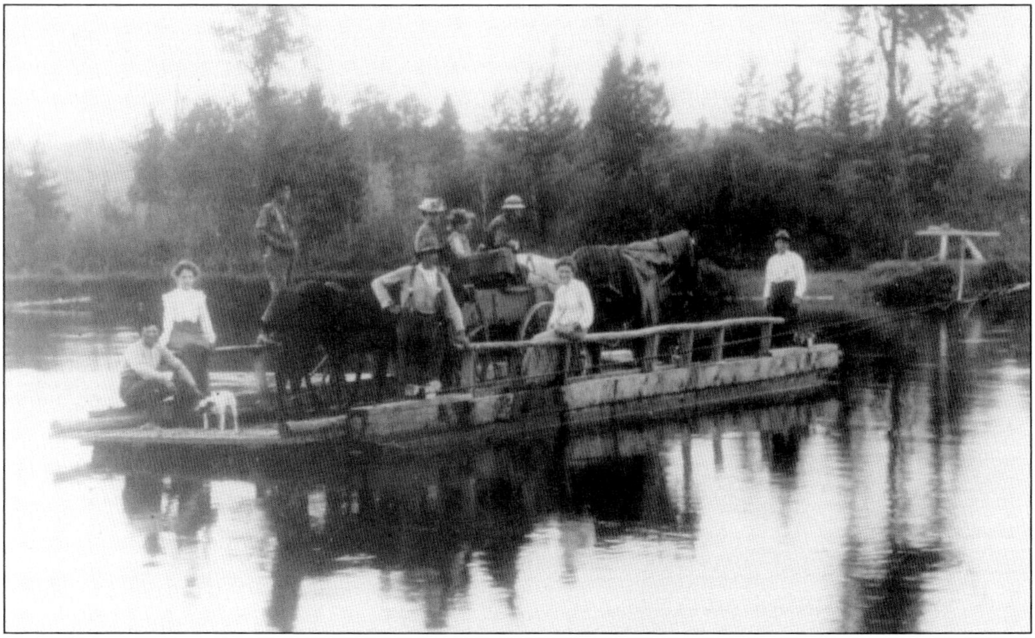

People in eastern Pine County usually traveled to Wisconsin to shop and conduct business. The Pansy Ferry crossed the St. Croix River and connected settlers to Wisconsin towns like Grantsburg. Residents could avoid the 20-mile trip by ordering supplies, which were transported to them by wagon or sled.

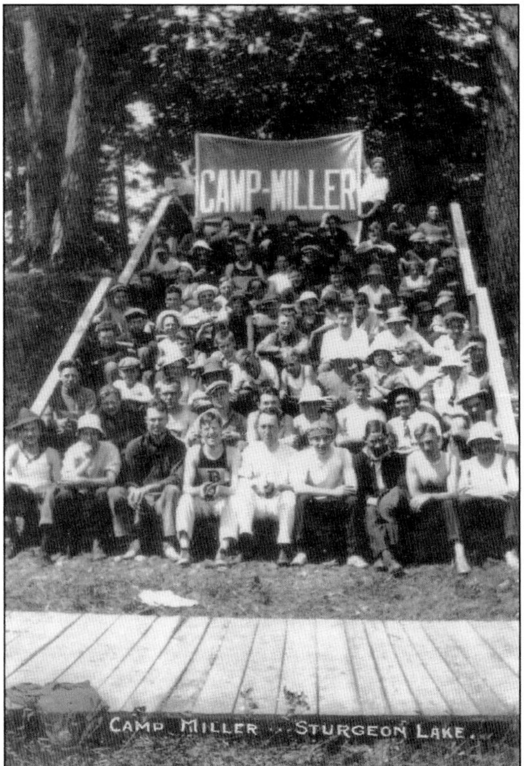

The Sturgeon Lake area has always been famous for its numerous camps and resorts that dot the shores of the region's lakes. These campers at Camp Miller took a little time from their activities to pose for a group photograph.

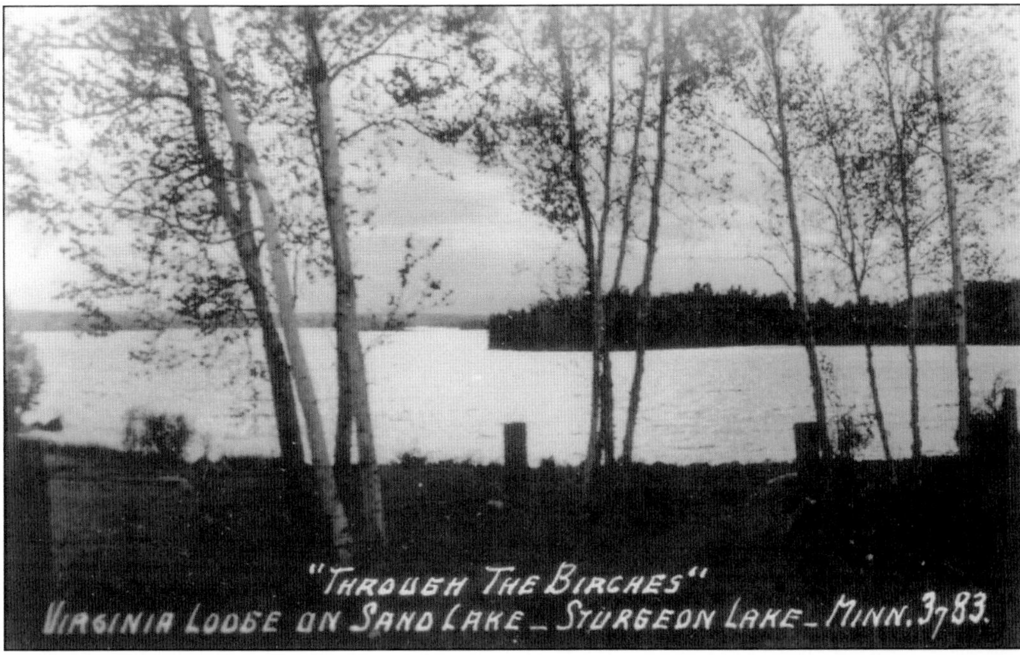

Virginia Lodge was located on Sand Lake, north of Sturgeon Lake, near Pine County's northern border.

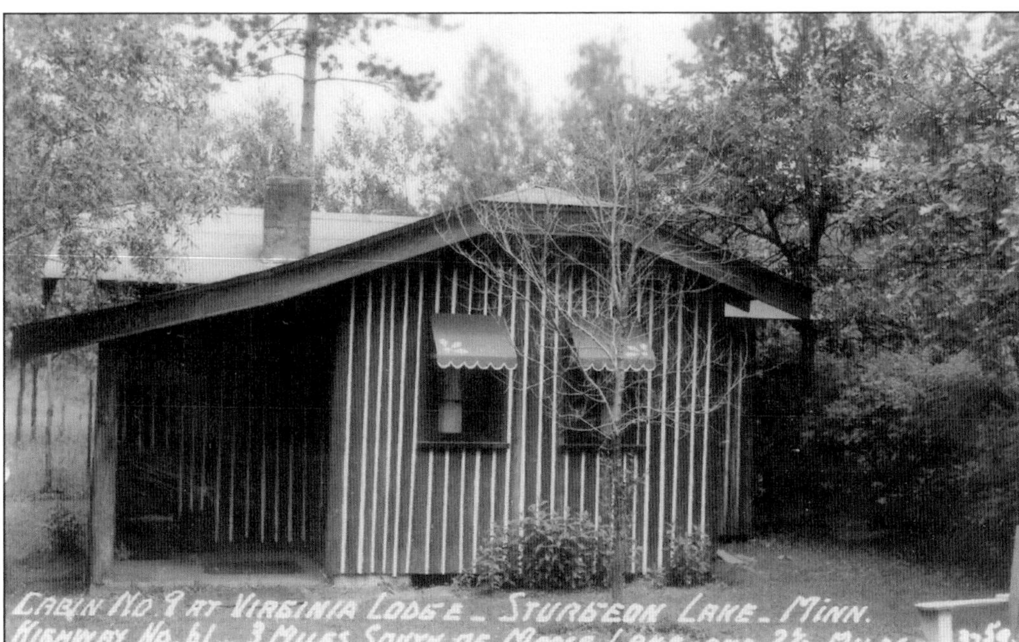

Virginia Lodge offered several cozy cabins for campers to rent so they could enjoy the great outdoors in comfort.

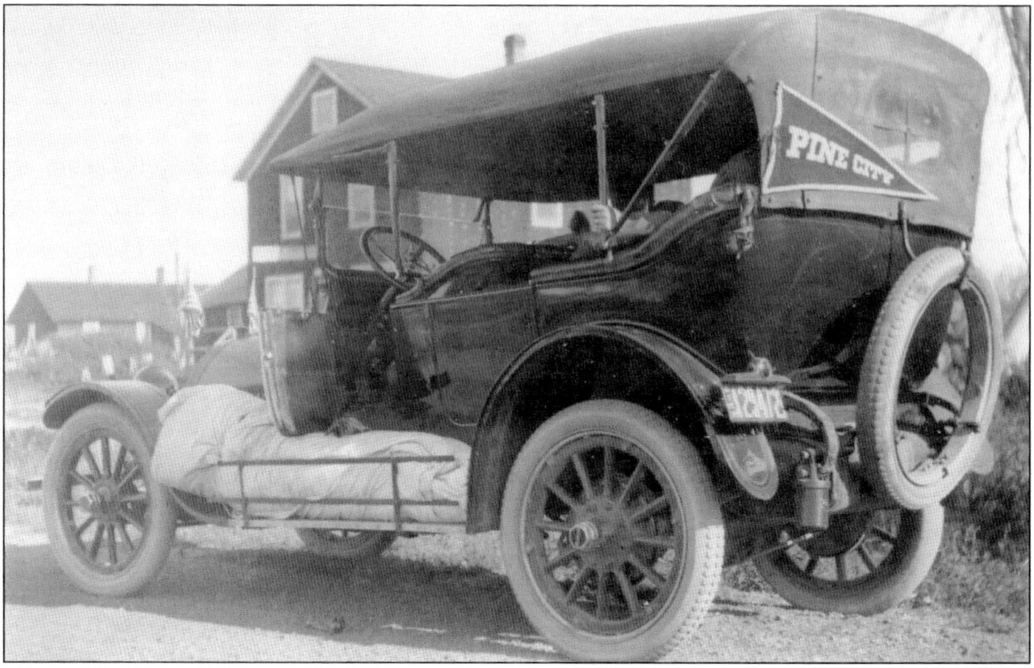

This car was all packed up and ready to head north on a camping trip. Before trunks or rear storage, supplies were bundled and secured to an automobile's running boards.

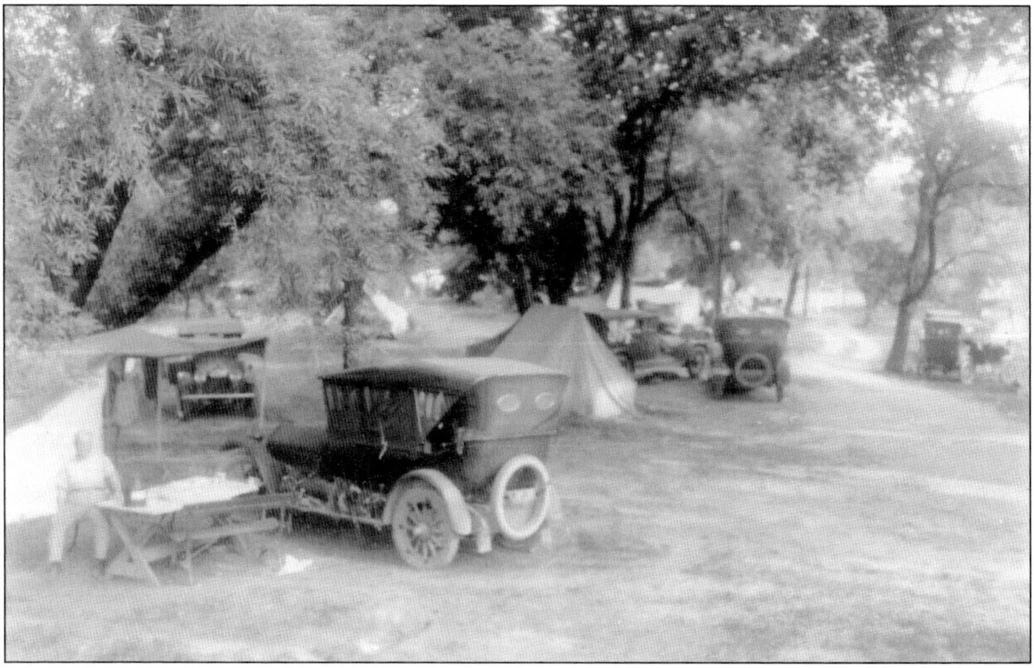

Camping was an enjoyable pastime for the people of Pine County. Numerous forests offered outdoor folk opportunities to hike, fish, hunt, and appreciate nature.

Melvin Nyberg was enjoying his day of fishing on Big Pine Lake in 1914 or 1915. Despite his flooded boat and single oar, he was catching fish. Perhaps he even caught a glimpse of the famous Pine Lake monster, which was said to lurk in the lake's depths. Some residents claimed that the monster was really a 12-foot sturgeon they affectionately named "Oscar."

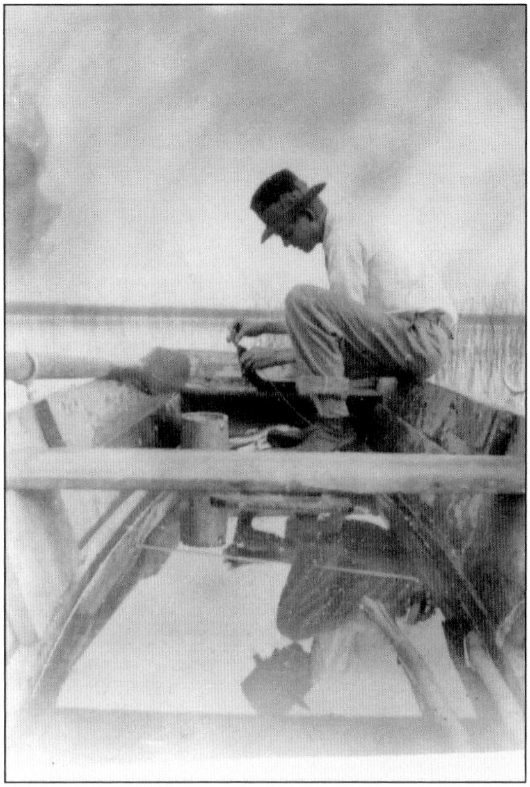

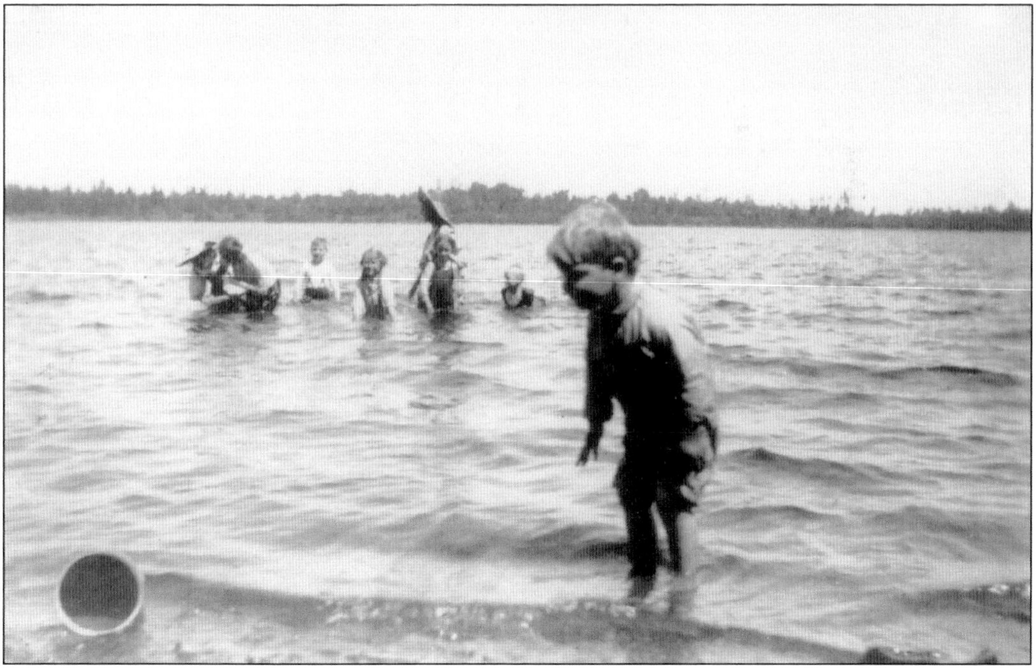

These children were playing in Grindstone Lake, about 5 miles west of Sandstone. Grindstone was the site of Indian villages and logging camps before it became a popular destination for tourists and fishermen.

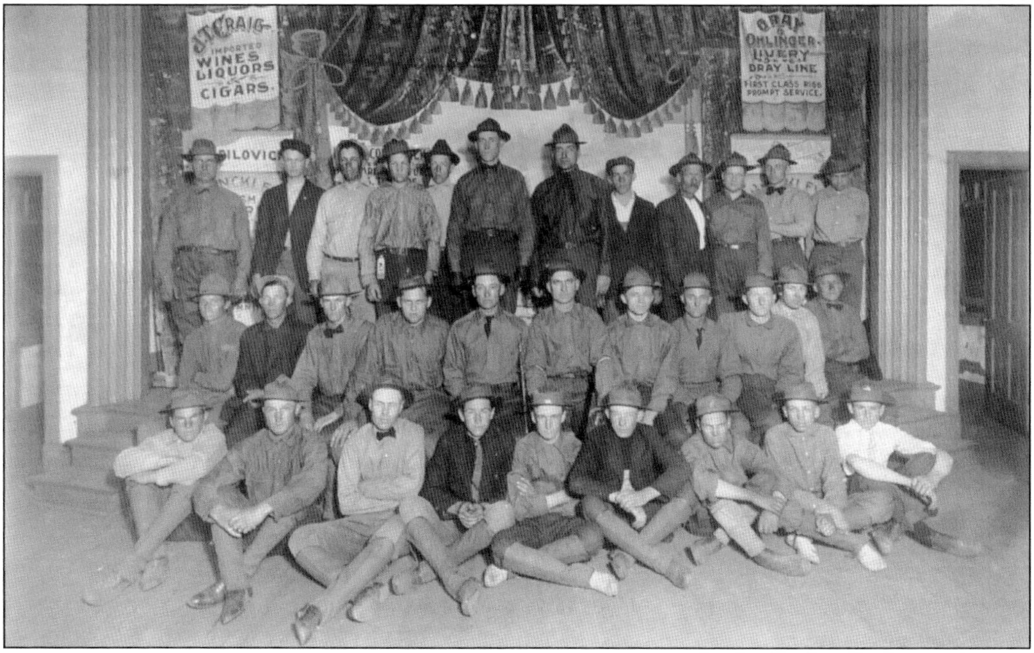

The Pine County Home Guard posed for its group photograph during World War I. Men from ages 18 to 60 were eligible to join the Home Guard and contribute to the war effort, even if they were unable to join the regular military. Their primary task was to guard bridges and railroads against enemy attacks and sabotage. According to the local newspaper, they also "stopped the spread of seditious speech" and broke up "disloyal" meetings.

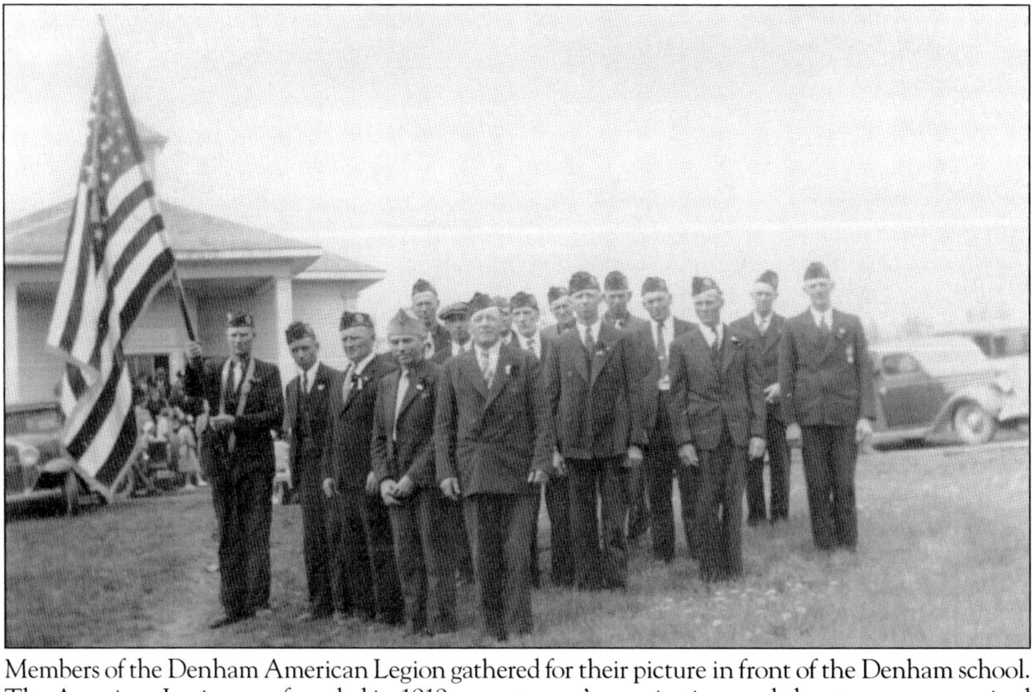

Members of the Denham American Legion gathered for their picture in front of the Denham school. The American Legion was founded in 1919 as a veterans' organization, and chapters were organized throughout the country to serve veterans, service men and women, and their communities.

Nine

Citizens and Families

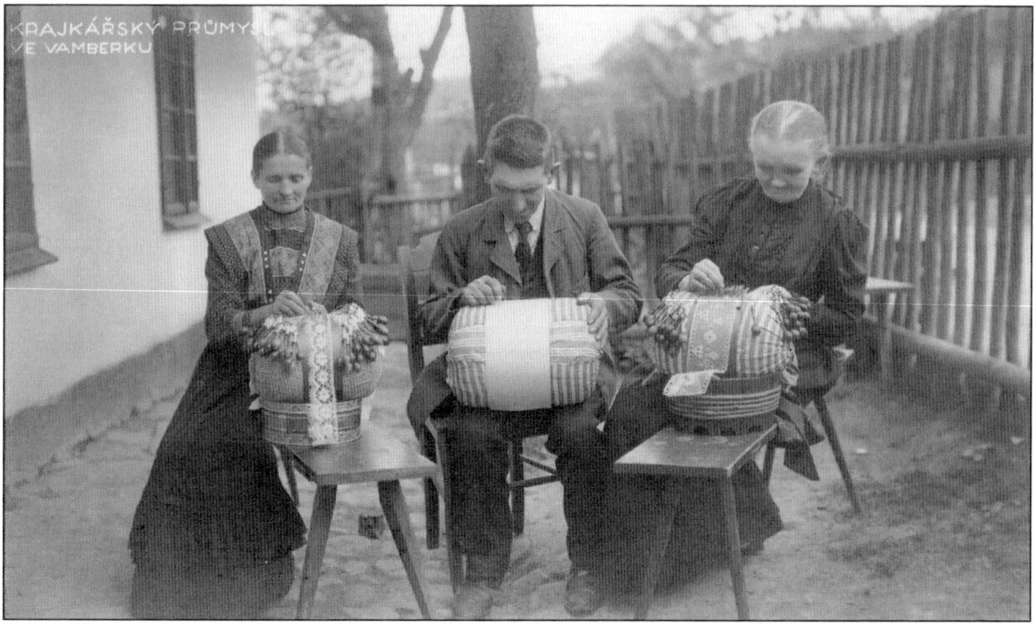

This Czech family was making bobbin or pillow lace. Several bobbins were wound with thread and then braided, woven, and twisted to make intricate and beautiful designs. While this type of lace-making began in Italy in the 16th century, it spread through Europe, and different nationalities developed their own variations. Immigrants brought their traditional skills with them to America.

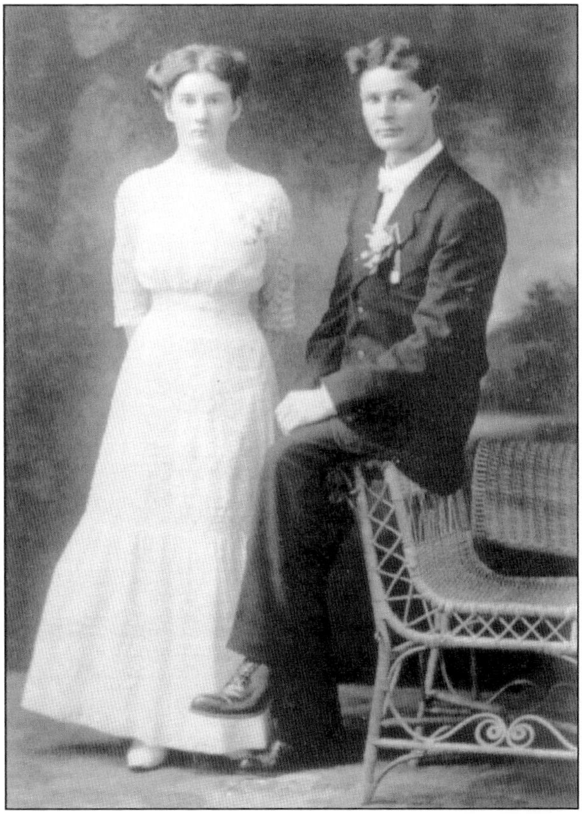

On September 19, 1911, Arthur Elroy Wood and Gertrude May Eaton, both of Willow River, were married at the 24th Annual Pine County Fair. At 3:00 in the afternoon, the couple was escorted onto the fair grounds by the local Boy Scout troop. They rode in style in two automobiles to the main stage where a large crowd had gathered.

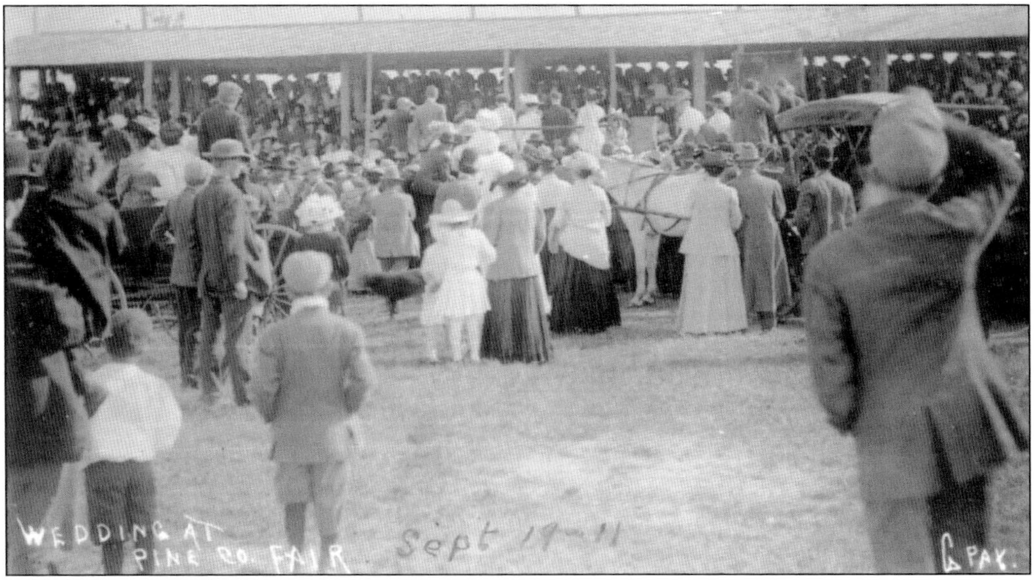

Minnesota governor E. O. Eberhart, who had just completed his speech, was on hand to give away the bride, and Rev. H. H. Parish conducted the ceremony. The newly married couple spent the rest of their afternoon enjoying the fair before catching a train for Hinckley. Other fair goers remained at the main stage to watch Mons Dubec and his troupe of trained dogs, cats, monkeys, apes, and rats.

Herman Trott was one of Pine County's founding fathers. He was instrumental in organizing Pine County and in promoting settlement in Chengwatana, the first county seat. While living in Chengwatana from 1856 to 1862, Trott was a prominent merchant, postmaster, and county commissioner. He later moved to St. Paul to serve as railroad commissioner for James J. Hill's Great Northern line.

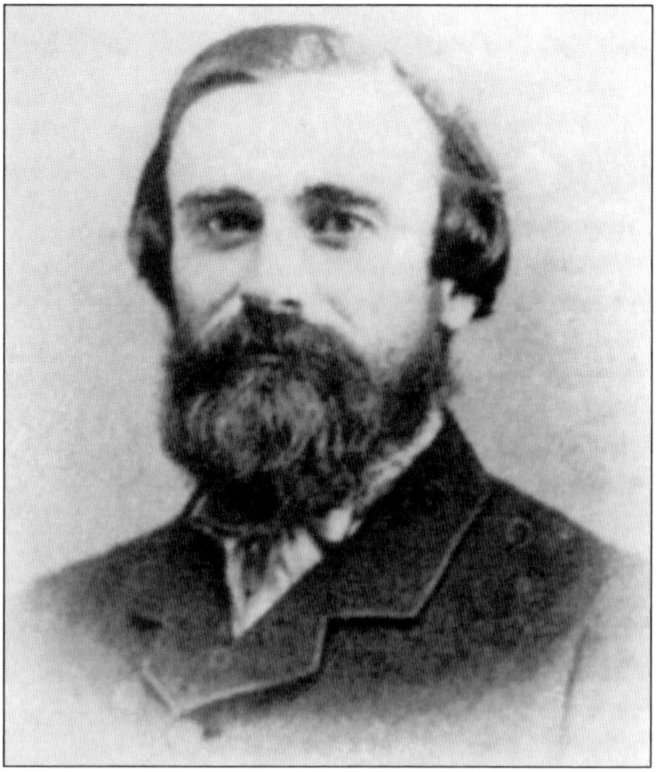

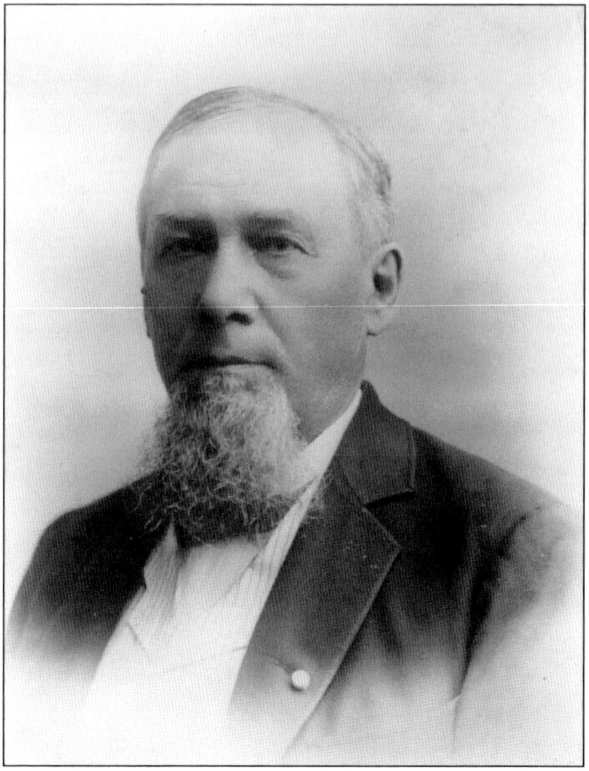

William Grant was an important figure in early Northern Pine County history. He discovered a formation of sandstone along the Kettle River in 1885 and founded the Kettle River Sandstone Company. Grant leased the quarry to the Minneapolis firm Ring and Tobin in 1887, for the project was too expensive for a single company, and then resigned in 1888 to focus on his banking career.

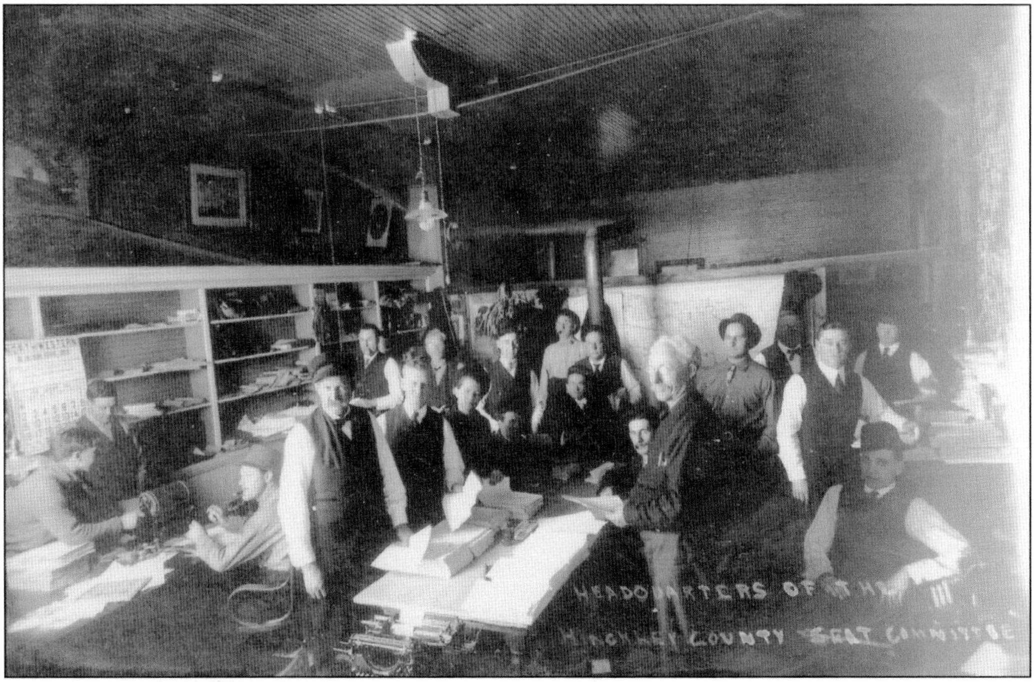

Pine County's people have been involved in numerous internal conflicts over the years. On several occasions, residents have contemplated splitting the county in two, north and south, to even out limited resources. This 1914 committee gathered to advocate transferring the county seat from Pine City to Hinckley. The move never happened.

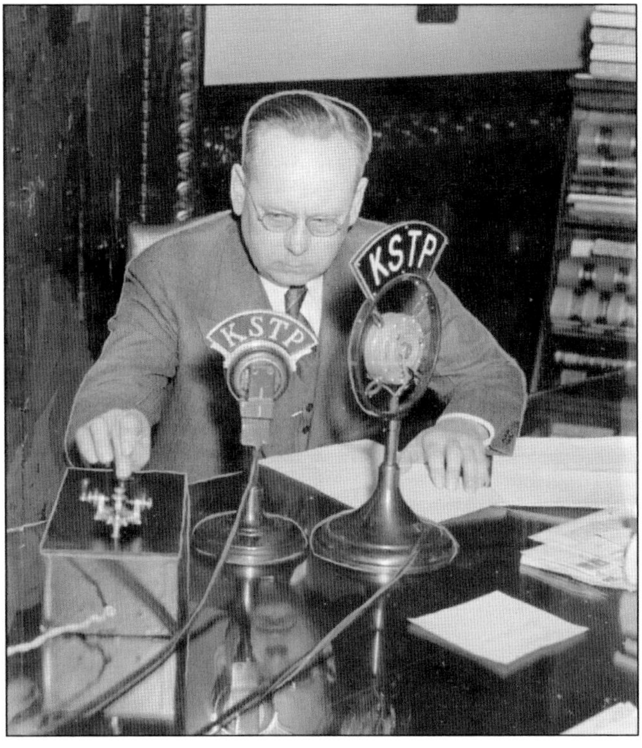

Hjalmar Petersen, the 23rd governor of Minnesota, was born in Eskildstrup, Denmark, in 1890 and immigrated to America as a child. He purchased the *Askov American* newspaper in 1914 and retained ownership until his death in 1968. Petersen was elected lieutenant governor in 1934. When Gov. Floyd B. Olson died of cancer in 1936, Petersen was sworn in as governor for the remaining two years of the term.

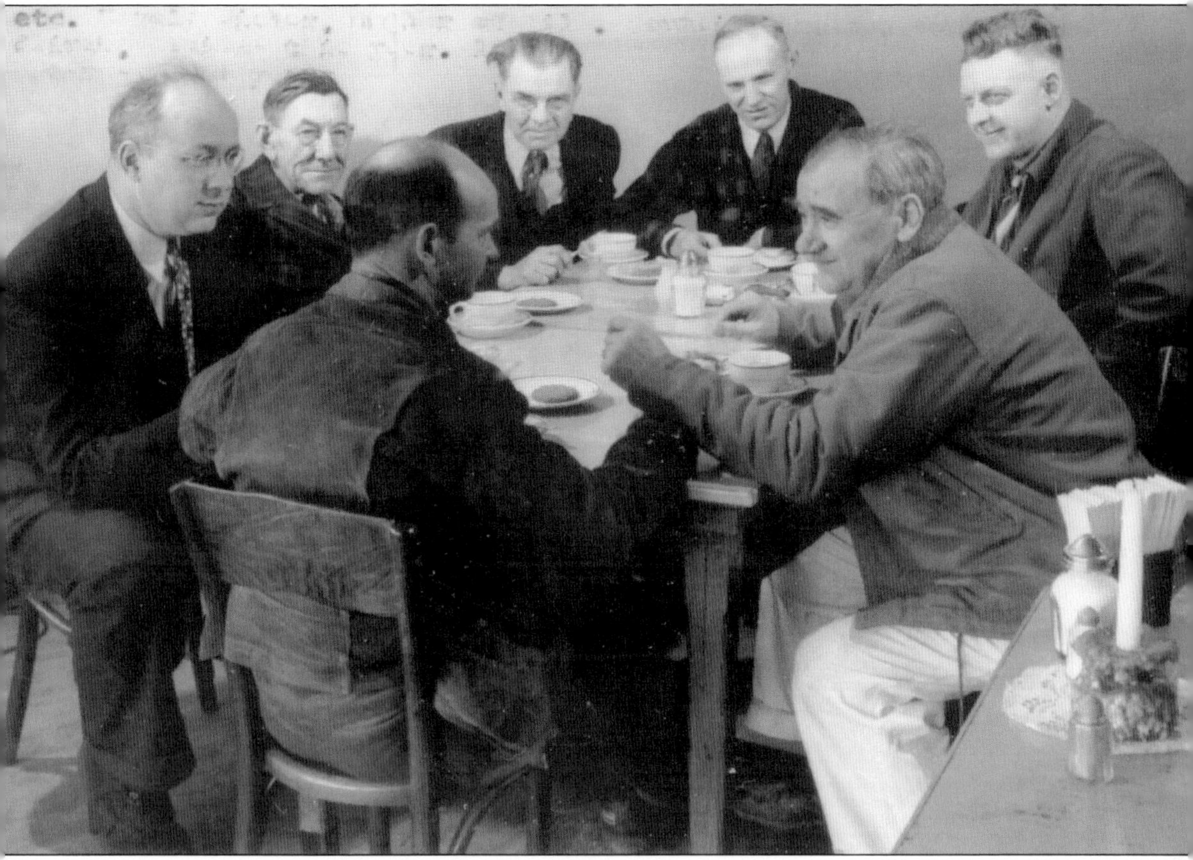

The Danish caption for this Askov photograph reads, "*Byens Faedre drøfter Problemerne over en Kop Kaffe. Fra v. Raadmand Harold Fischer, H. B. Miller, Bagermester Conrad Christensen, Borgmester Mosbaek, Kontorist A. G. Danielsson, Skoleforstander Harold Ause og Brandchef Clarence Mogensen.*" Translated, that means, "City fathers discuss problems over a cup of coffee. From left, Alderman Harold Fischer, H. B. Miller, bakery owner Conrad Christensen, Mayor Mosbaek, clerk A. G. Danielsson, school superintendent Harold Ause, and fire chief Clarence Mogensen."

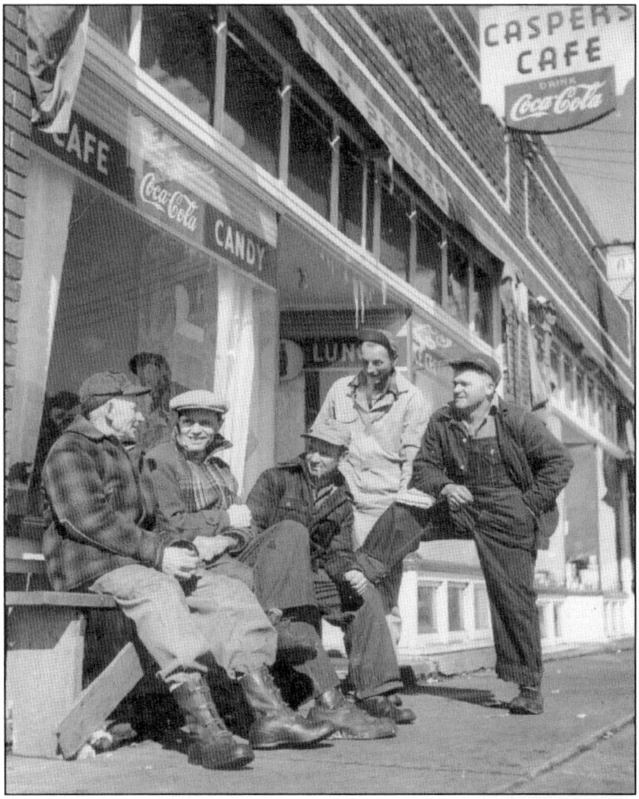

These Askov men gathered outside the local café to discuss the latest news. This scene was common throughout Northern Pine County. From left to right are Lawrence Paulsen, Chris Molgaard, Harold Fisher, Henry Kari, and Thorvald "Ted" Jensen.

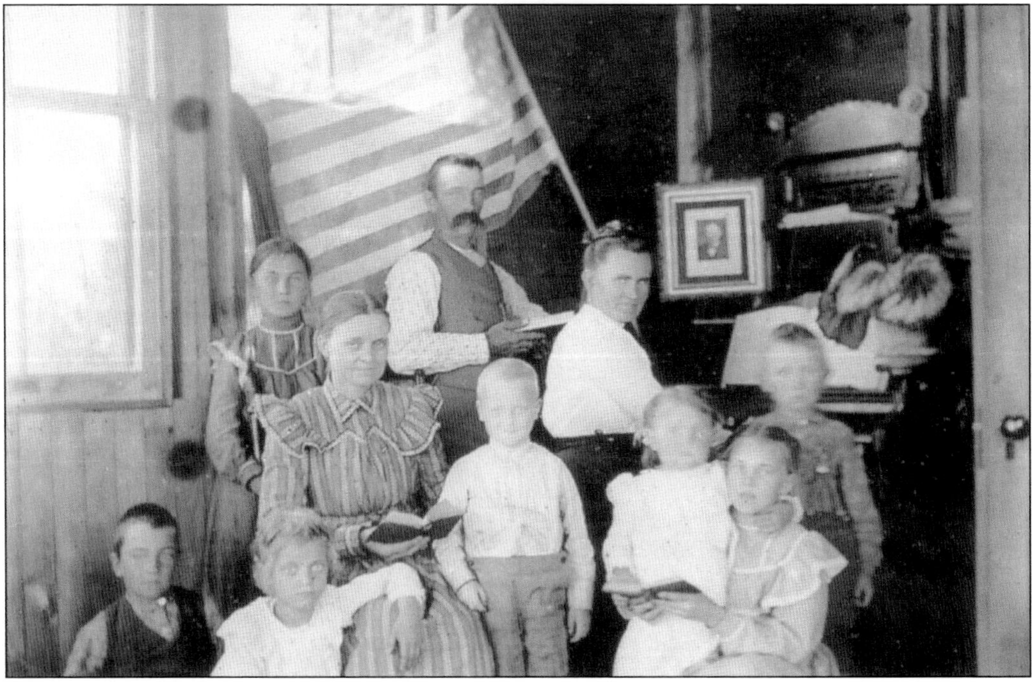

This Northern Pine County family proudly displayed the American flag in this photograph. They seemed to be enjoying a sing-along.

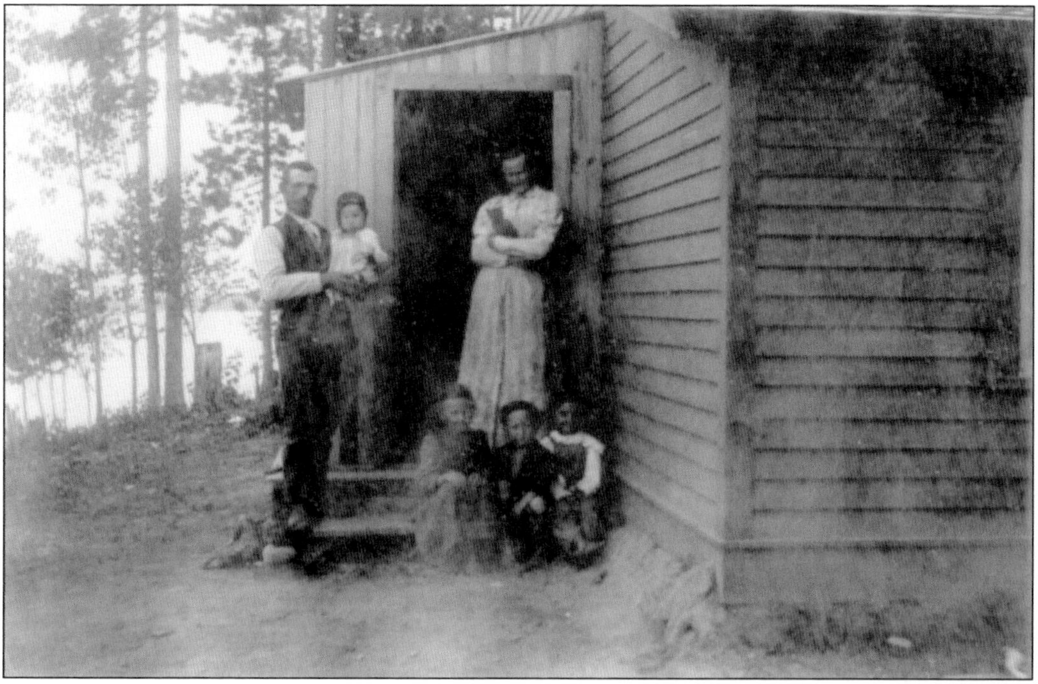

A couple, their four children, and a pet kitten posed beside their home on one of Northern Pine County's beautiful lakeshores.

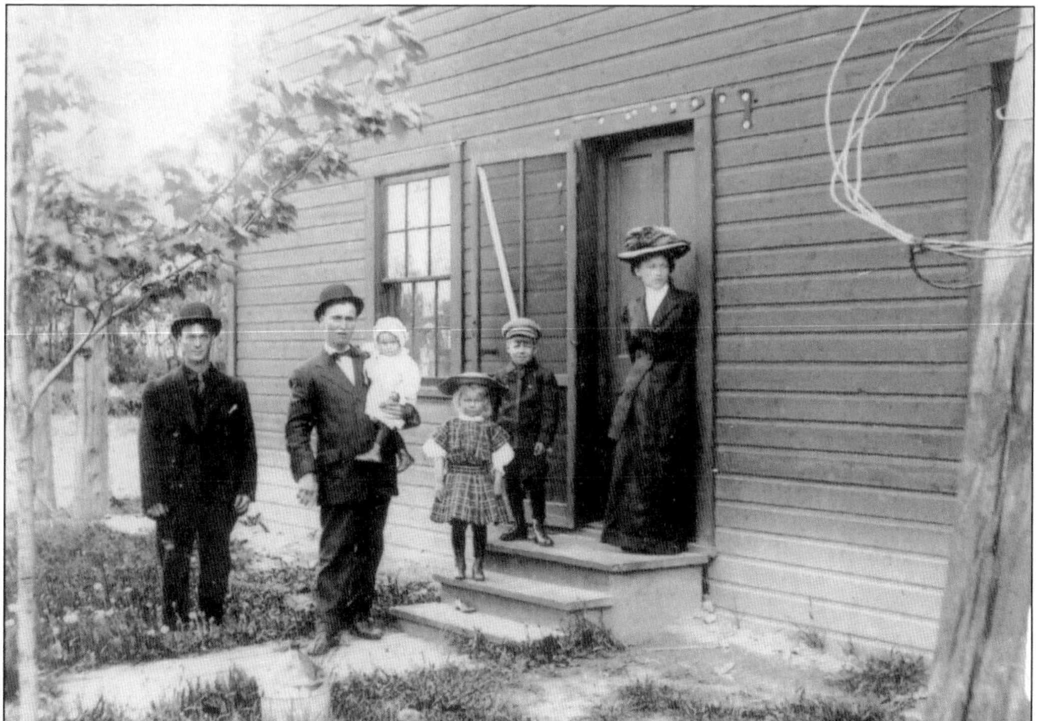

George Beaudry (left), John Lungren (beside him), and John's family were dressed in their Sunday best when they paused for this photograph. The Lungrens lived in Askov's railroad section house.

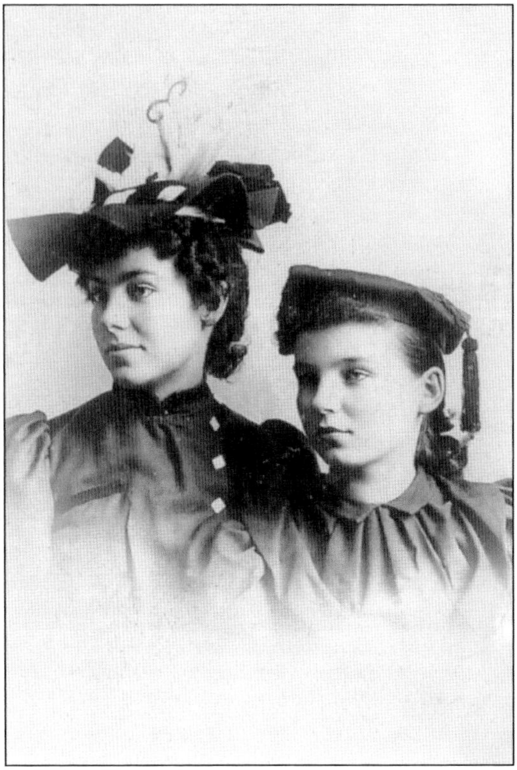

Catherine (left) and Ellen Linehan lived in Sandstone at the time of the 1894 fire. They were 16 and 13 years old, respectively. Their father, Ed, had been the quarry superintendent until the Panic of 1893 forced the quarry to close for several months. The girls, along with the rest of their family, saved themselves in the Kettle River on the day the firestorm swept through their town.

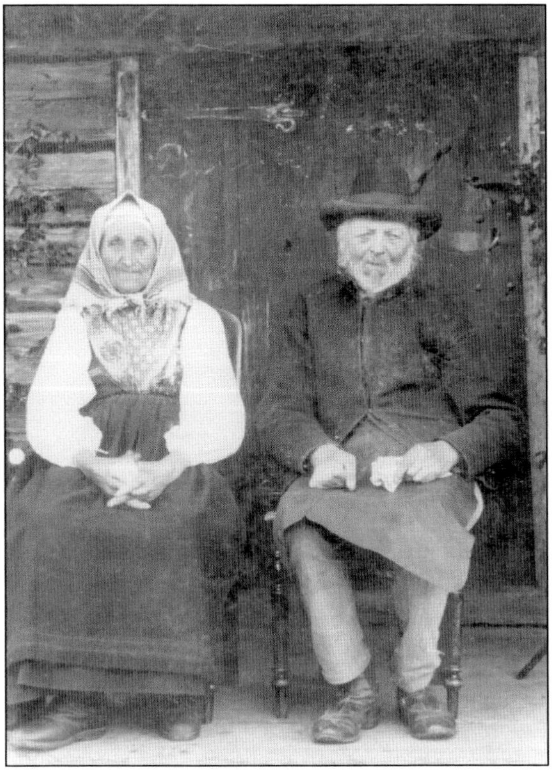

Dan and Christine Nelson were from Vilstad, a small community between Askov and Bruno. The village was little more than a Swedish church, which had been established by nearby homesteaders in 1899 and named for Vilstad, Sweden. Vilstad means "place of rest" in Swedish.

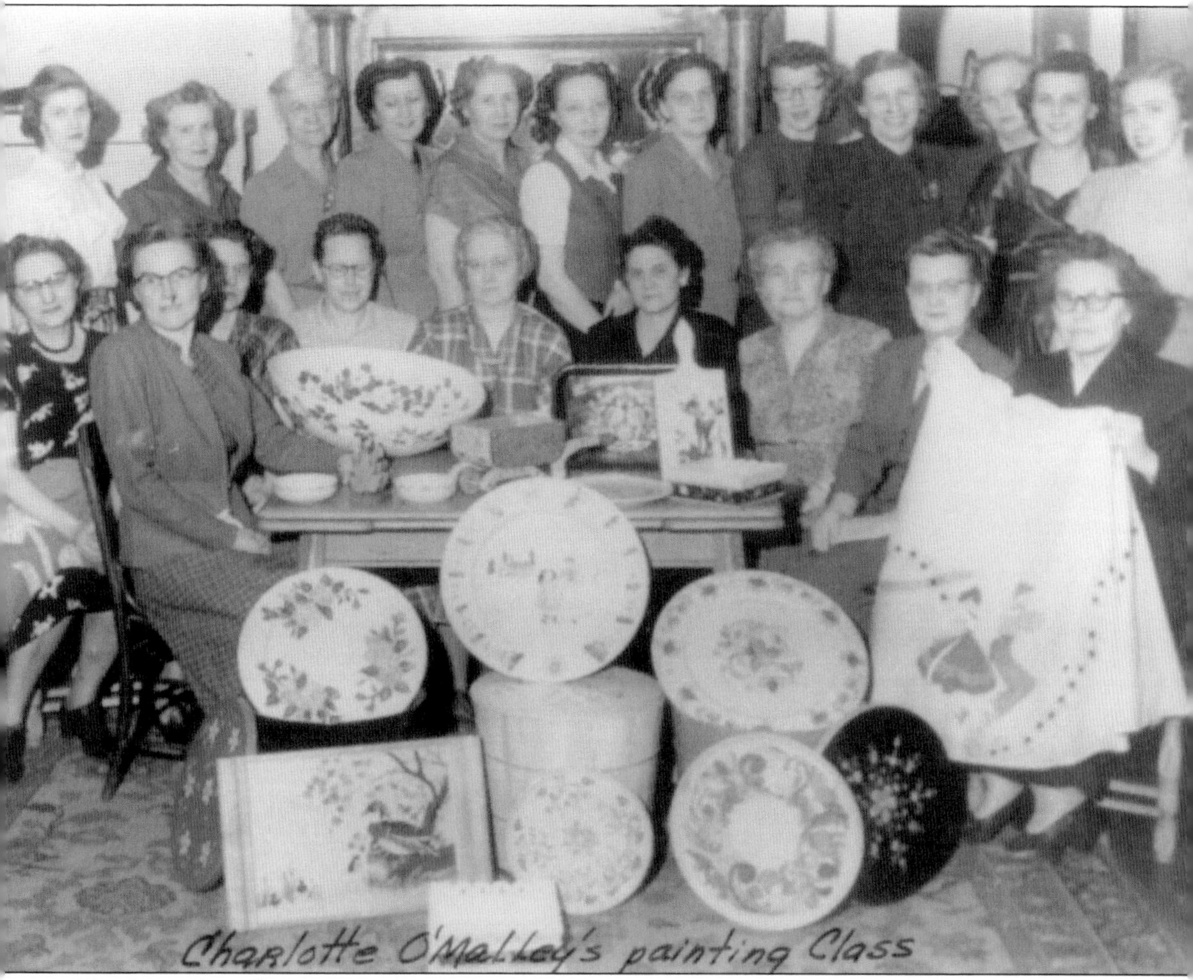

Charlotte O'Malley's art students proudly displayed their painted artworks in this Hinckley photograph. Class members included Mrs. Wilson Welles, Jane Danger, Dora Von Rueden, Gert Hope, Ethel Jackson, Helen Brant Miller, Edith Swanson, Betty Anlie, Helen Peterson, Irene Halvorson, Donna Peterson, Doris O'Malley, Elizabeth Shade, Neva Ellstrom, Ellen Frye, H. Soens, Olga Kluck, Mrs. Emil Besch, and Ann Mann.

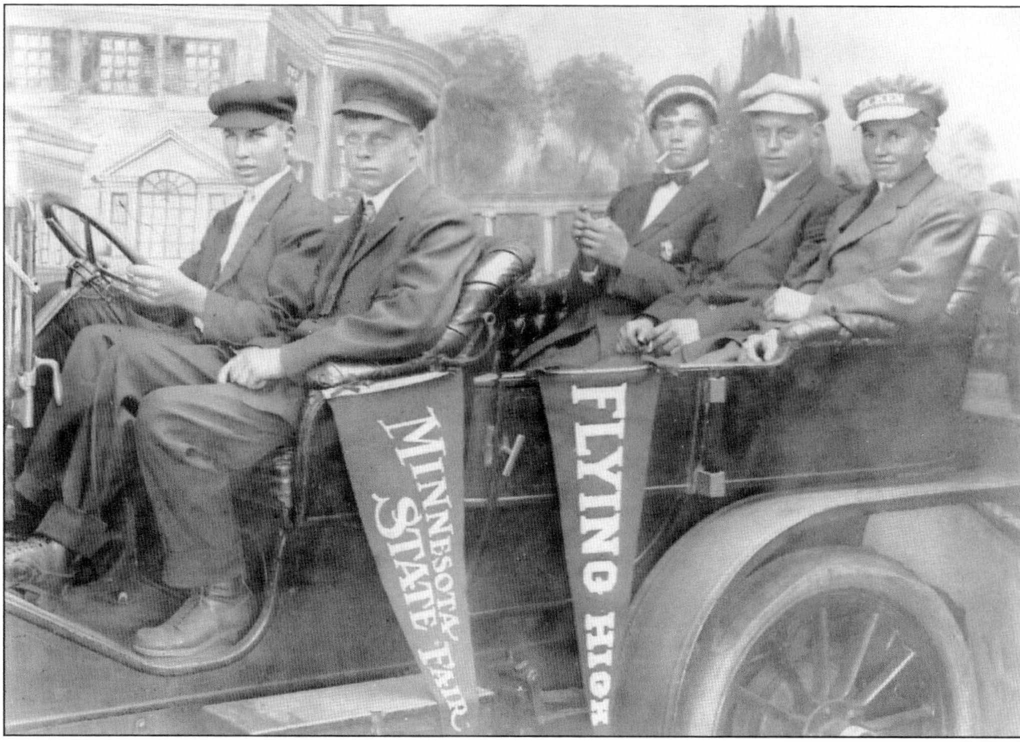

These Sandstone fellows, Al Olson, Oscar Bjorklund, Ted Thurin, Harry Halvorson, and Charlie Sukola, posed for their picture in an early automobile at the Minnesota State Fair.

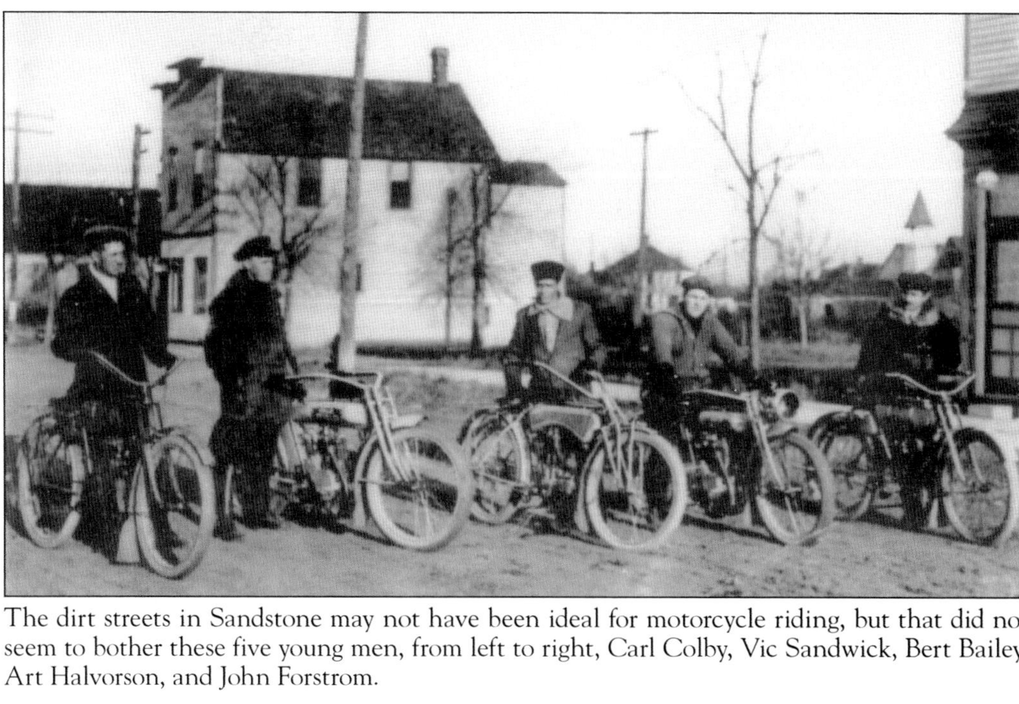

The dirt streets in Sandstone may not have been ideal for motorcycle riding, but that did not seem to bother these five young men, from left to right, Carl Colby, Vic Sandwick, Bert Bailey, Art Halvorson, and John Forstrom.

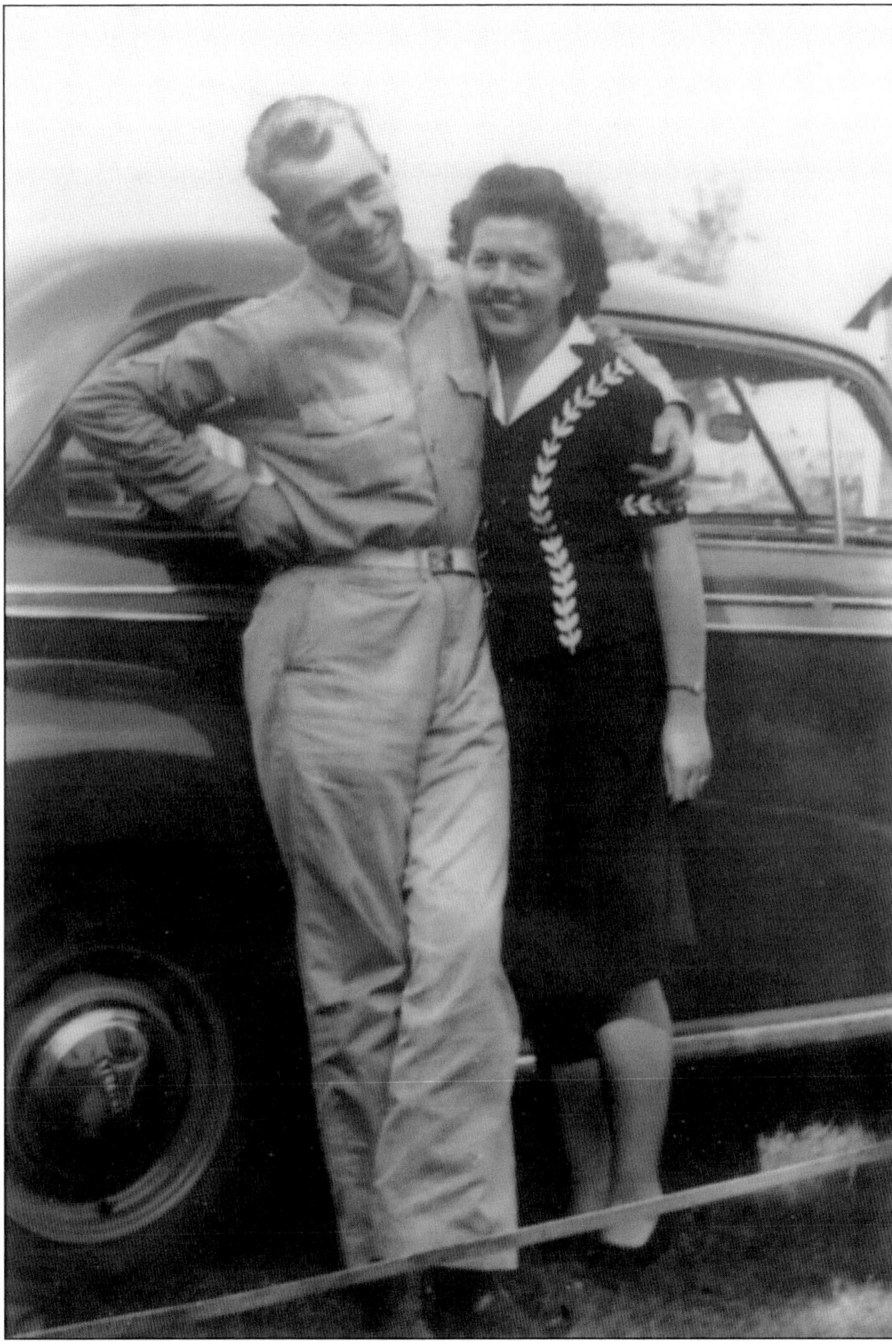

Earl and Dorotha Foster were married on December 23, 1941, and posed for this photograph on the Leo Stoffel farm in the summer of 1942. Earl was born in Pine City in 1921 and joined the National Guard in 1937. When the Guard was activated in 1941, he shipped out with two brothers, one cousin, and an uncle. After the war, Earl and Dorotha returned to Pine City and bought a home on Woodpecker Ridge. Earl passed away in 1995, still living in the same home. Dorotha passed in 2004. The photographs in this book, along with many others, are being collected to honor Earl and Dorotha's memory.

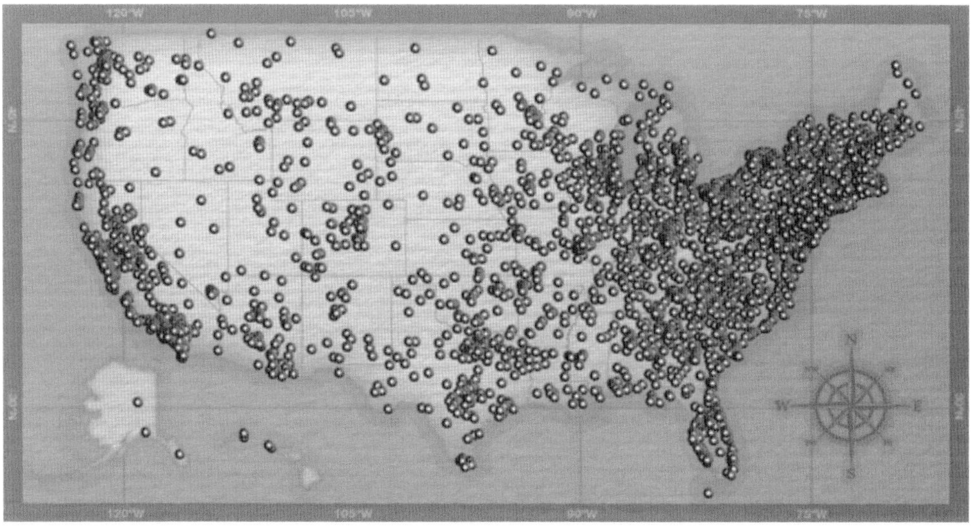